AF594601

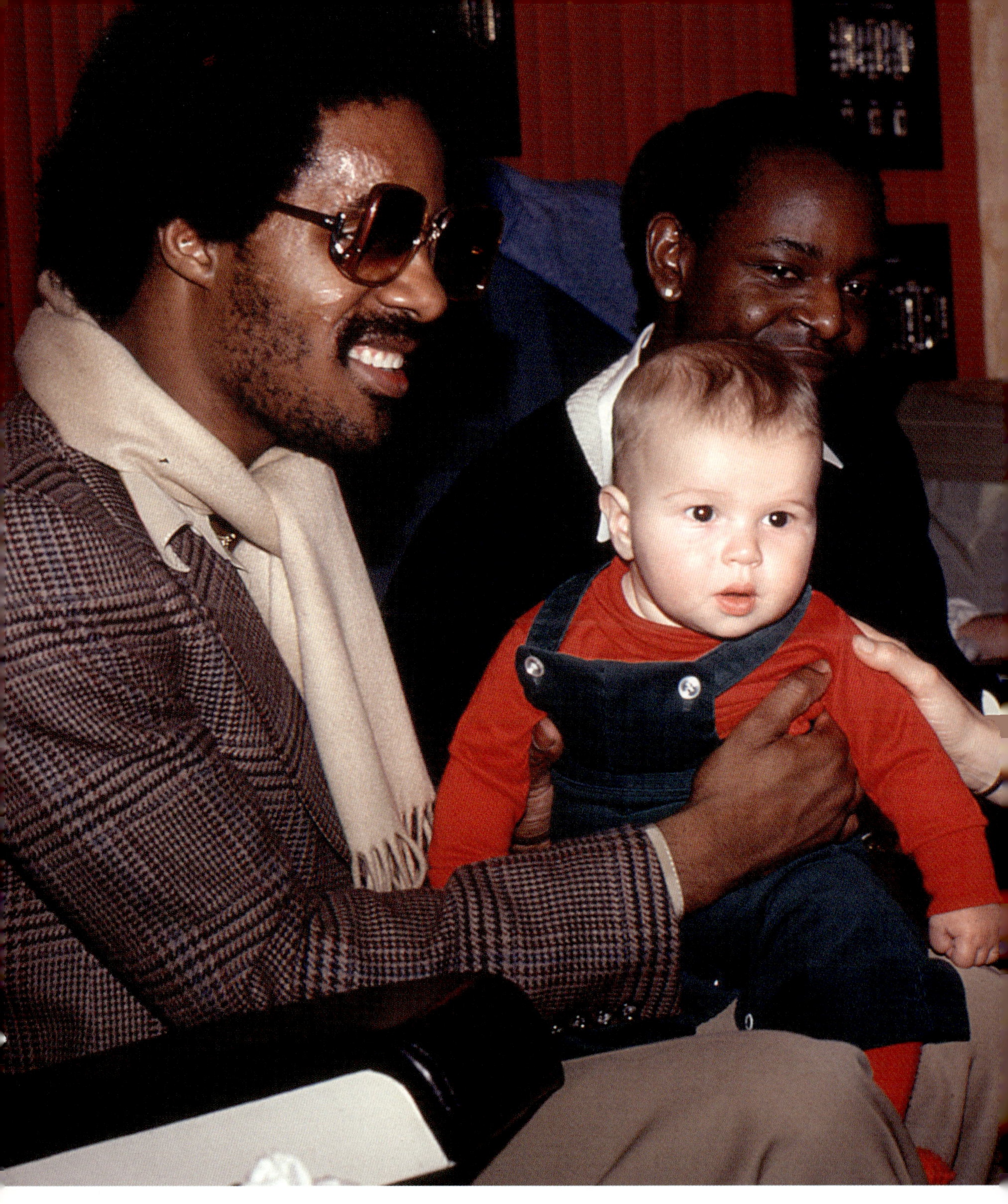

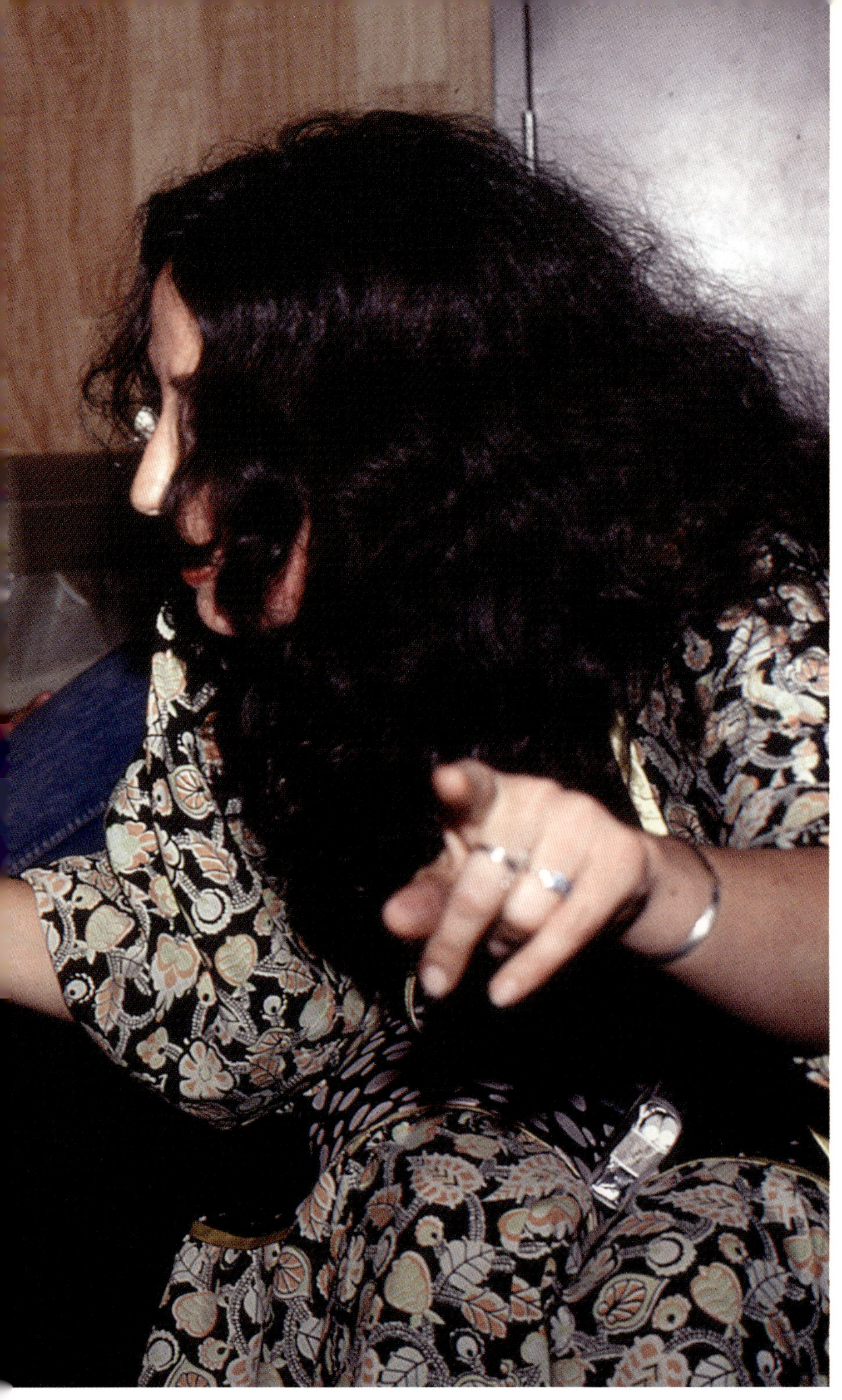

Maria Muldaur with the legendary Stevie Wonder, keyboardist / songwriter Reverend Patrick Henderson, and Ethan Nichtern, whose father, David, wrote Maria's hit song "Midnight at the Oasis." Ethan and David became Buddhist teachers, inspired by Chögyam Trungpa who founded the Naropa Institute in Boulder, CO—known not only for Buddhist teachings, but also for the Jack Kerouac School of Disembodied Poetics with professors Anne Waldman and Allen Ginsberg at the helm.

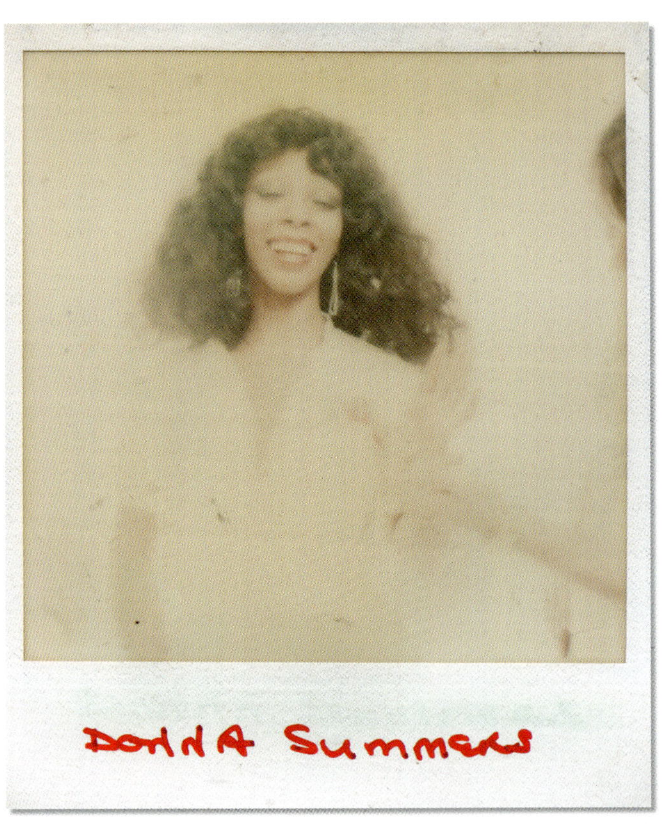

↑ *Donna Summer*

➳ *Alice Cooper*

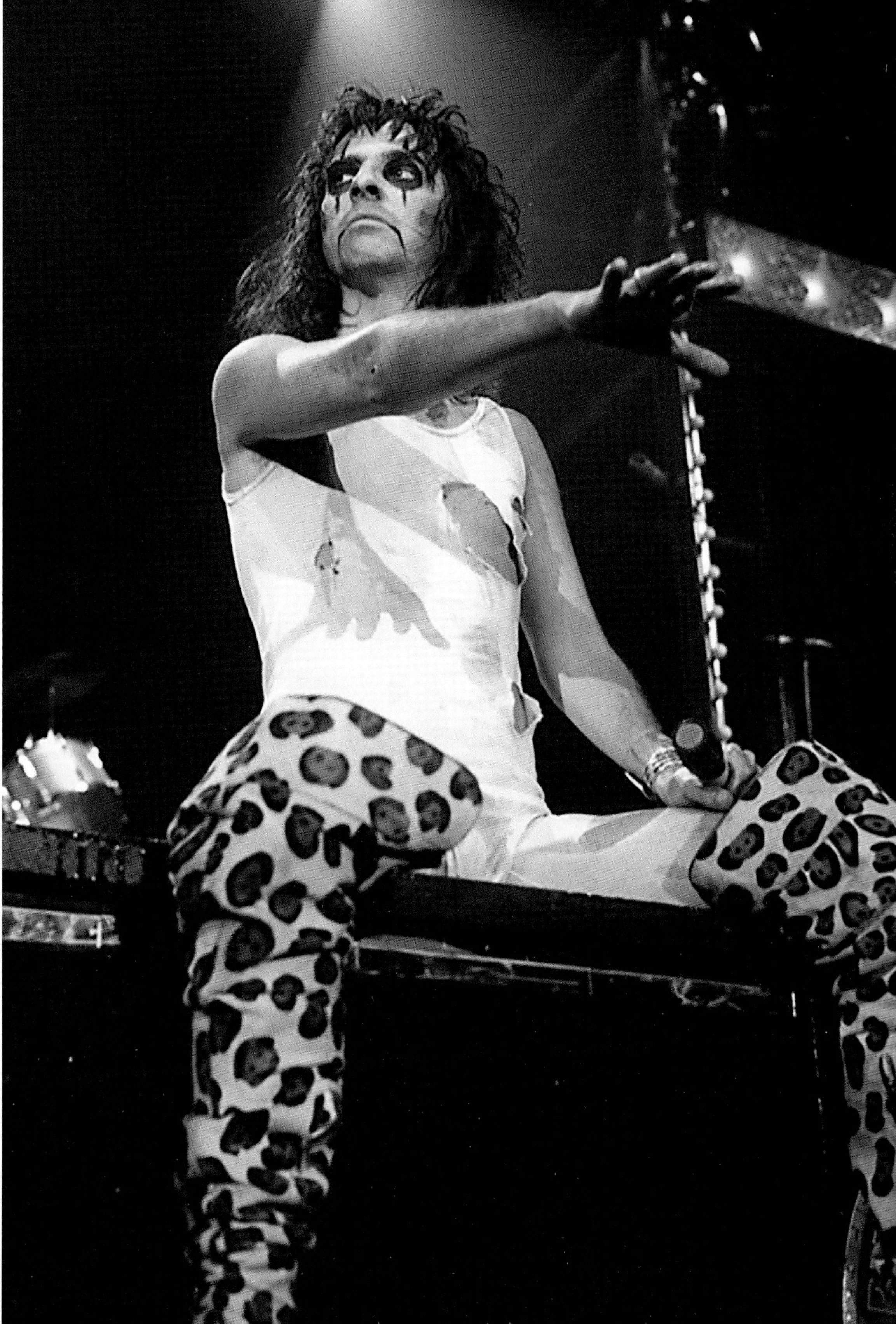

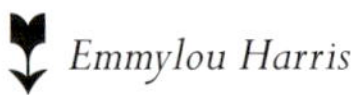

Emmylou Harris

Maxayn Lewis. At the time of this photo, she was recording for Capricorn Records (best known for their classic Allman Brothers albums). In recent times, she performed much of the singing of Ma Rainey (on behalf of actress Viola Davis) in the movie Ma Rainey's Black Bottom.

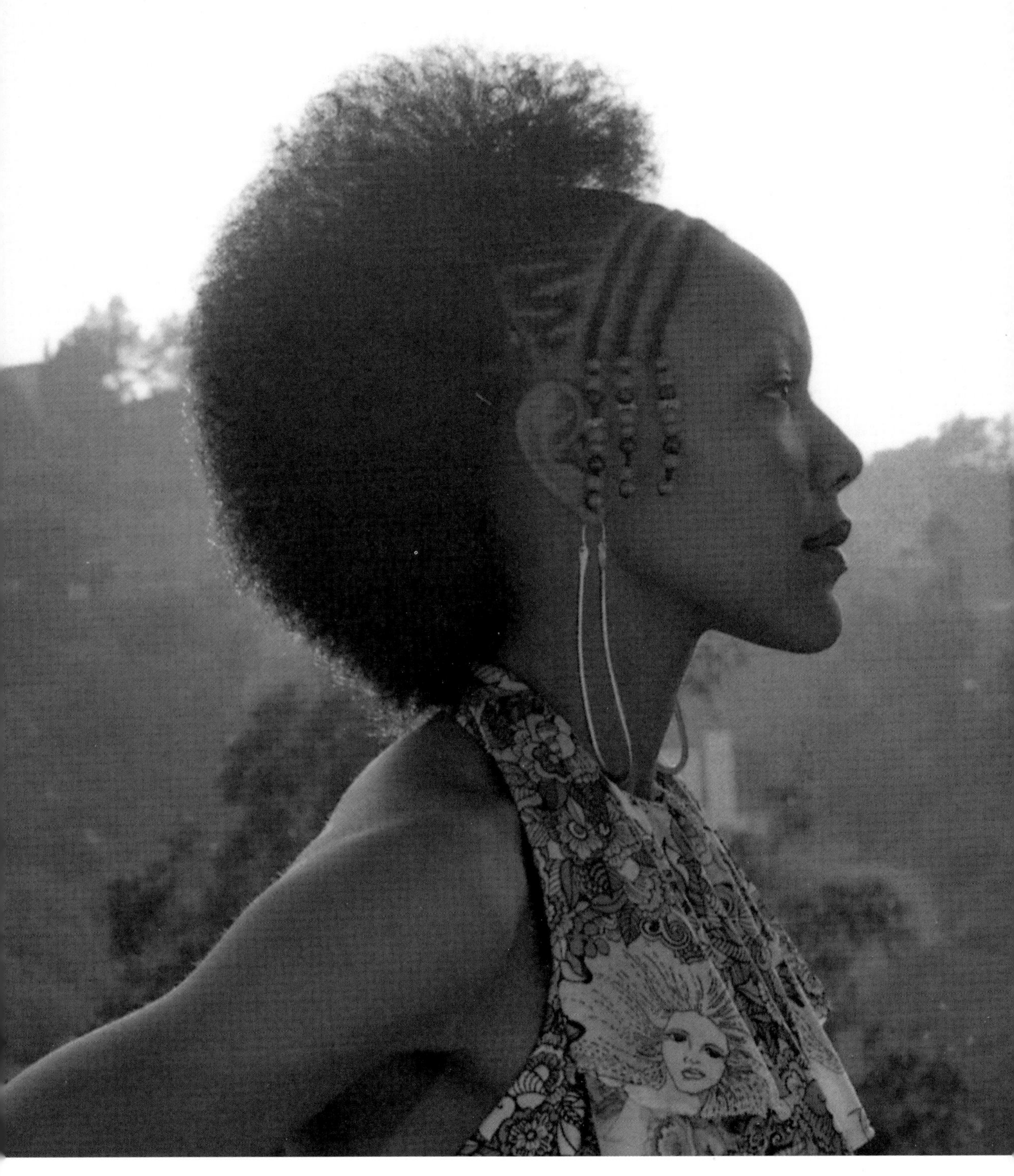

➛ *(pg. 8) Gram Parsons*

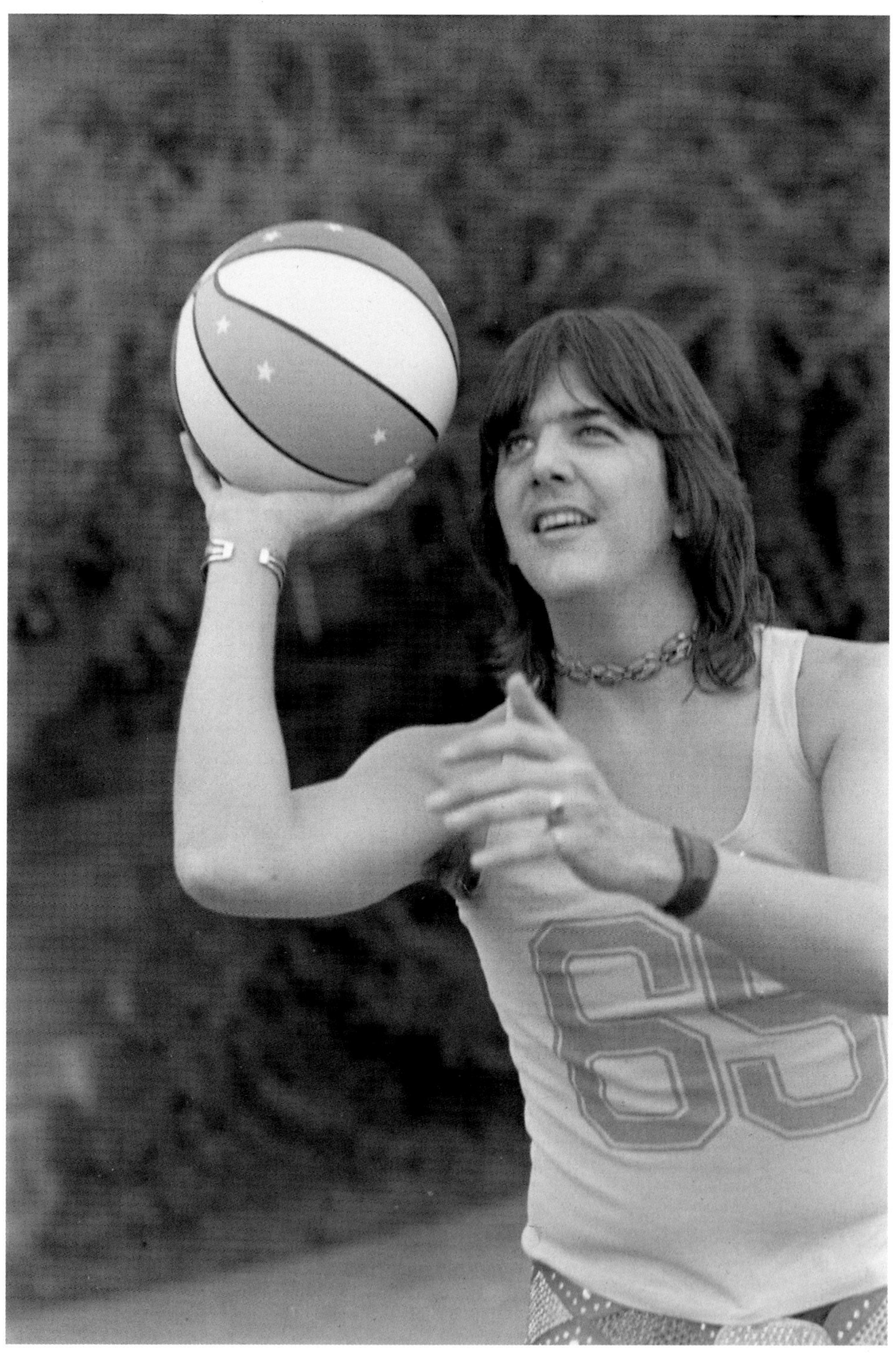
65

GRIEVOUS ANGELS, TROUT MASKS, AND AMERICAN BEAUTIES

1970s ROCK & ROLL PHOTOGRAPHY BY

GINNY WINN

FANTAGRAPHICS
UNDERGROUND

Jerry Garcia playing with Old & In the Way, circa 1973. Jerry Garcia (Banjo), Peter Rowan (Guitar), Richard Greene (Fiddle), David Grisman (Mandolin), and John Kahn (String Bass).

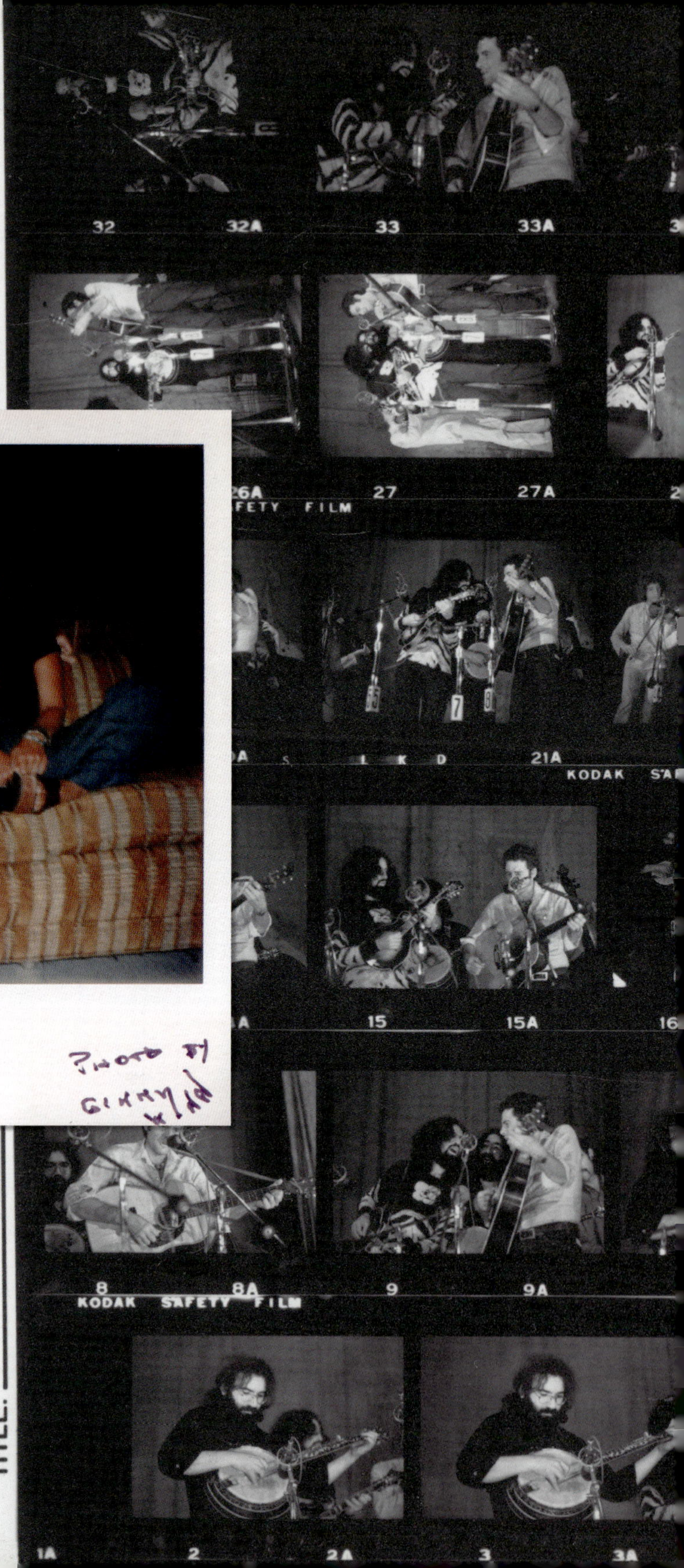

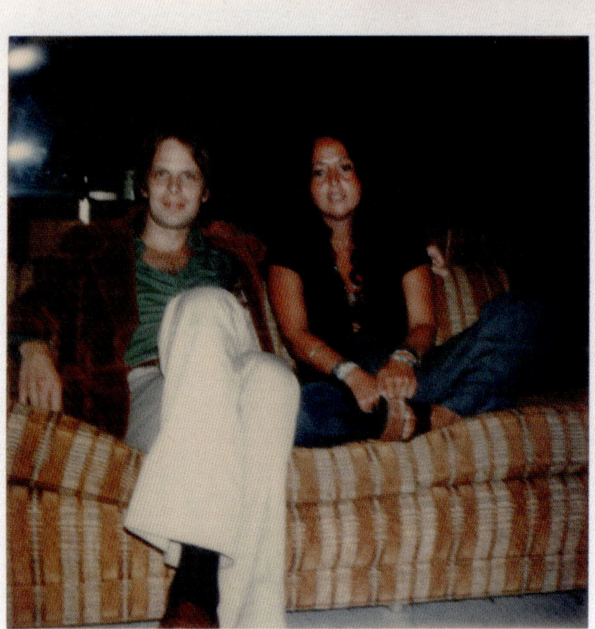

Producer Joe Boyd & Maria Muldaur. Joe worked with Maria on "Midnight at the Oasis," and he's known amongst Fairport Convention, Nick Drake, and Richard & Linda Thompson fans for his mythological recordings with them.

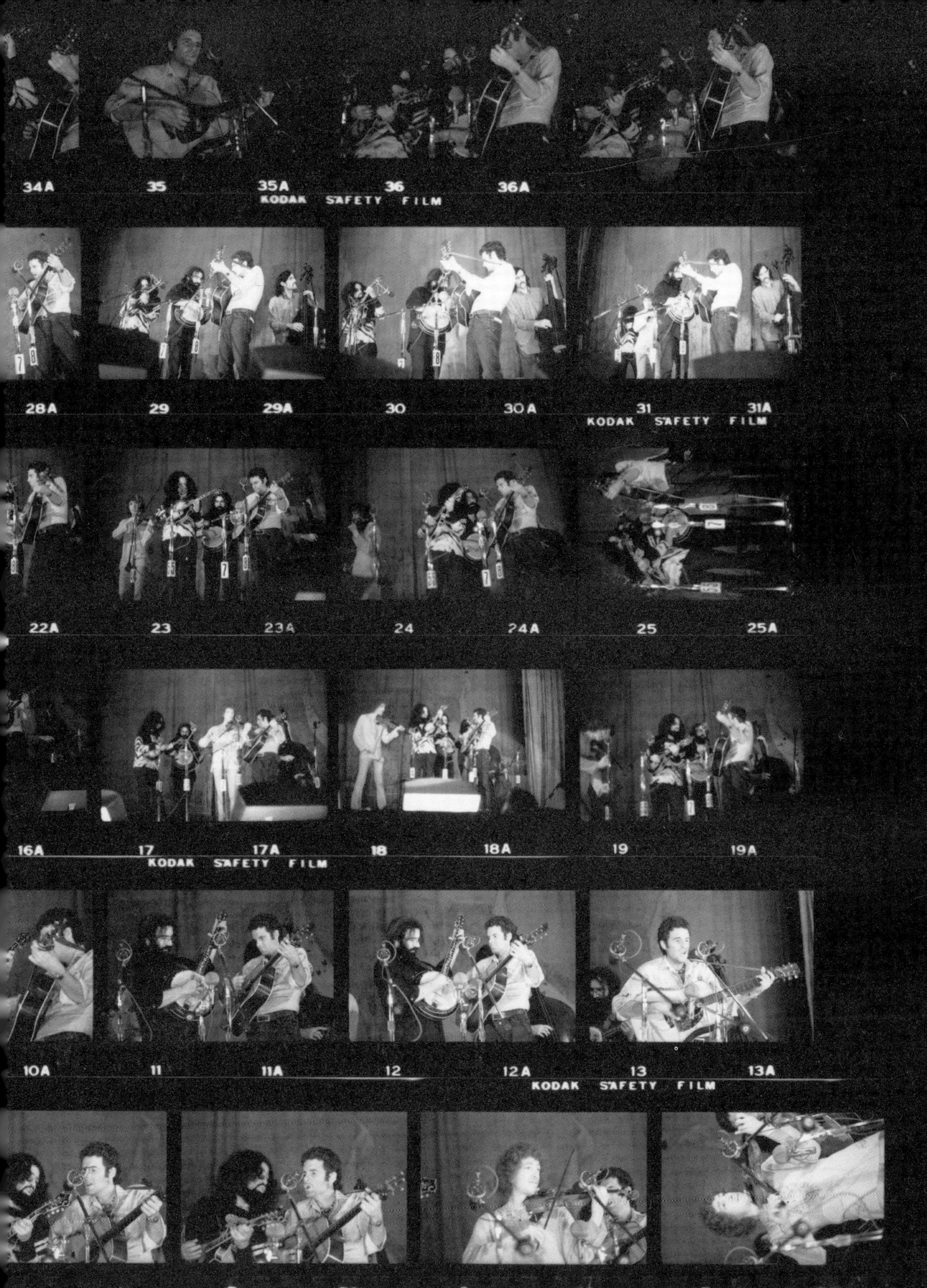
34A 35 35A 36 36A
KODAK SAFETY FILM
28A 29 29A 30 30A 31 31A
KODAK SAFETY FILM
22A 23 23A 24 24A 25 25A
16A 17 17A 18 18A 19 19A
KODAK SAFETY FILM
10A 11 11A 12 12A 13 13A
KODAK SAFETY FILM
4A 5 5A 6 6A 7 7A

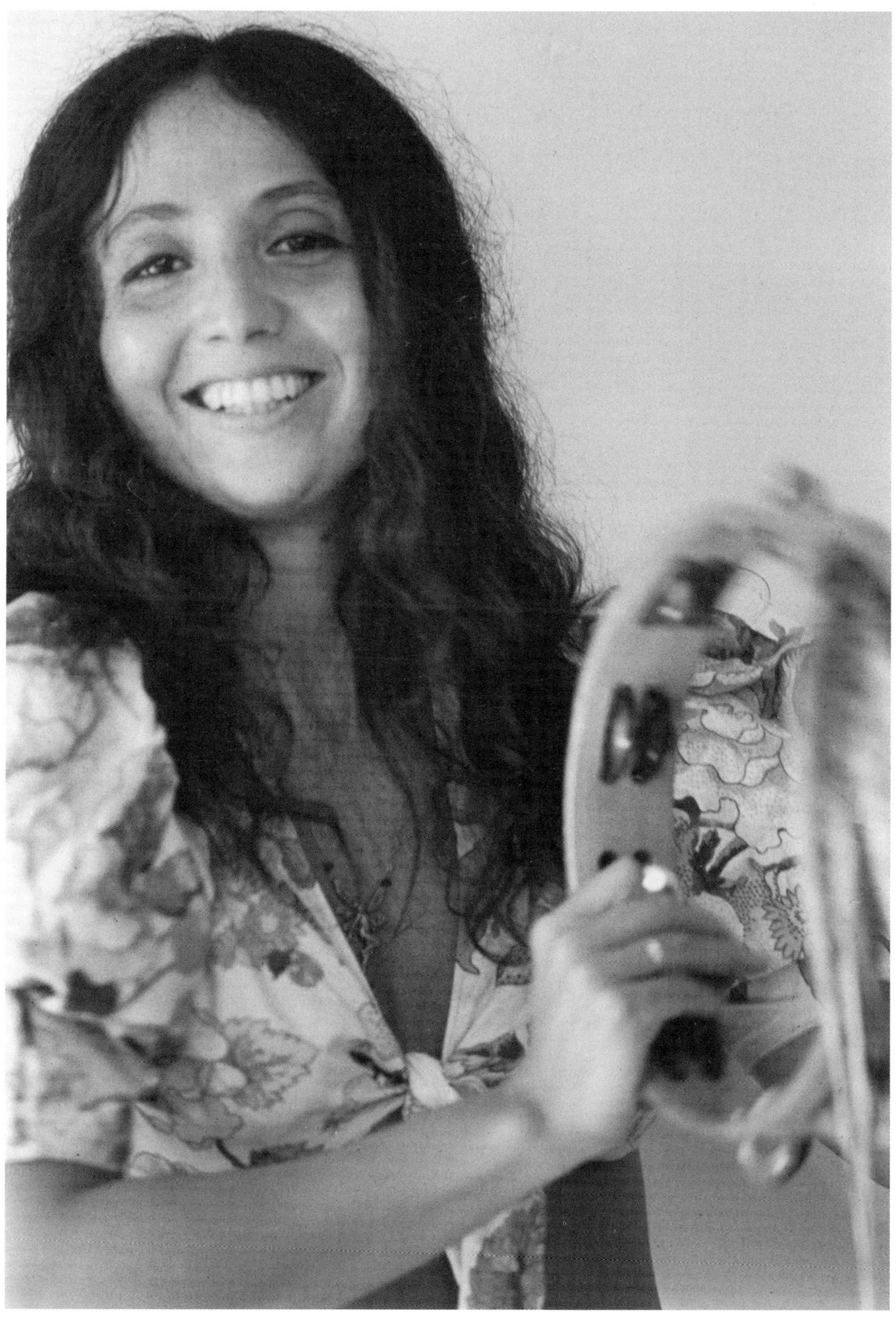

"That a photo is worth 1,000 words is so true. When people look at my photos, what they say is that there's a kind of immediacy. And I'm always looking for something when I'm shooting. I get close. I always want to see the pupils in their eyes. I focus on the eyes and in that way, you're really looking in—soul to soul. I wanted to connect with my subjects in a 'soulful' way."

← *Maria Muldaur*

➔ *Vocalist Charlie Allen of Pacific Gas & Electric, an L.A.-based psychedelic soul band, best known for their 1970 hit "Are You Ready?"*

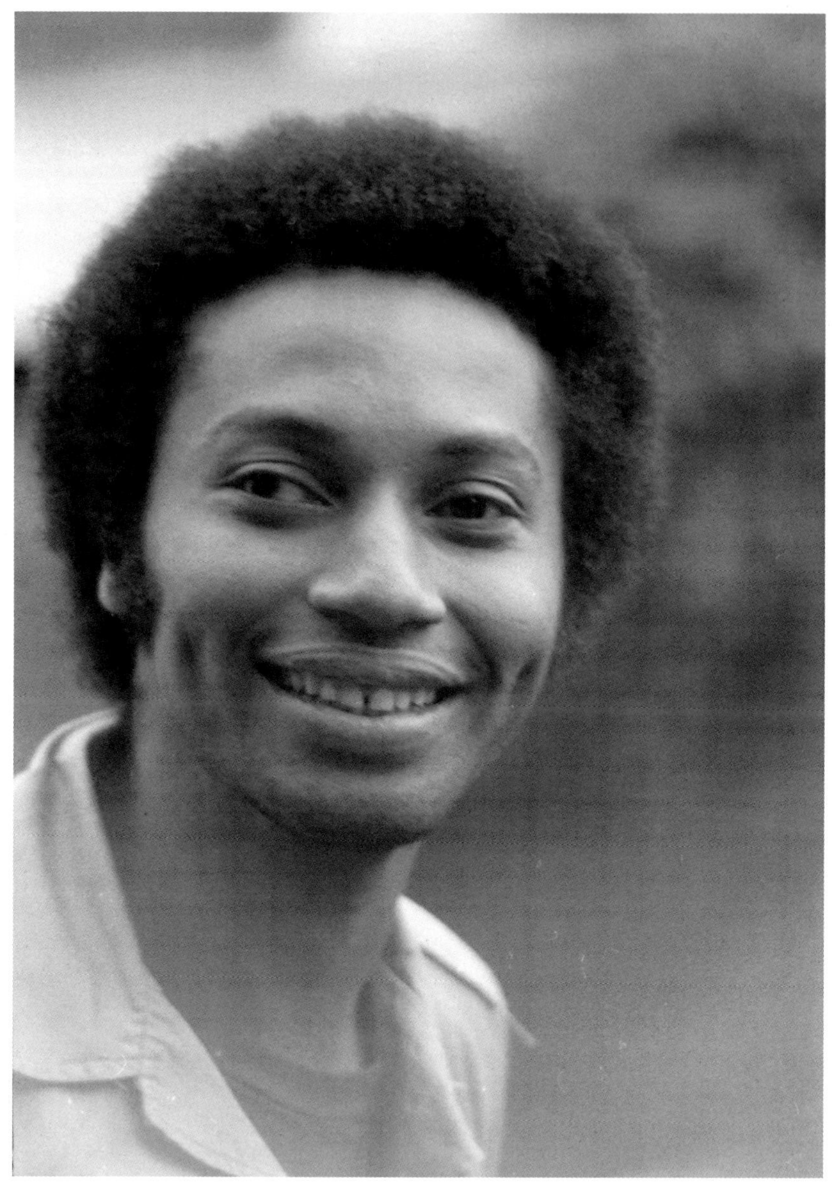

➔ Rolling Stone *magazine photographer Annie Leibovitz*

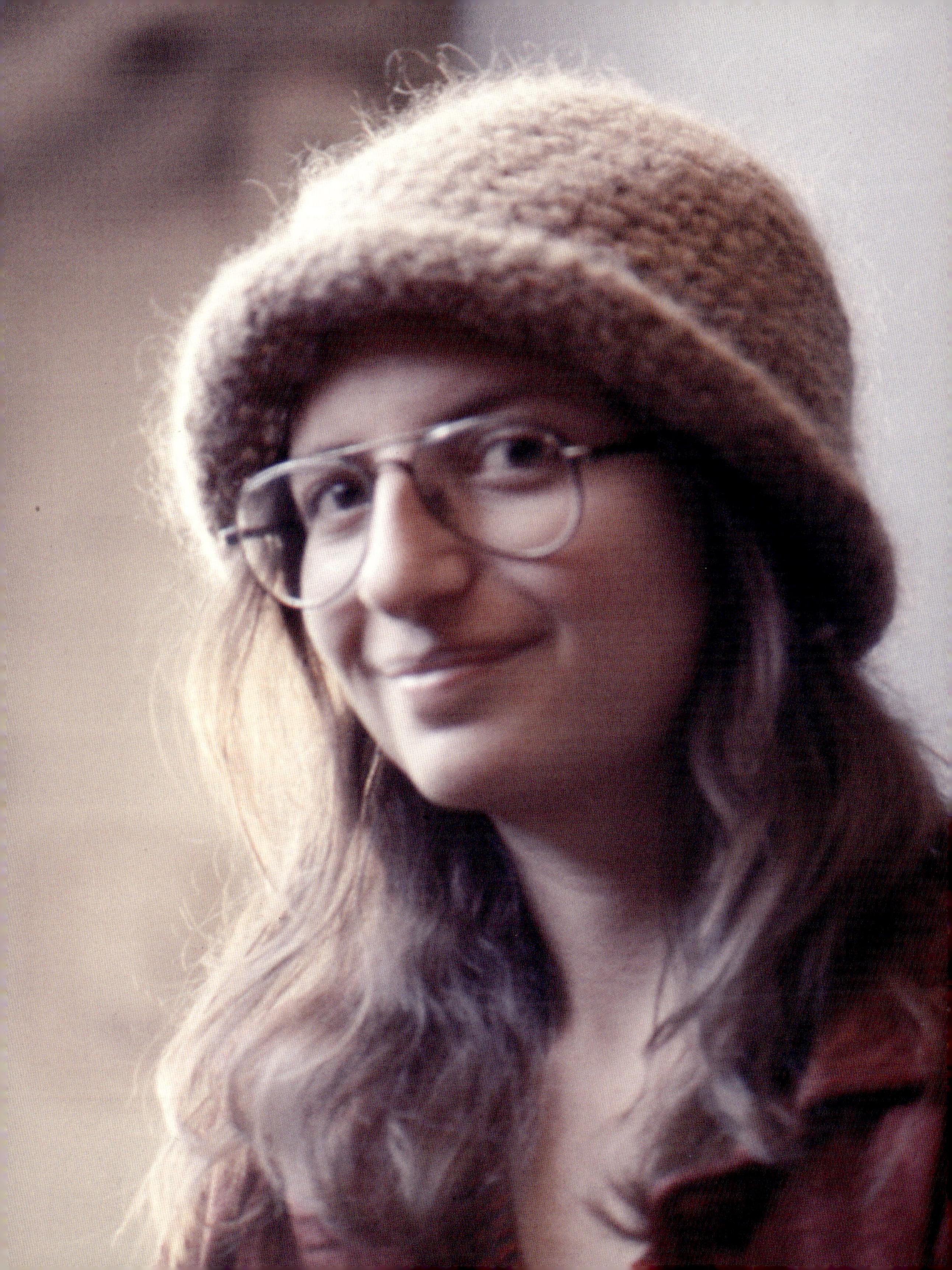

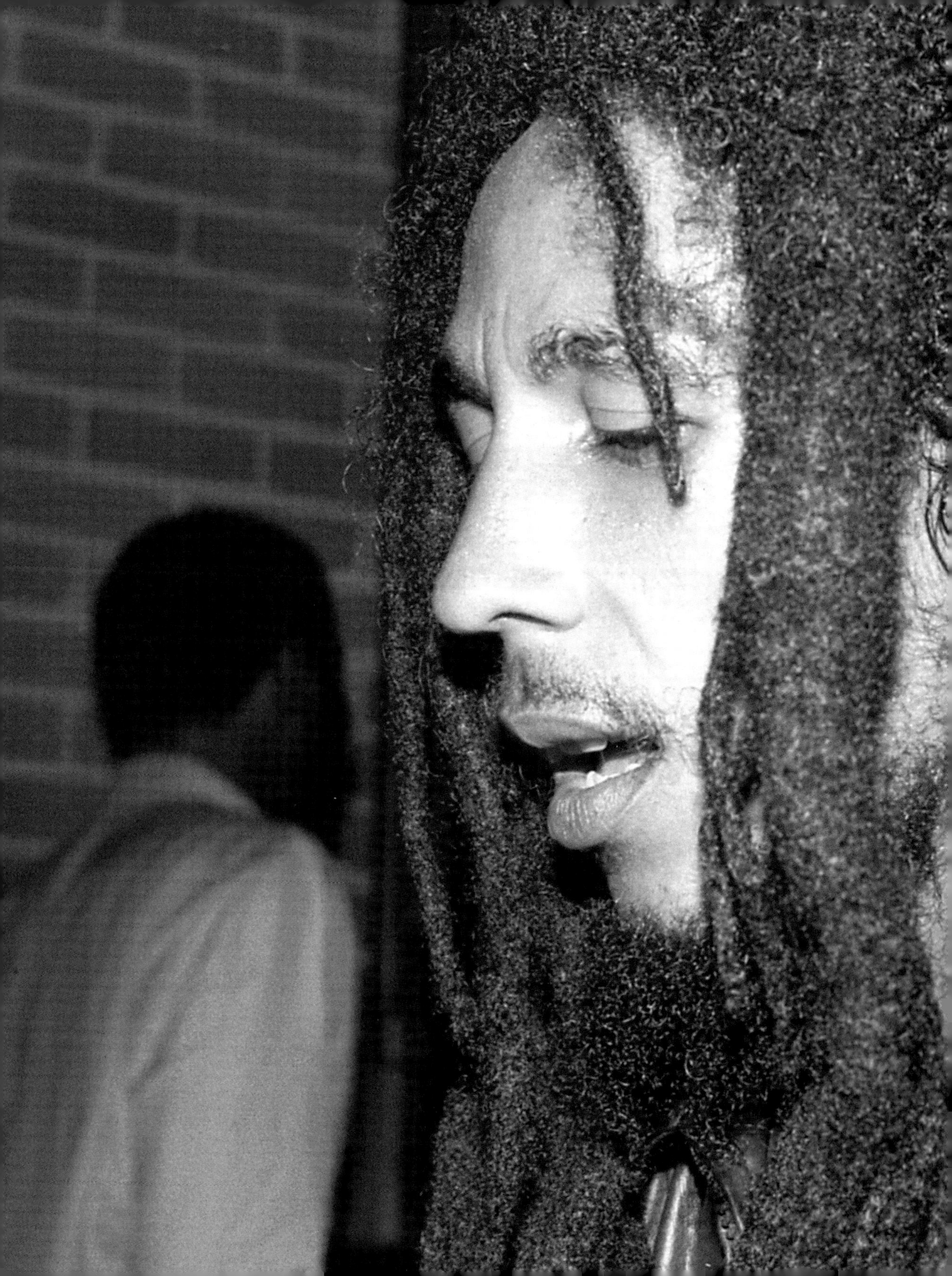

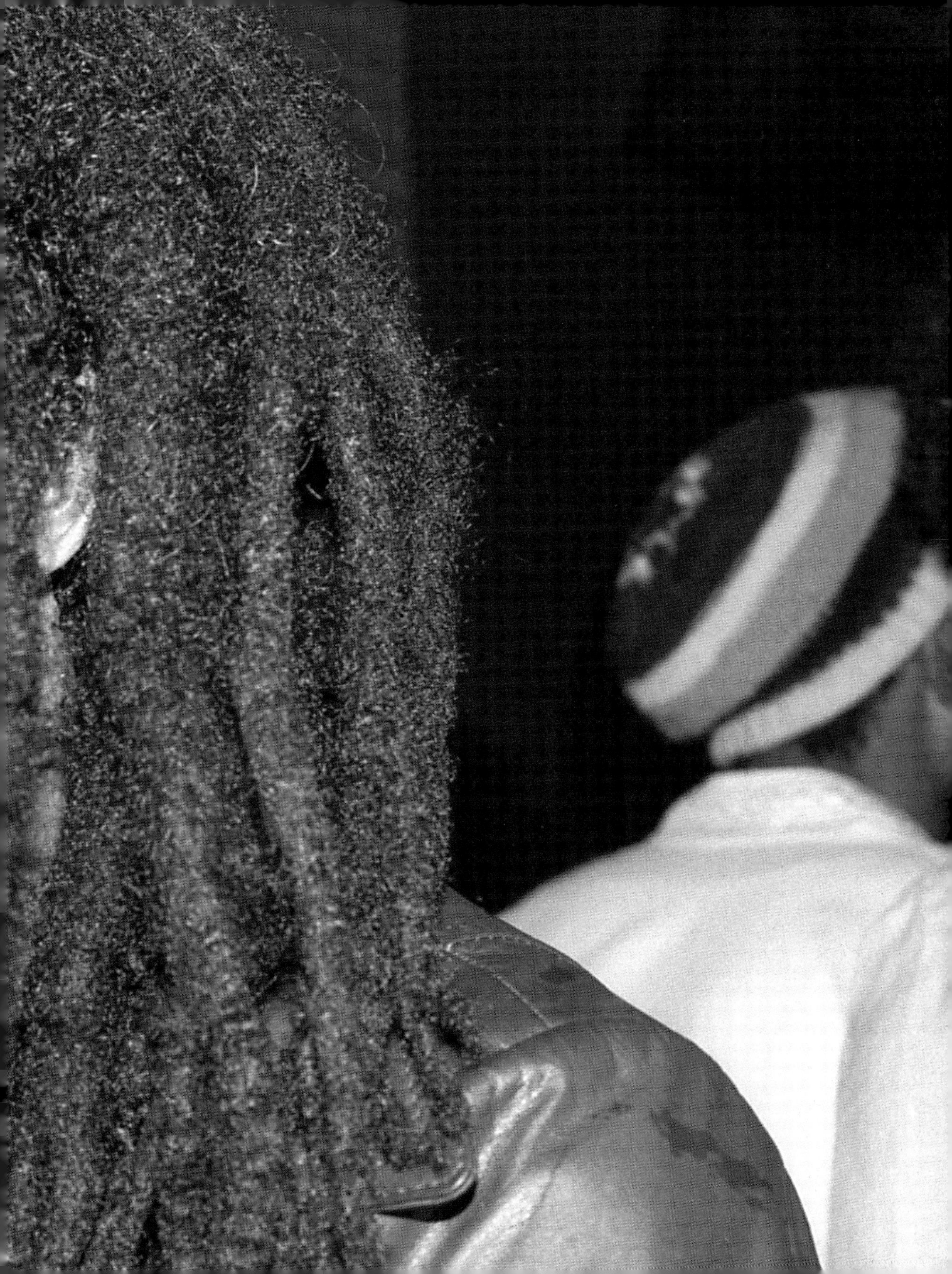

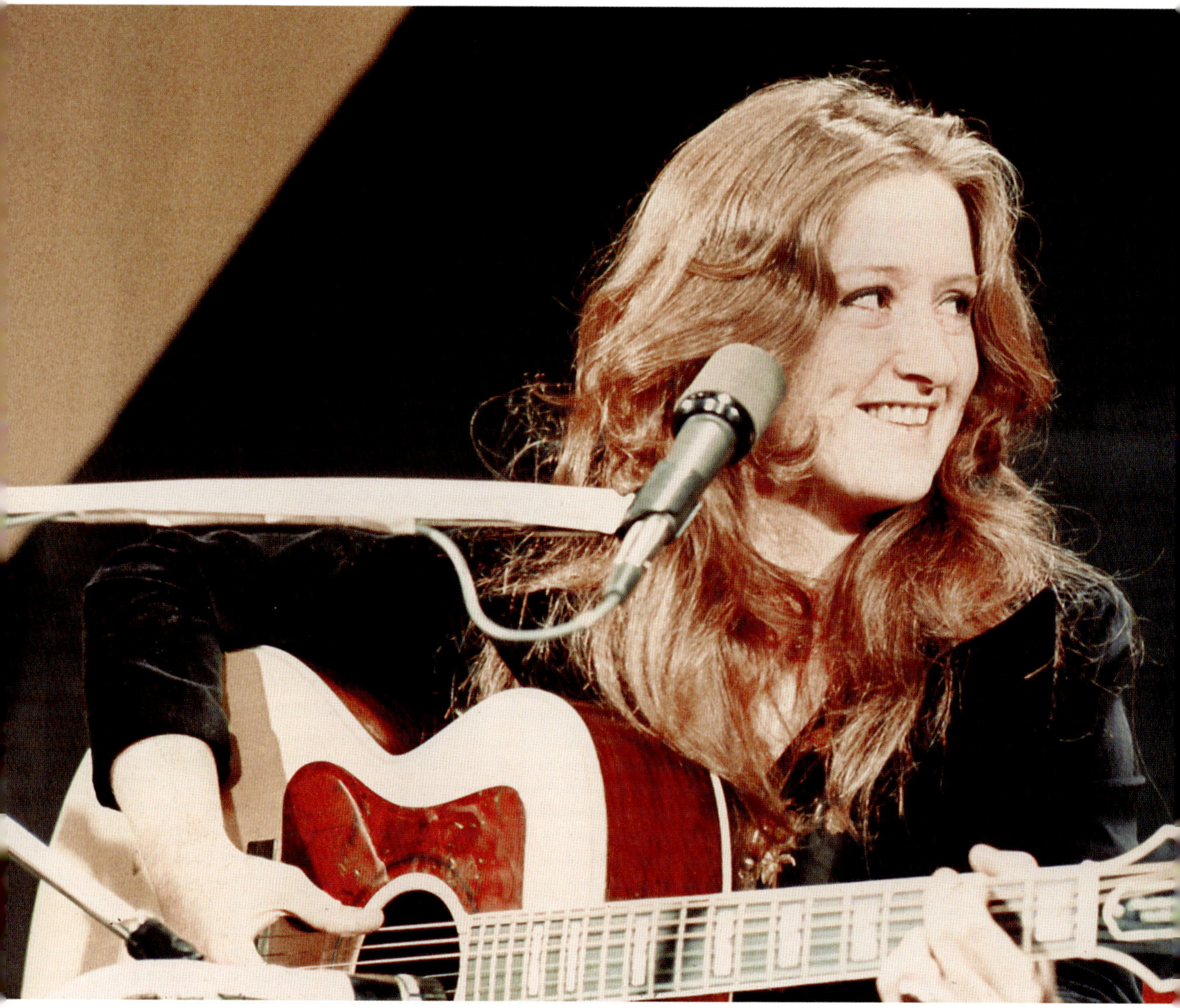

(pg. 16–17) *Bob Marley*

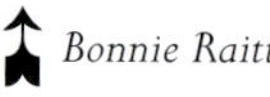

Bonnie Raitt

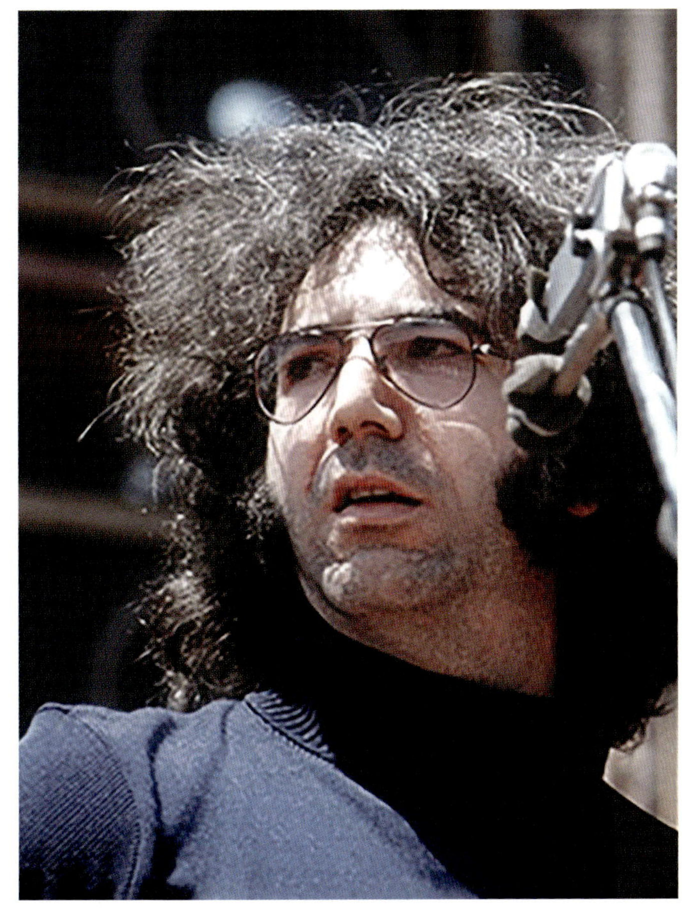

➽ *Jerry Garcia*

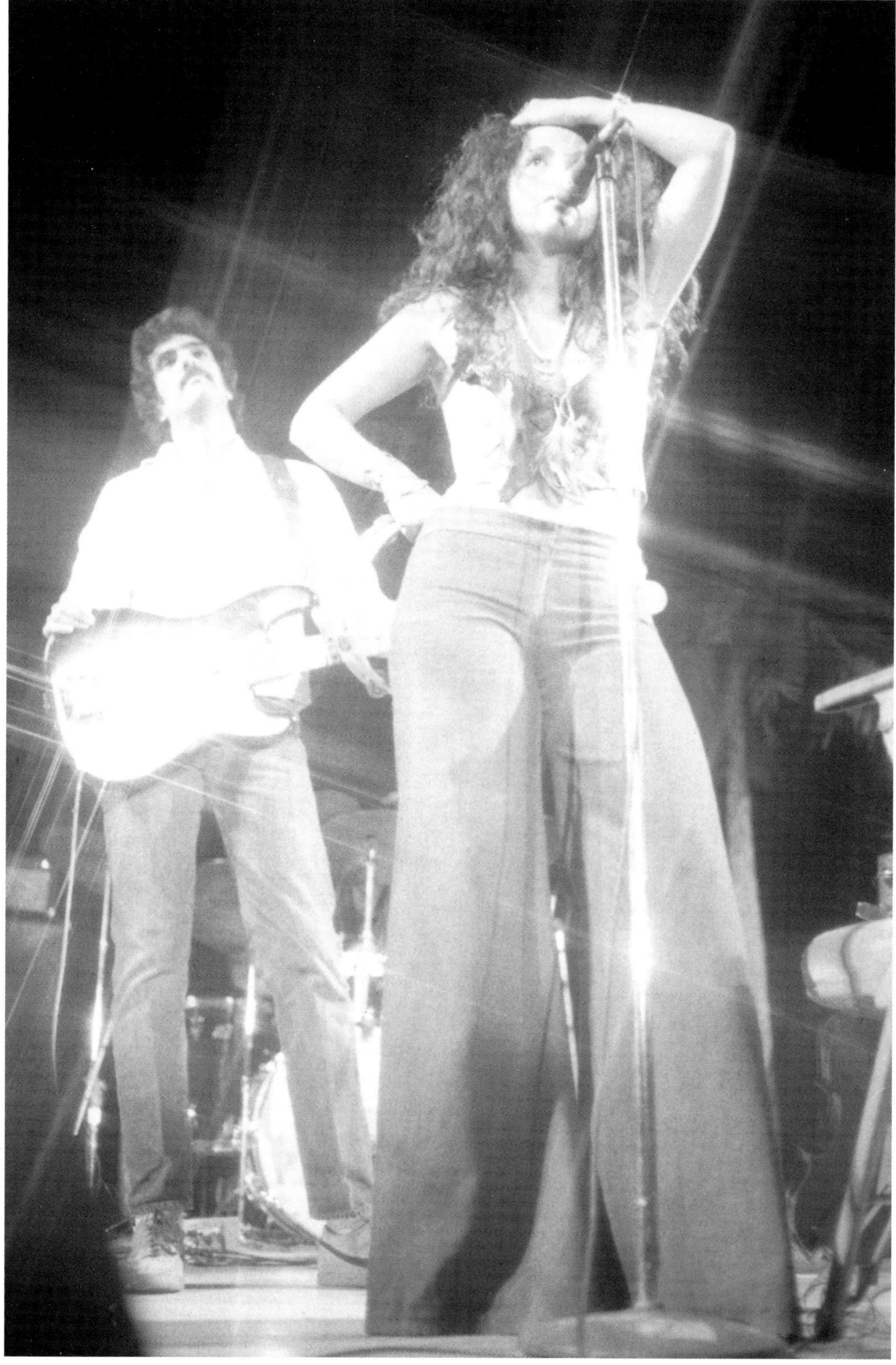

Foreword

Empathetic Imagery

In 1973, as a newly single mom of a 7-year-old daughter, I found myself transported from the laid-back little country community of Woodstock, New York, to Hollywood, where I had been given the opportunity to make my first solo album for Warner Bros. Records. To say that this young hippie mom felt completely like a fish out of water in those radically different surroundings would be an understatement.

One day while sitting in the offices of my producer, Lenny Waronker, I saw a woman rushing by who I immediately felt was a kindred spirit. Her blondish hair was fluffed out in the "permed" look of the day, she wore a hand-embroidered peasant blouse over *very* short denim cutoffs, had well-tanned, long slender legs, and wore the de rigueur pair of tan Kork-Ease platform sandals which even further elongated her leggy look. She emanated a bristling energy, and upon asking who she was, I was told her name was Ginny Winn, the official staff photographer for Warner Bros. The next time I saw her rushing by Lenny's office I called out to her, "Hey! I hear you're the photographer around here! I need a photo taken for my album cover! Can we get together?"

When we met to discuss ideas for my photo shoot, I discovered that she had recently moved from Woodstock herself with her two young children and that we now lived only three doors away from each other in Laurel Canyon. We had so much in common, and bonded immediately, remaining dear friends to this day! I'm not one that loves to have her photo taken, but photo shoots with Ginny were always a fun, casual, spontaneous and creative adventure.

I never felt like I was "posing" for the camera with her...just hanging out in a very natural way. We shot my cover photo on the back steps of my bungalow. Far from being "gussied up," I wore a plain black shirt tied around my waist, a long denim skirt, and minimal makeup. The night before the shoot we'd all been to a great party at my friend Jonathan Taplin's house, and somehow, I'd ended up with actor Michael Pollard's black velvet Borsalino fedora. (I think I'd admired it and he'd insisted on giving it to me!) Ginny suggested I try it on, and it completed my "look" for the shoot.

For my first Warner Bros. album, I had the pleasure and privilege of being surrounded by so many of my musical heroes—

Maria Muldaur with bassist John Kahn

Ry Cooder, David Lindley, Dr. John, Clarence White, Richard Greene, and Jim Keltner, to name but a few. These were not just "session musicians" but amazing artists, and I strongly felt that their photos should also be part of the album package. Ginny turned out to be a master of nimbly and deftly being able to get candid shots of musicians in action, without being intrusive in any way. She somehow gracefully and almost invisibly floated around the studio without interrupting the flow of musical energy and we ended up with wonderful candid shots of all the musicians, as well as other people I considered to be an important part of my life—my daughter Jenni, my mother's helper, Lenny, etc. Ginny wanted to extend her creative vision beyond the wonderful photos she'd taken, and suggested we collaborate with Michael Wood, an artist friend of hers, and the result was a marvelous magical iconic album cover that remains unique to this day.

I think Ginny Winn's ability to blend in and become an empathetic part of the Musical Energy taking place is what made her such a successful music photographer; a dearly loved and always welcome presence by many of the top artists of the 70s. Her vast body of work from that era captures musicians at their best, most natural moments—whether live on stage, hard at work in the studio, or just relaxing. Her photos all have a very organic feel to them. Looking at these wonderful photos now, I feel a nostalgia for the natural, laid-back, spontaneous, uncontrived "vibe" we enjoyed in the 70s.

—*Maria Muldaur, Singer/Songwriter*

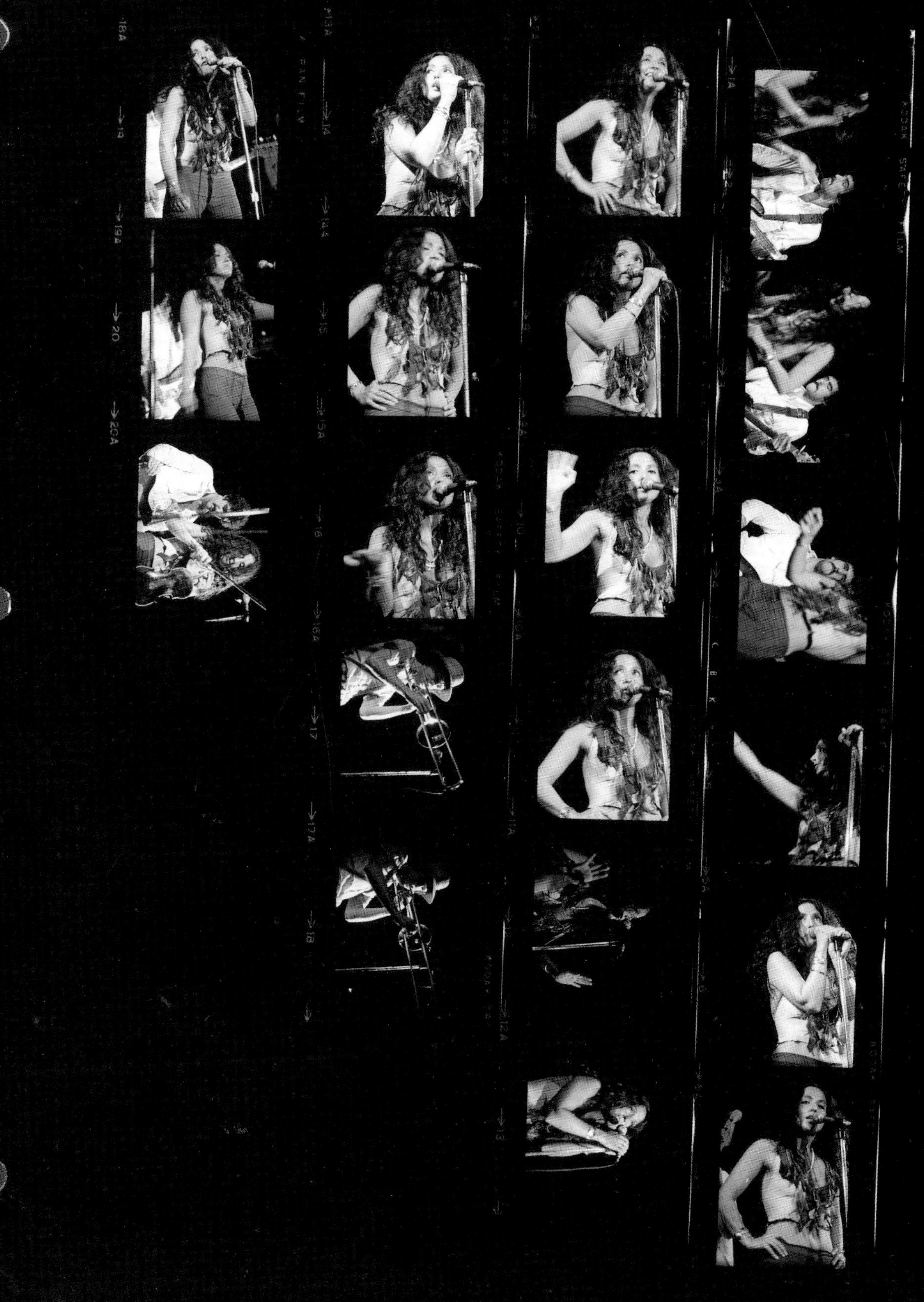

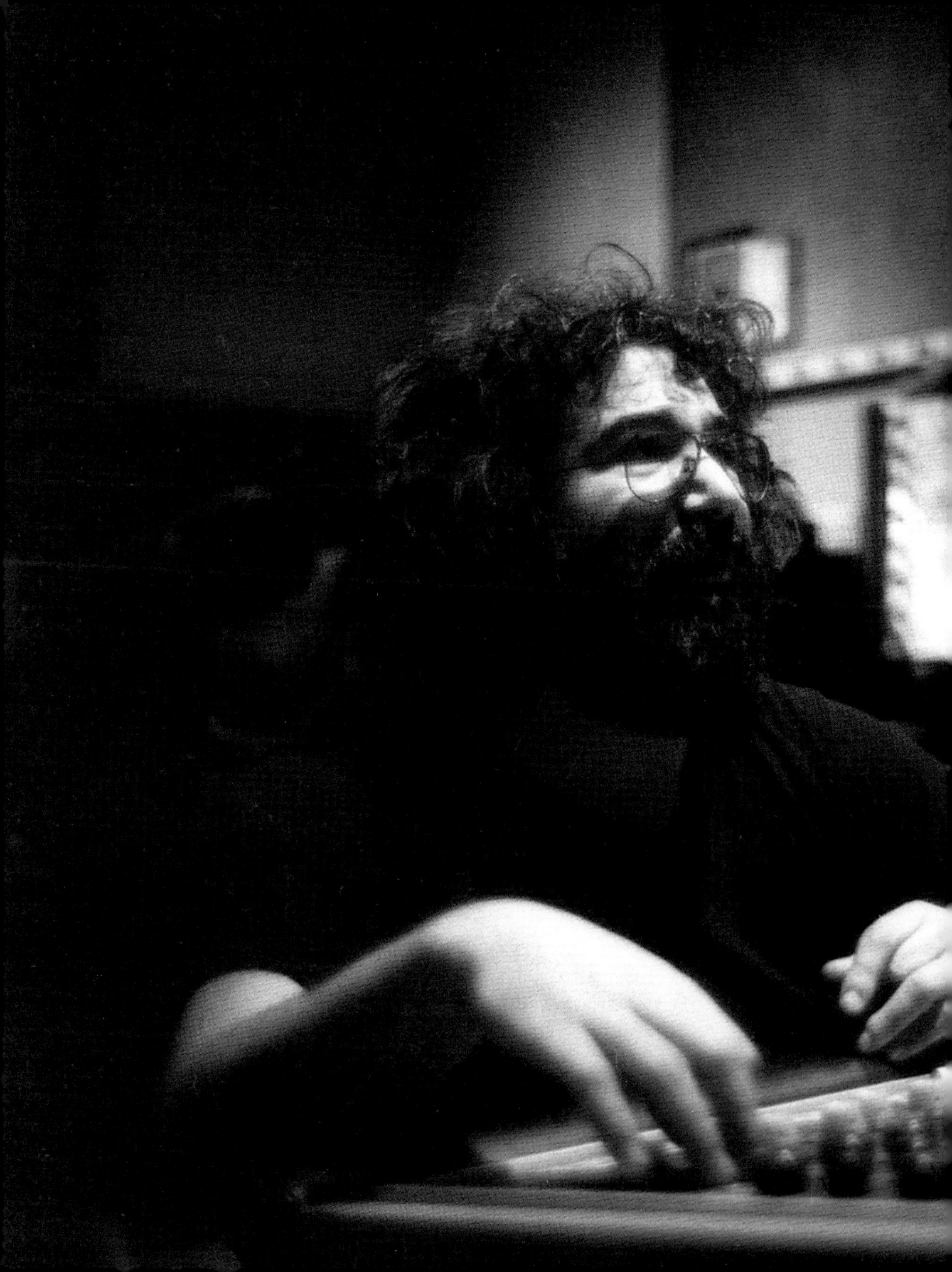

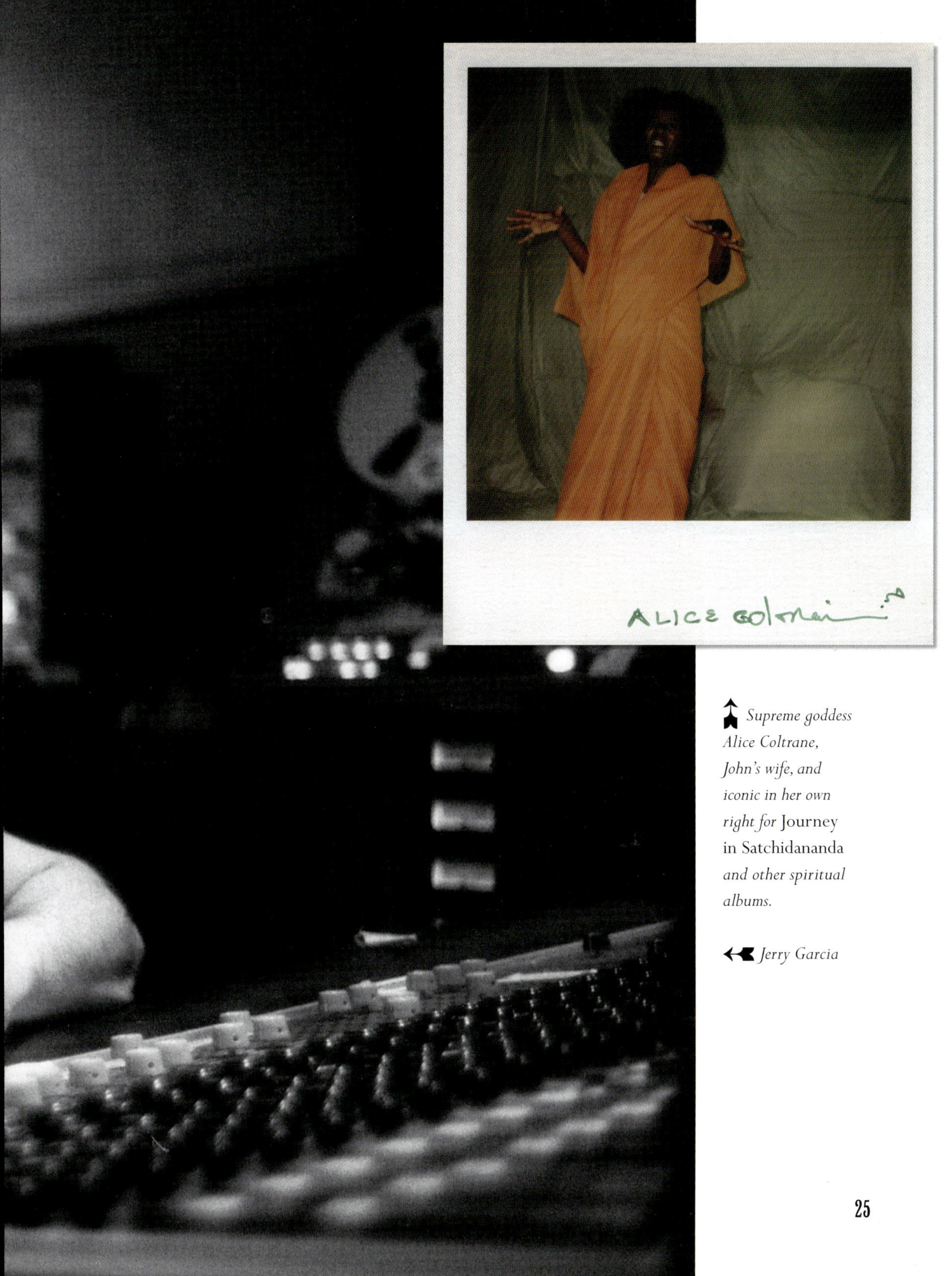

Supreme goddess Alice Coltrane, John's wife, and iconic in her own right for Journey in Satchidananda *and other spiritual albums.*

Jerry Garcia

Ginny Winn on
The Grateful Dead

On a "day in the life" shoot that Warner Brothers sent me to do, I spent a day with Mickey Hart at the Grateful Dead ranch in Novato. In the morning, we went down by the horses. There was a bottle of liquid Owsley acid. Each of us had a drop. I'm shooting for Warner Brothers and I have a brand-new camera that I've never seen a roll of film from. And I had dropped the brand-new camera in the airport. But I encouraged myself to trust the process and get the shot; I had a kind of heightened awareness all day. And I got the shot! The most fun part of the day at the ranch was getting to hear the "Live Europe" mixes in the studio that night. I was there in the studio, listening to them doing the mix, and thinking, "This is as good as it gets." Amazing sound! It was a really great time. Mellow and such incredible music.

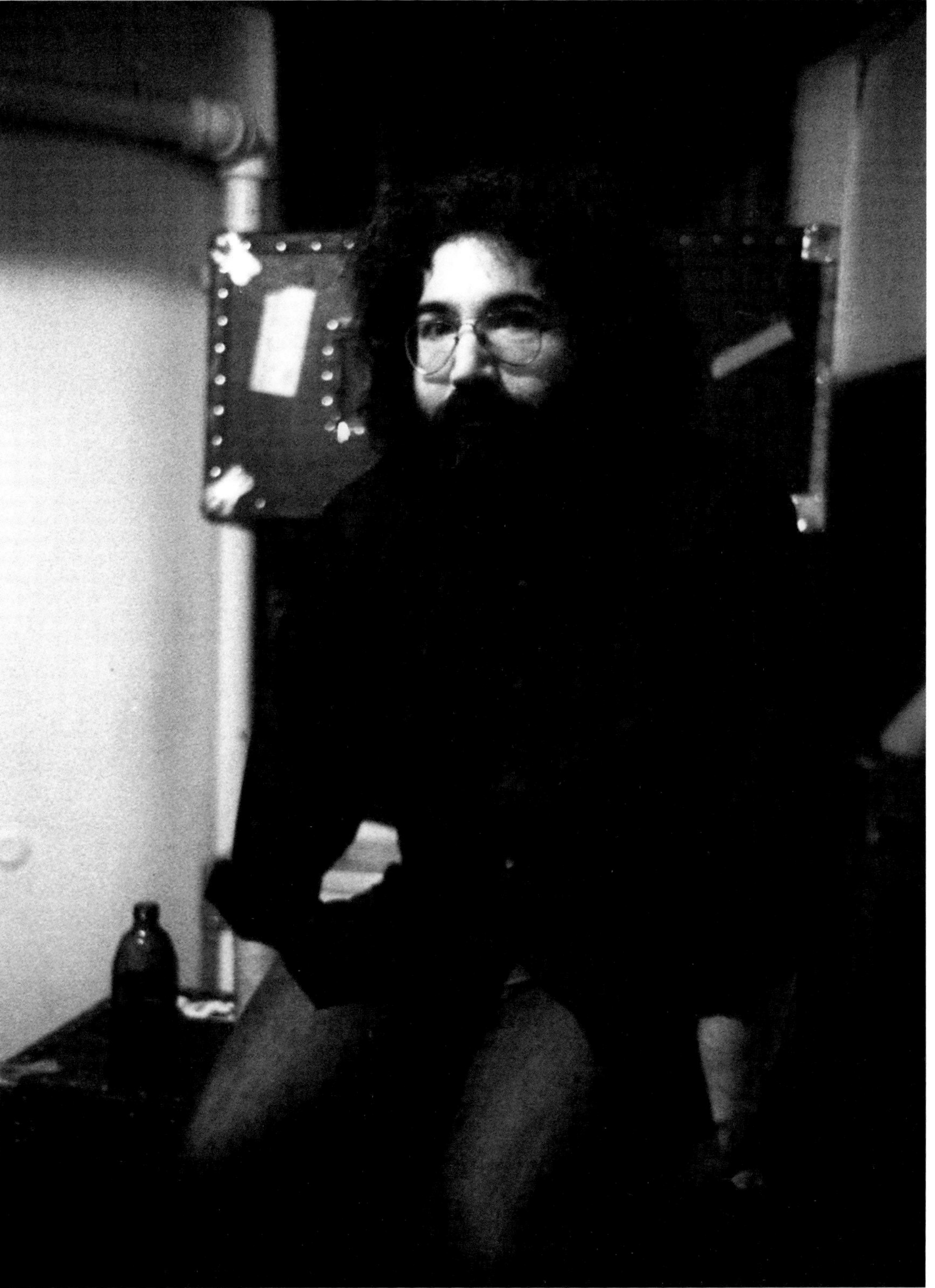

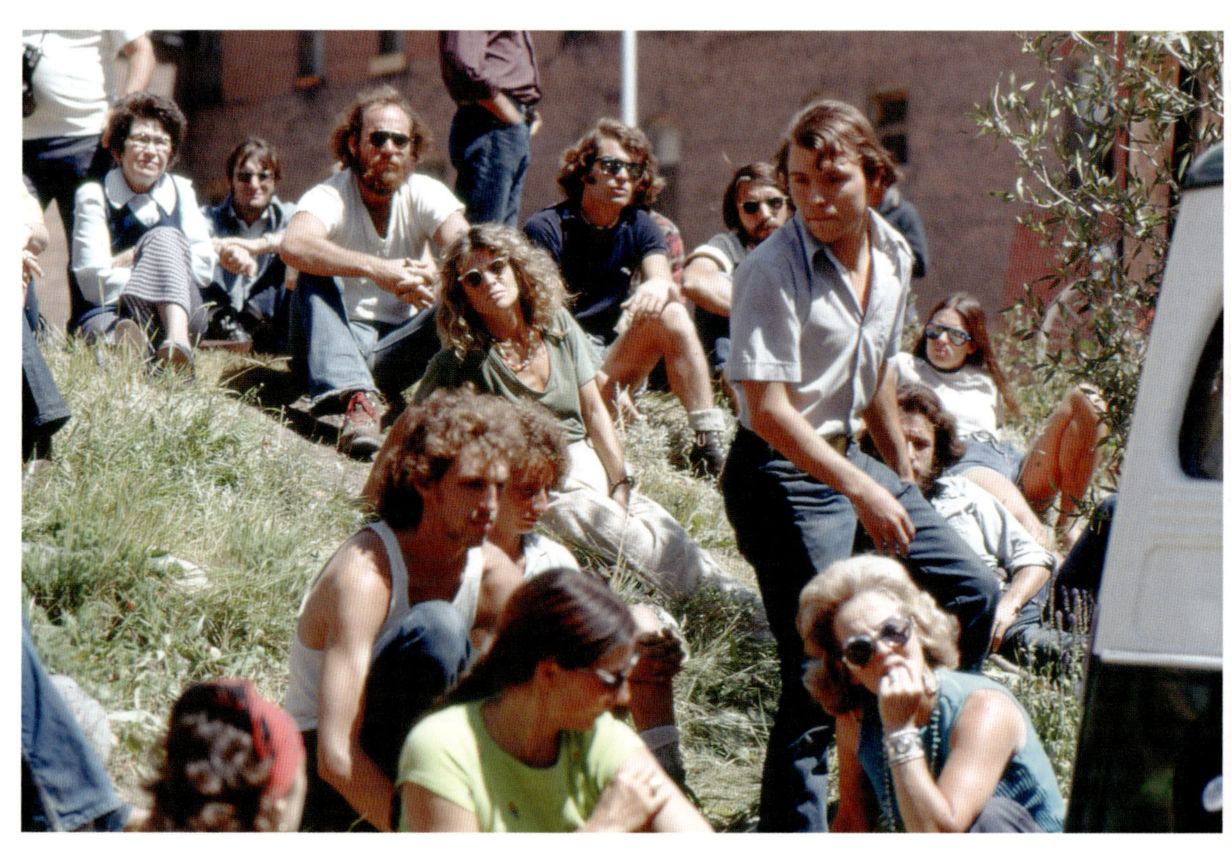

↑ *Telluride Festival with actress Julie Christie*

→ *Freebo of Bonnie Raitt's band*

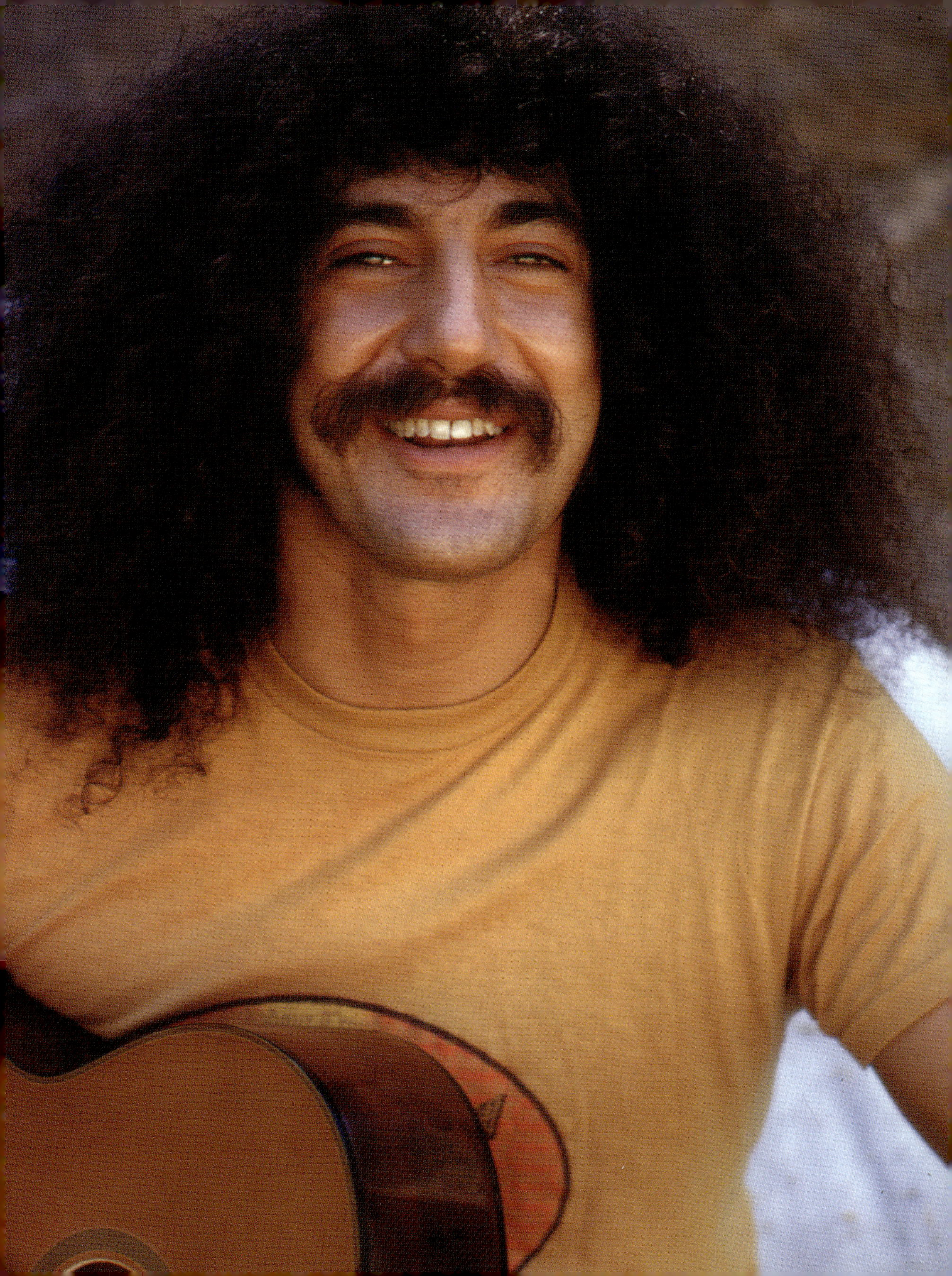

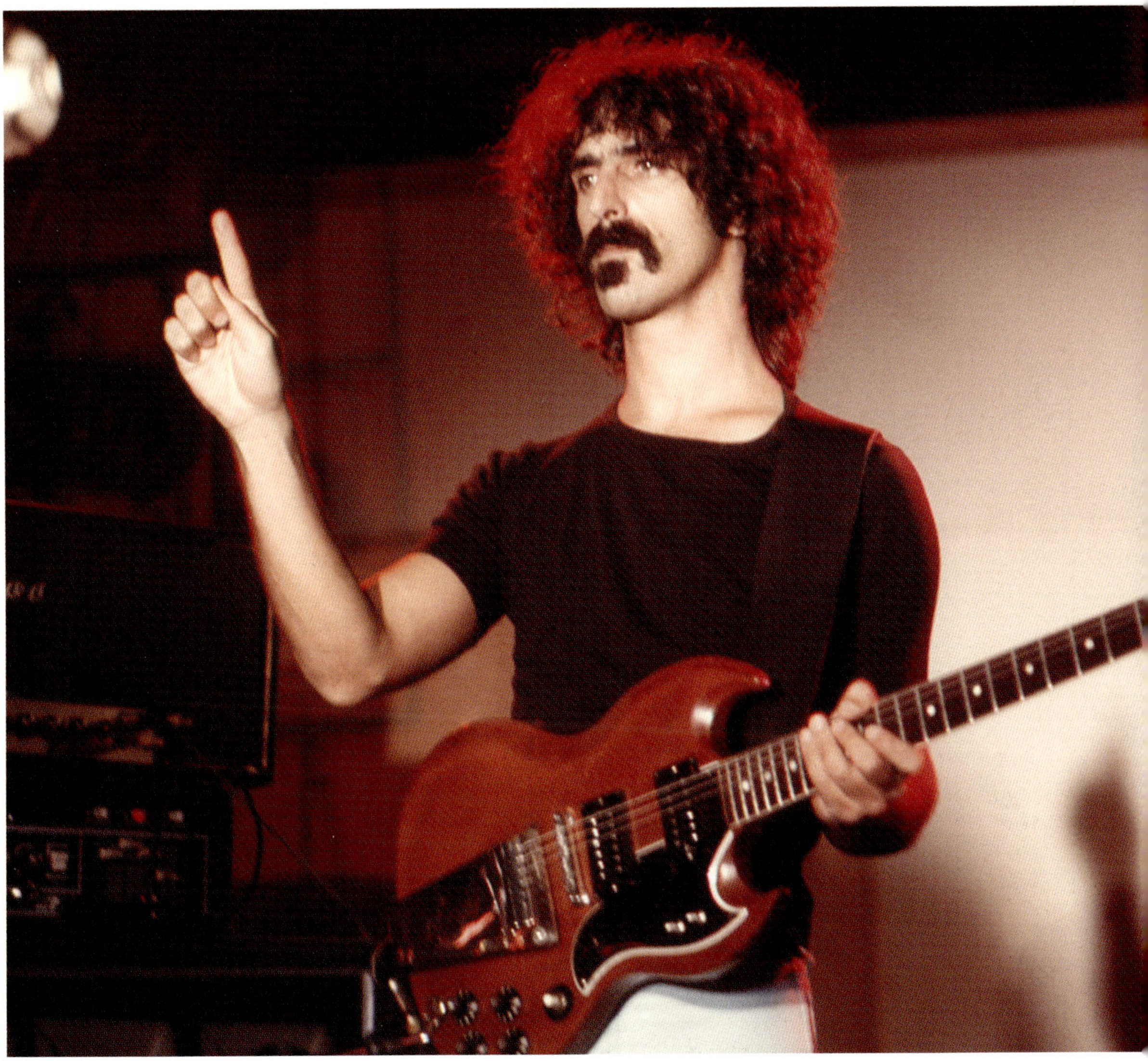

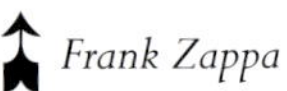

Frank Zappa

The late great Canadian singer/songwriter Kate McGarrigle of the sublime McGarrigle Sisters (along with Anna), who recorded several albums on Warner/Reprise produced by Joe Boyd.

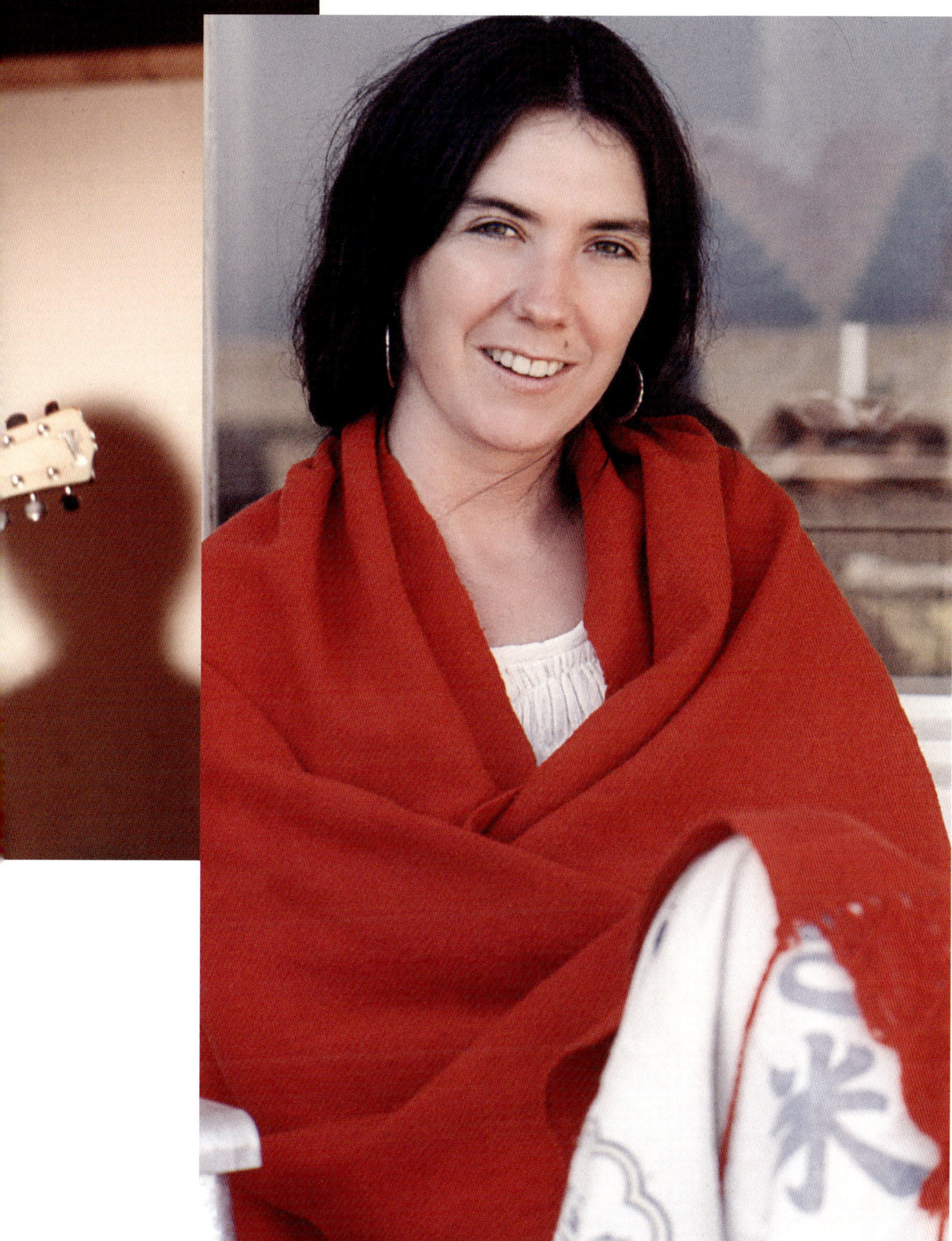

Ginny Winn on
Frank Zappa

Frank Zappa. He had a studio. He would direct me and have me climb around in the lighting and rafters. He would let me hang out. Normally, he didn't like people photographing, and he didn't like that whole kind of scene. But, to me, he was just nice and welcoming.

➔ *Frank Zappa*

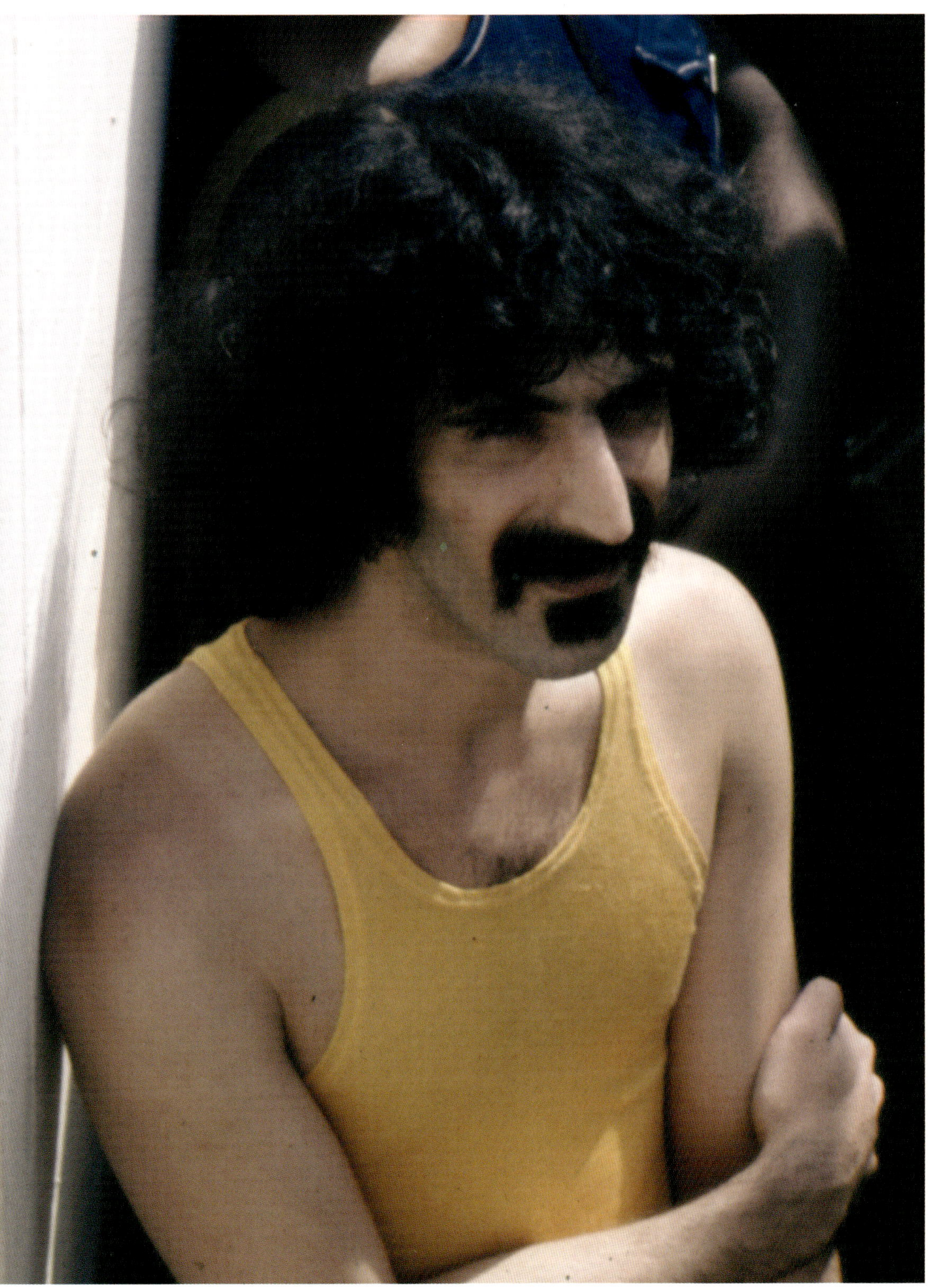

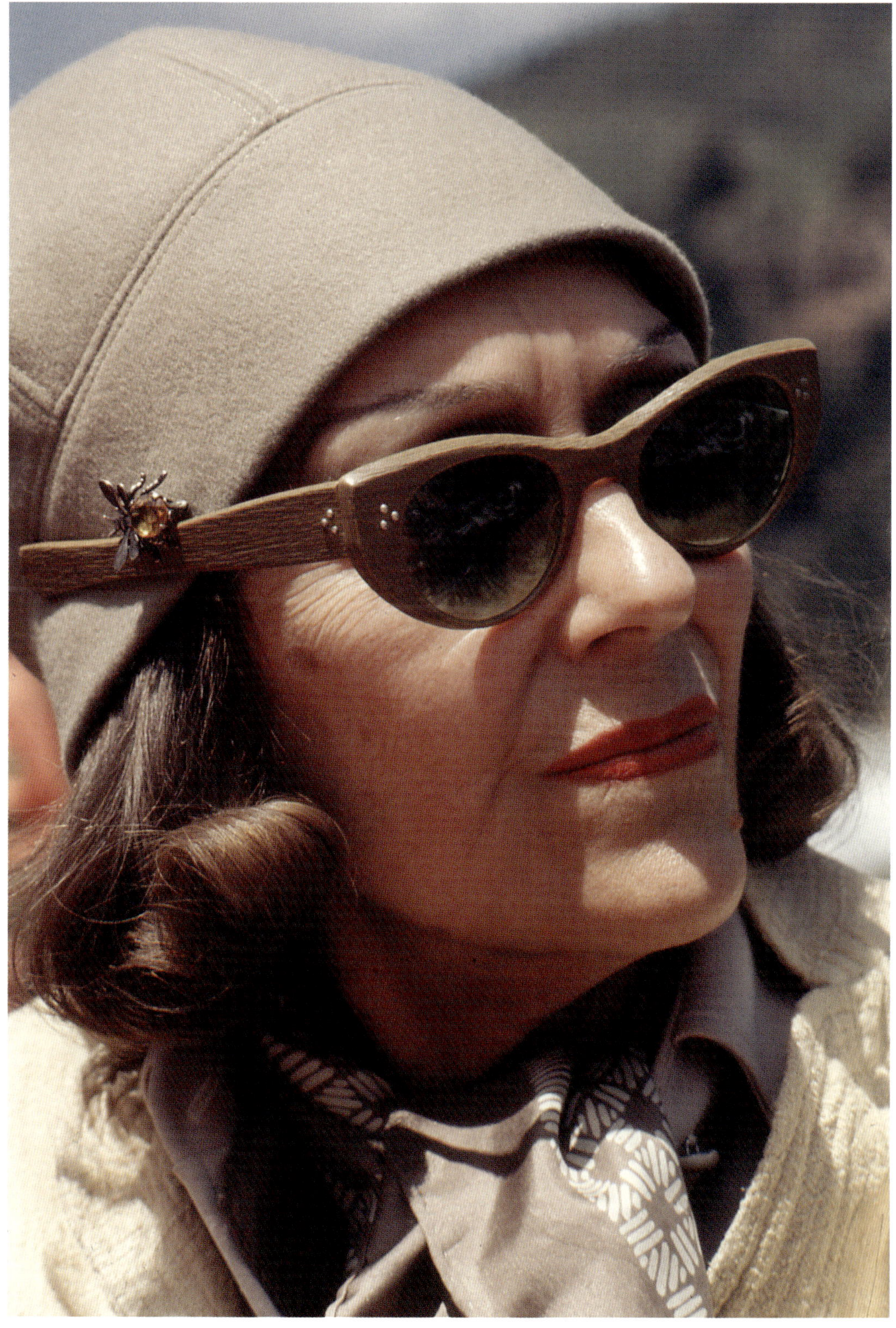

A Fly on the Wall

The Photography of Ginny Winn

Throughout the 1960s, the monolithic Warner/Reprise Records—despite working with such iconic musicians as Jimi Hendrix, The Kinks, Jethro Tull, and Neil Young—did not employ an in-house staff photographer. All of that changed in the early 1970s, when a young woman named Ginny Winn arrived on the scene. Clad in a hand-crocheted ensemble of her own design and bursting with unbridled enthusiasm for the work, Winn quickly made herself indispensable. In addition to taking photographs of artists, she created an array of visual press materials for Warner Brothers—films, press kits, sales slideshows and more—working in a male-dominated field with a cheerful pluck and singular vision. "As a photographer, you get to be like a fly on the wall," Winn remembers. "And since I was a staff photographer at Warner, they would call me in to shoot meetings and it was fun. I remember thinking, 'This is cool. I get to hear this stuff that no one's hearing and see the stuff no one else is seeing.'"

Winn's uniquely intimate documentation of now legendary artists was a result of her developing close and lasting relationships with many of the Warner/Reprise roster. Winn was an admirer, but not a groupie; prolific, but not part of the "hungry for blood" press corps. Instead, she was a collaborator, creating aesthetic templates and a visual look and feel for some of the most iconic artists of the time. As a result, she gained special access; for instance, photographing Captain Beefheart at his Northern California home, or shooting countless photos with Gram Parsons, only a handful of which have ever been seen.

Her archives also house rarely seen photos of the Grateful Dead in the studio, of the Beach Boys during their bearded hippy phase—as well as the eclectic John Cale, a vibrant Bob Marley, chanteuse Maria Muldaur, and the legendary Van Morrison. Each artist was captured on film during a brief but golden era, a moment when the Warner/Reprise catalog represented the cream of the West Coast counterculture music scene.

Later in the 1970s, Winn left Warner Brothers to work alongside photographer Norman Seeff at his studio—a position that gave her direct access to a heady mix of both rock icons and silver-screen idols. "It was a totally different part of what I call the 'Los Angeles Experience' because it was

Actress Gloria Swanson

more of this glamorous thing, with a lot of movie stars, some of the biggest music stars coming through. So that environment at Seeff's was a very different environment than Warner's." Here, Winn relied on her handy Polaroid to capture relaxed, informal moments with everyone from Joni Mitchell to James Taylor, Gloria Swanson to Penelope Spheeris to Jodie Foster.

It's safe to say no other photographer has captured this era with such cheerful intimacy, Winn's camera documenting the exact moment when the West Coast counterculture collided with glistening "Walk of Fame" glamor. Her photographs record a fascinating narrative of 1970s Los Angeles, meshing the stories of two very different sides of both the city and the industries that fuel it.

Winn retired her camera in the 1980s, to become a family therapist, and her photos have remained largely unpublished and unseen for the last 40 years. "I'm just so grateful I have these memories and these connections, all through my photos," she explains. "When you look at these images, you reconnect with the people in them. With photography, you're keeping your subjects alive in some way, capturing a moment in time that lives on—forever."

—Pat Thomas & Jessica Hundley with Ginny Winn, Los Angeles, California, 2023

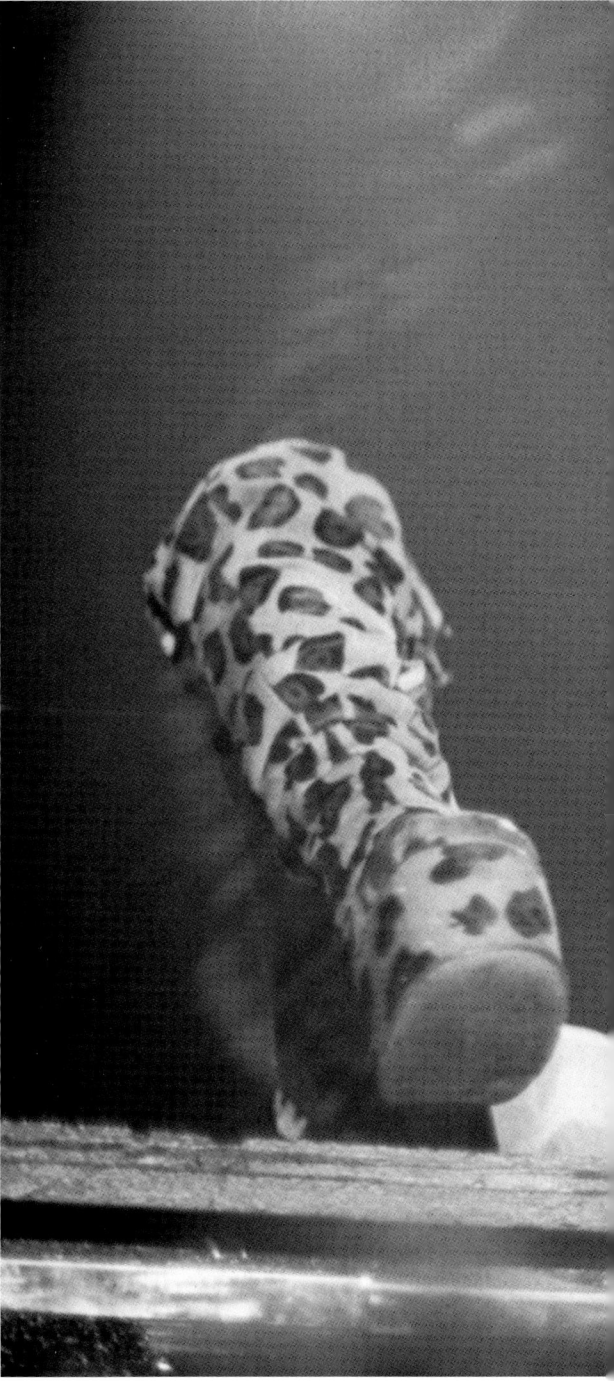

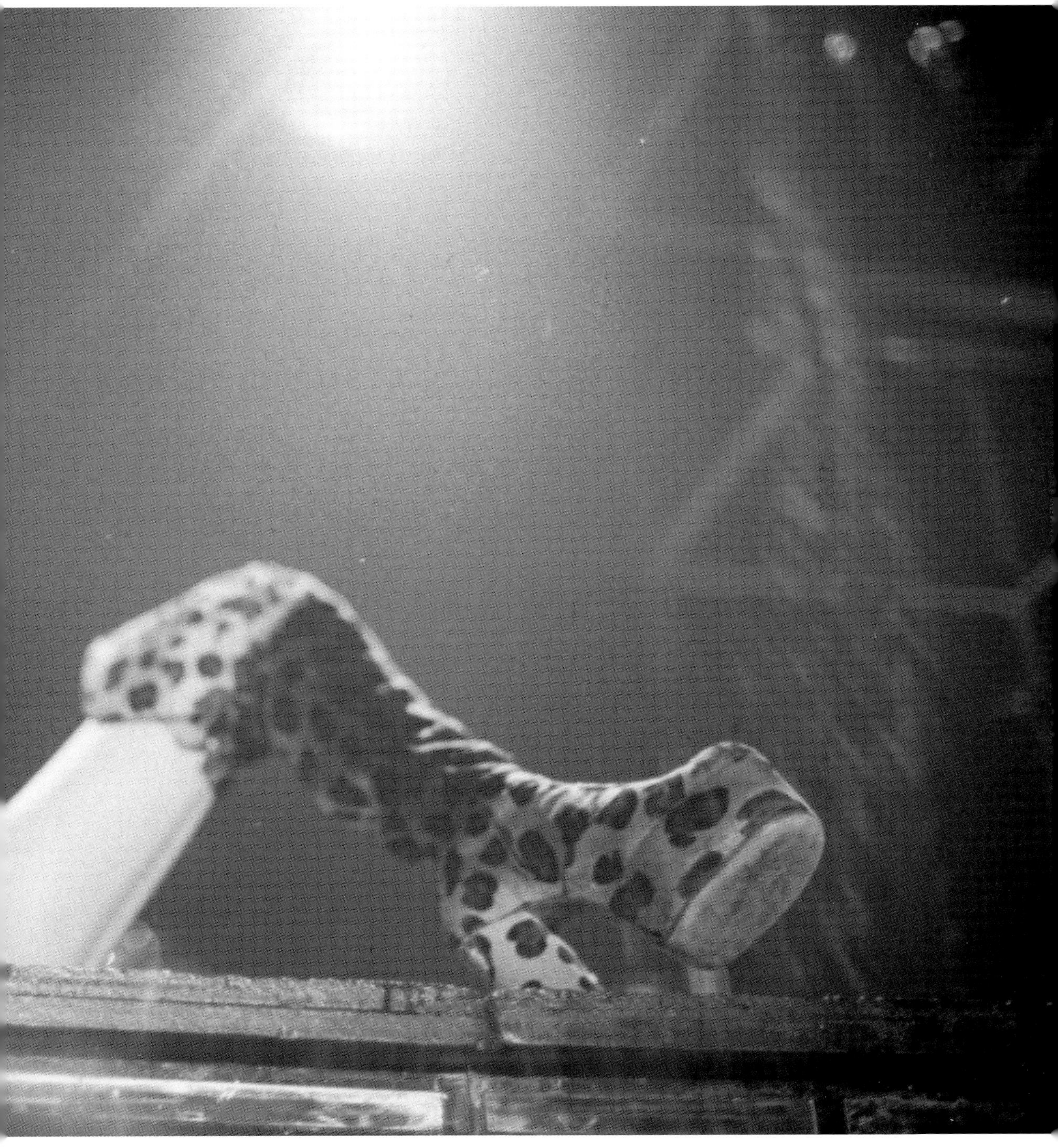

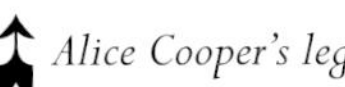
Alice Cooper's legs

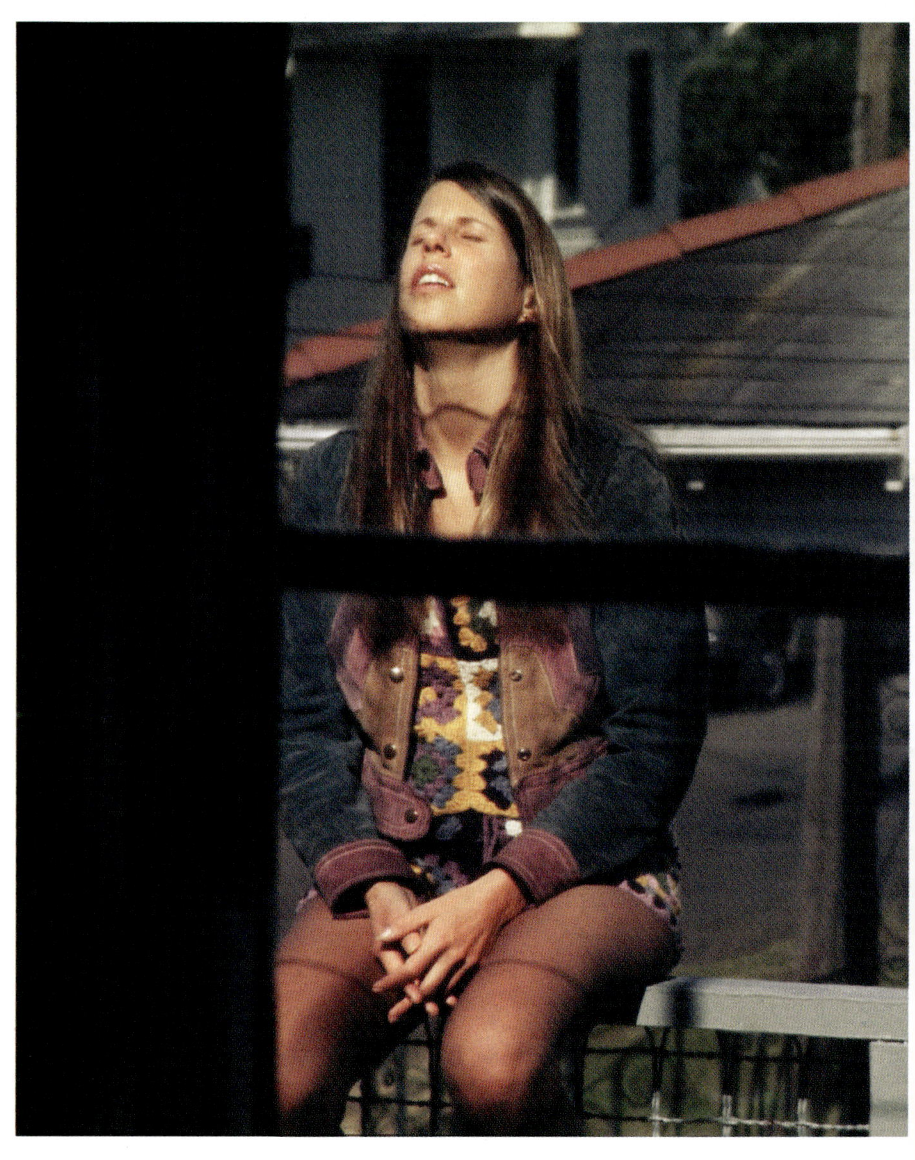

Ginny basking in the sun, New Orleans, late 1960s

The Maxayn Lewis Group

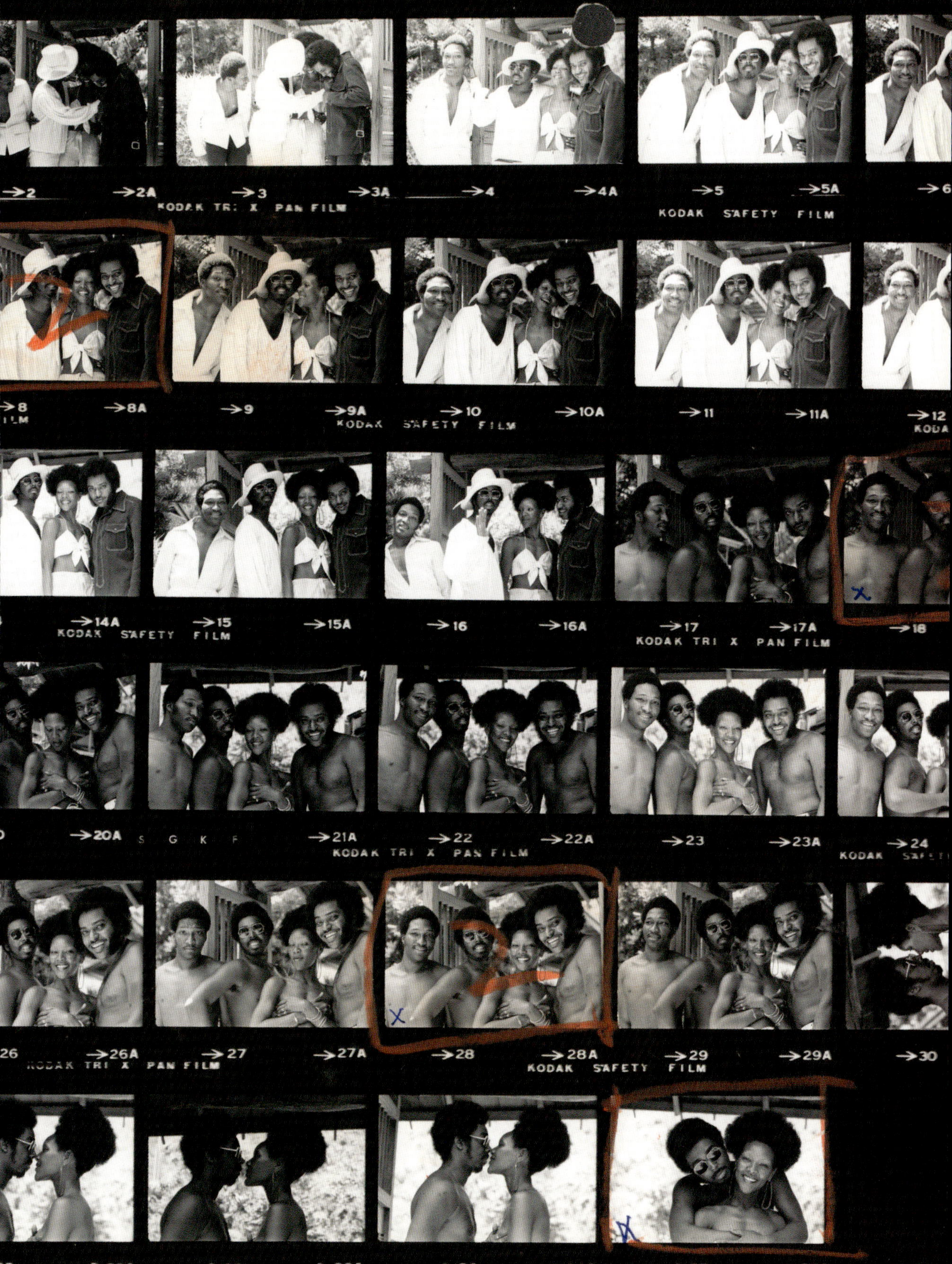

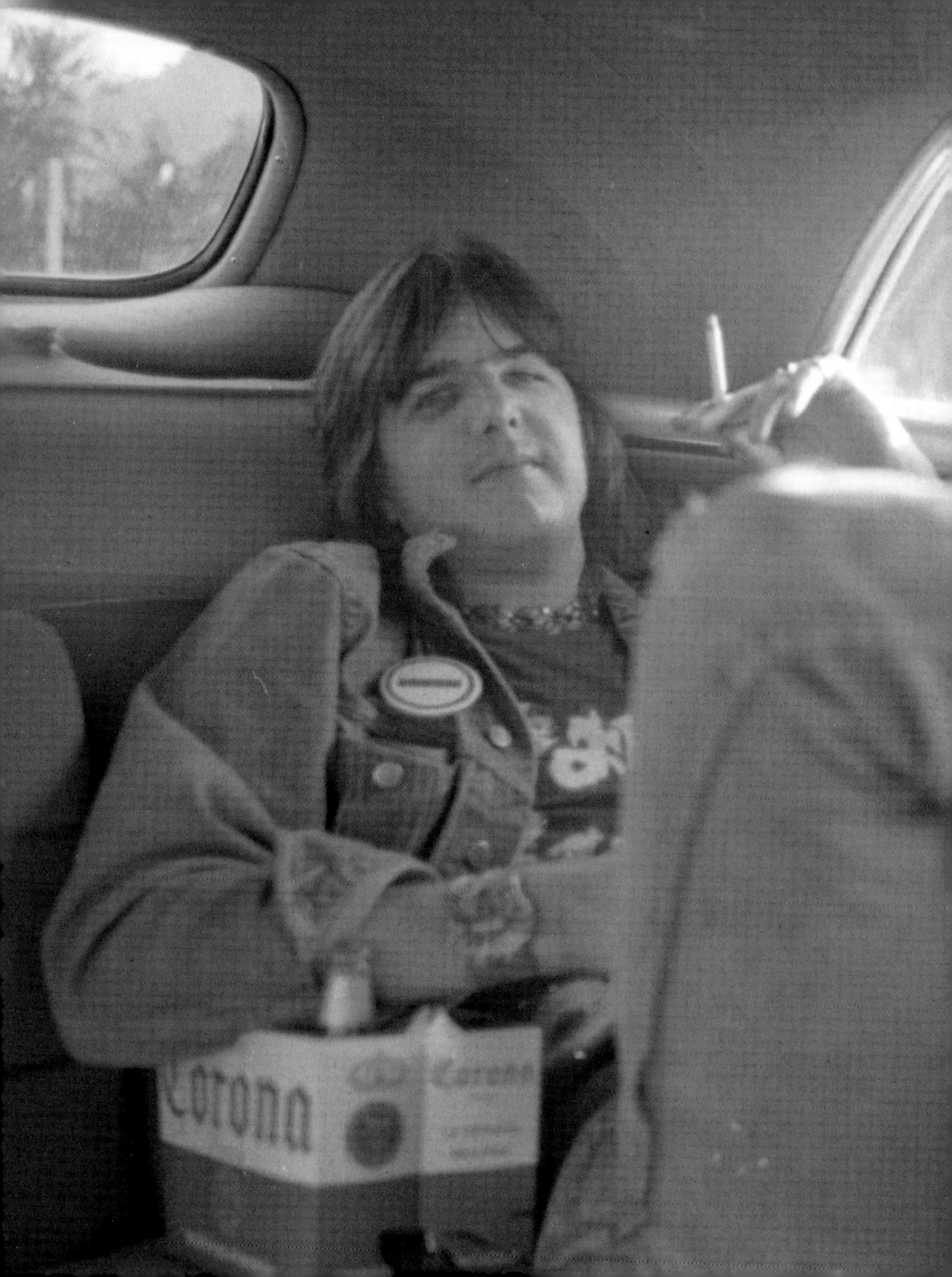
Corona

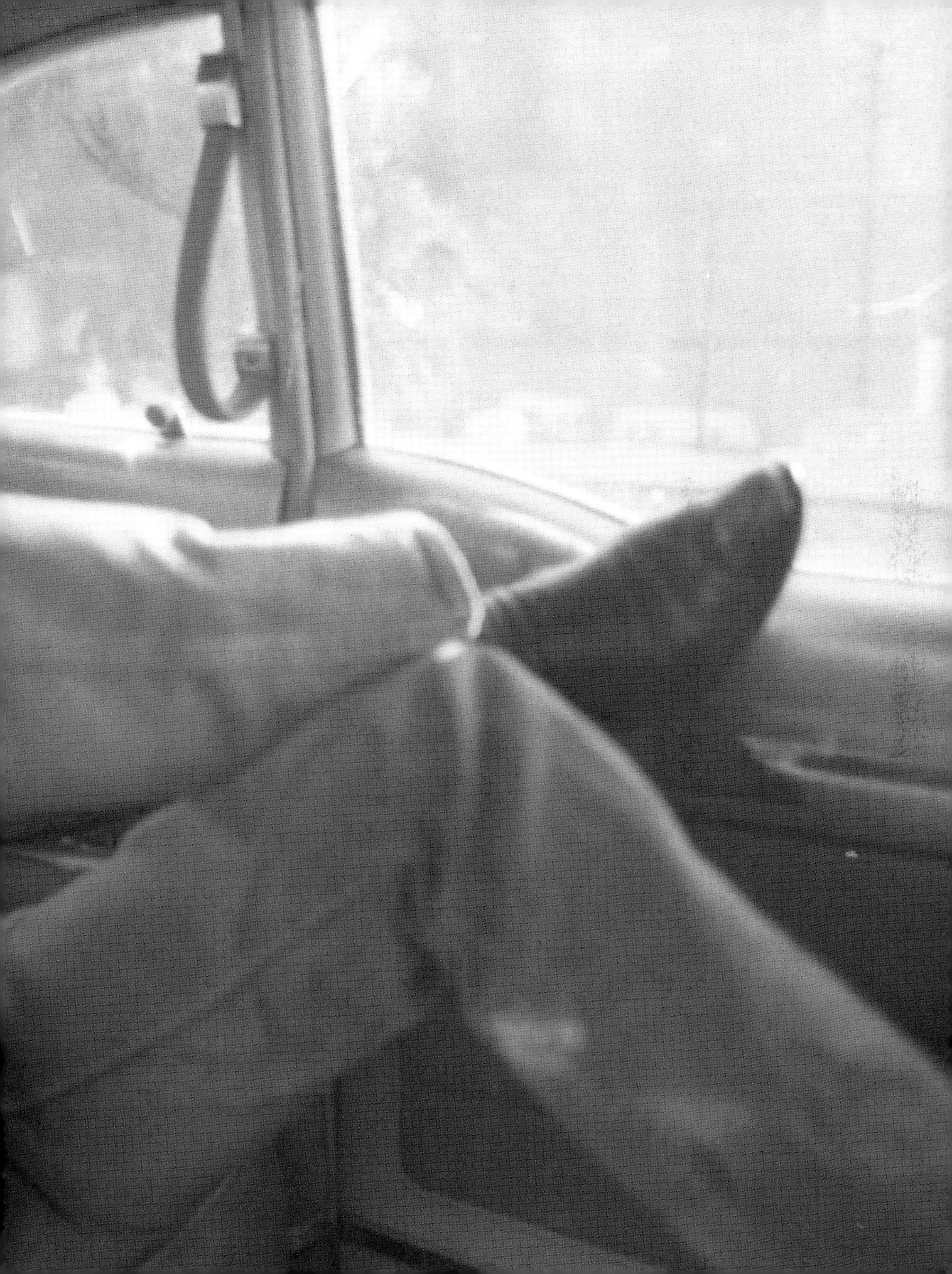

Ginny Winn on Gram Parsons

Gram Parsons, I can't remember how I first met him. But I remember being at his house and playing basketball. When I was in high school and starting college, my first true love was basketball. Gram was always trying to give me extra points because I'm left-handed. He thought that I should have a handicap point. I didn't! He was very sweet when we were together. I shot a lot of pictures of him. He was special. I felt a connection with the calm, positive, good side of him, when we were shooting photos. There was a calm that would happen, where you're just sitting shooting and you're comfortable. The camera becomes unintrusive. There is a trust.

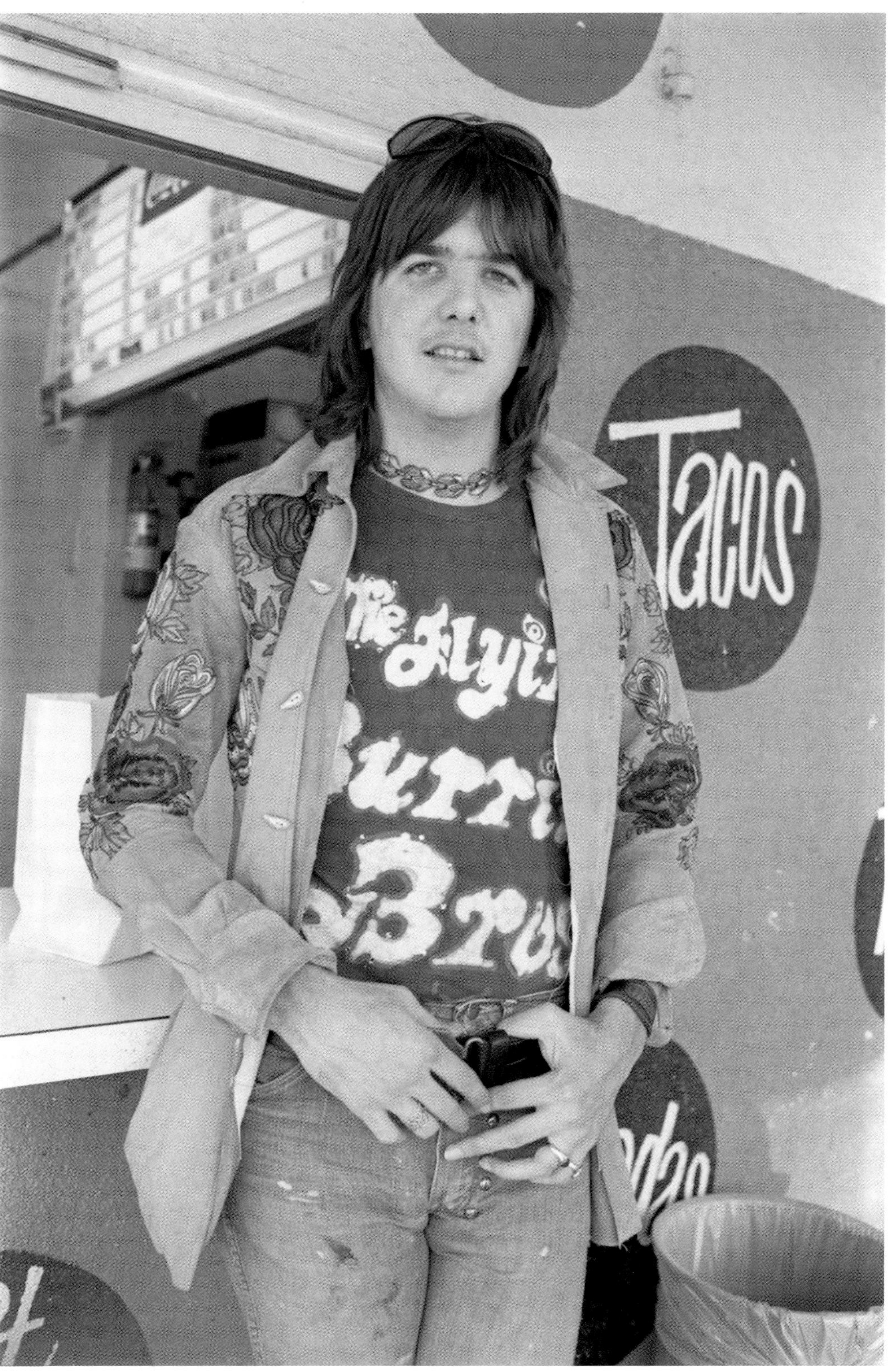
Tacos

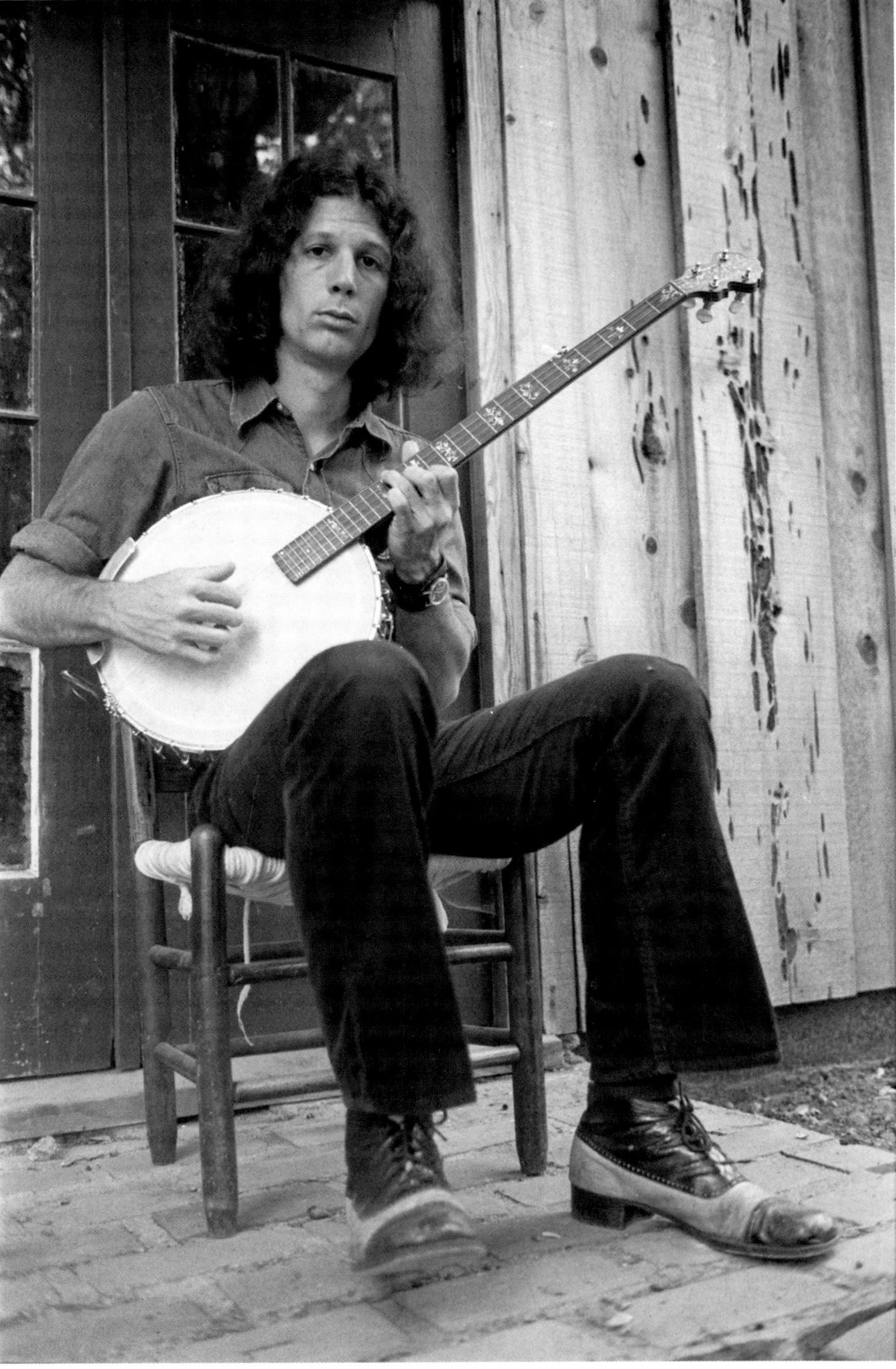

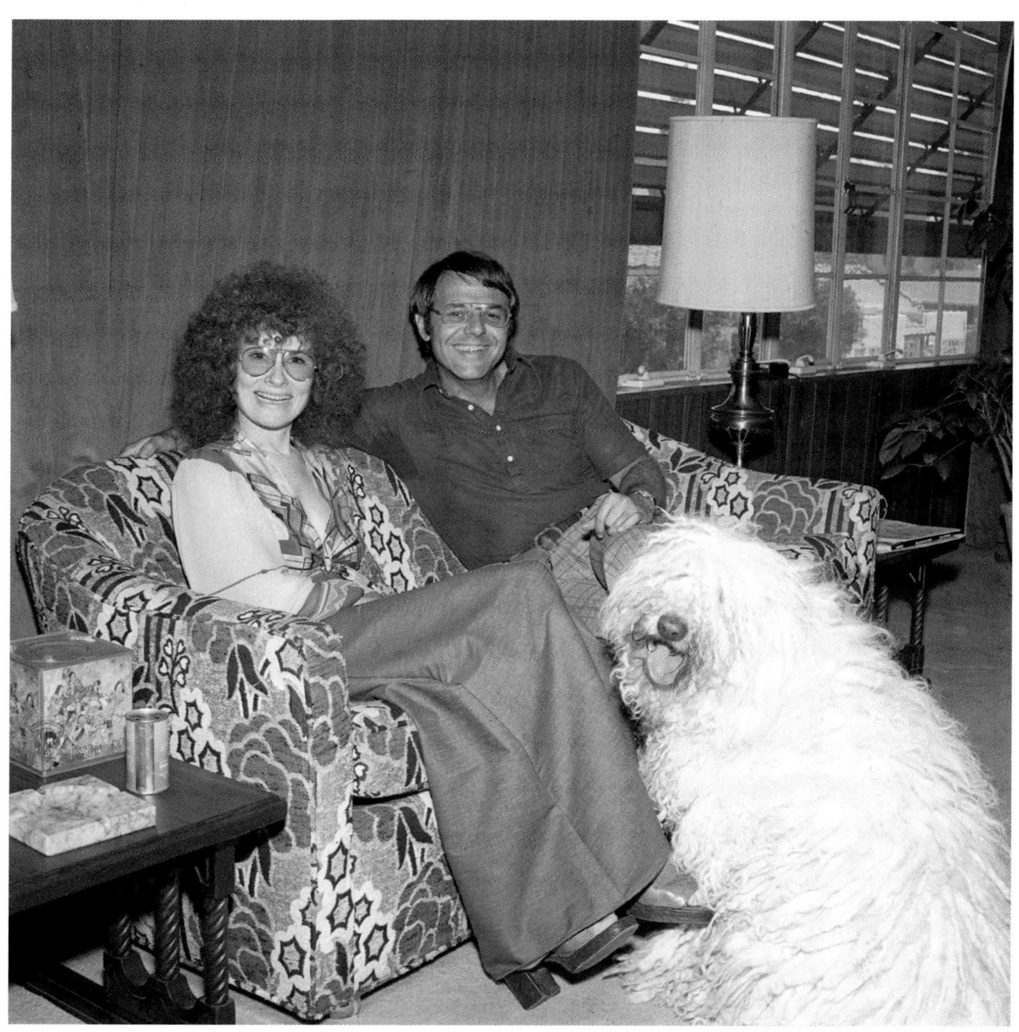

Folk/Country/ Bluegrass musician John Hartford, composer of "Gentle on My Mind" which was turned into a massively popular song by Glen Campbell.

Singer-songwriter Dory Previn with record executive Joe Smith of Warner/Reprise. Ideally, Dory's 1970s albums should be discussed as compelling masterpieces in the same breath as those of Judee Sill, Joni Mitchell, and Tim Buckley.

"When I was young, I had a little Brownie camera, and I was just very fascinated by it. I can still remember that first Brownie camera. It was so cool. It was what made me interested in photography initially—this very easy-to-use point and shoot, a comfortable way to communicate, to receive and give back."

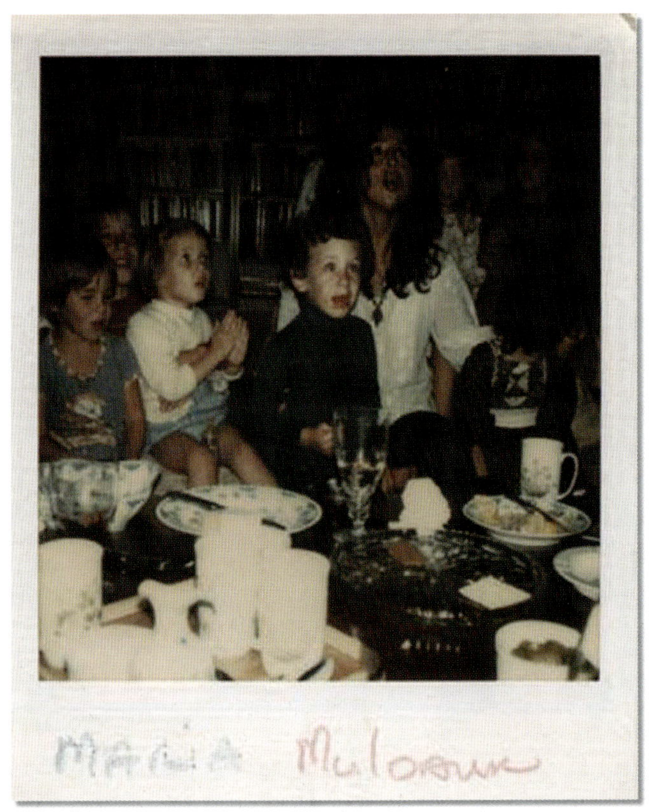

Maria Muldaur

Maria Muldaur plus Old & In the Way with fiddler Richard Greene

Tim Buckley

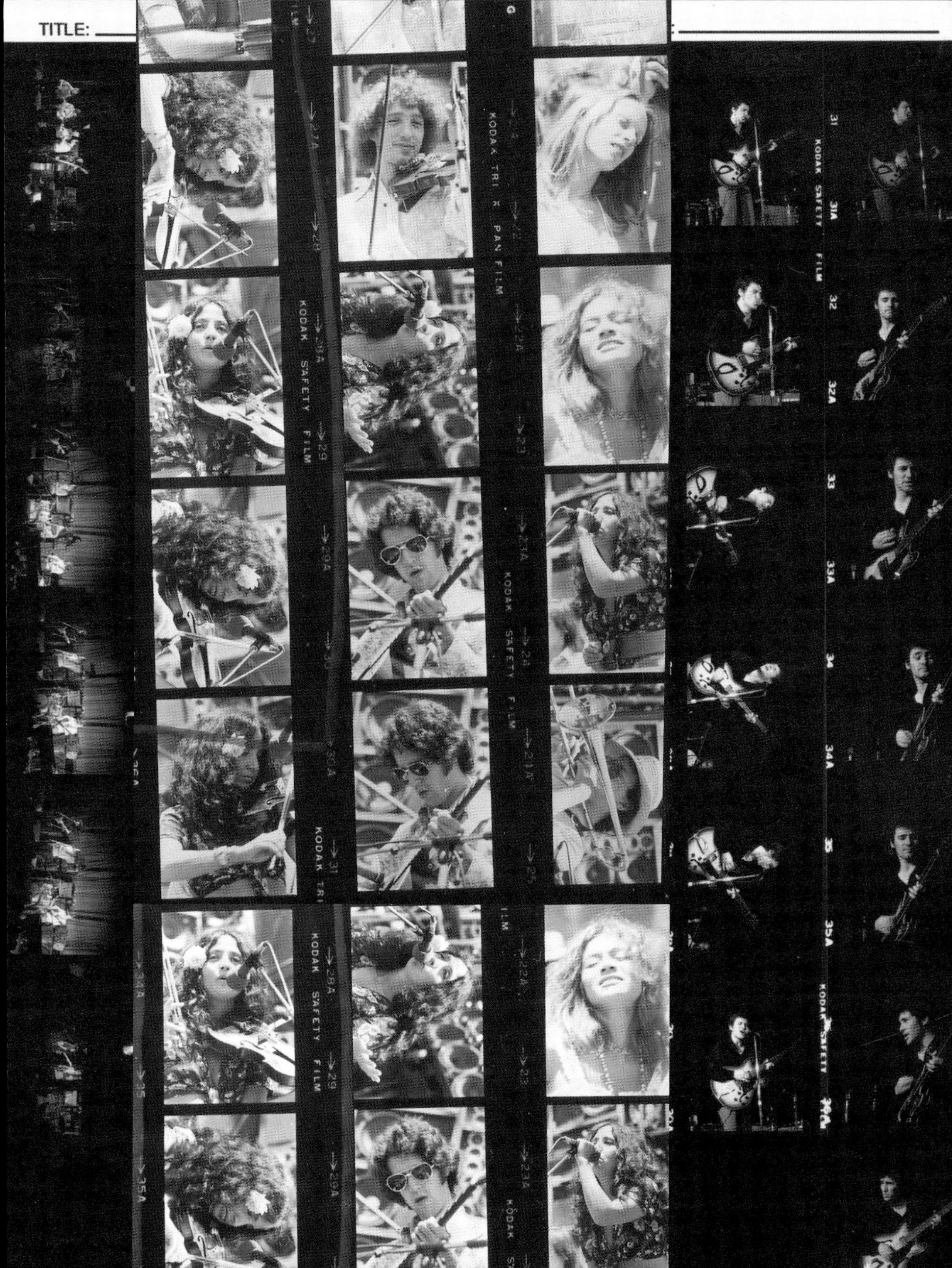
TITLE:
KODAK TRI X PAN FILM
KODAK SAFETY FILM

Al Green

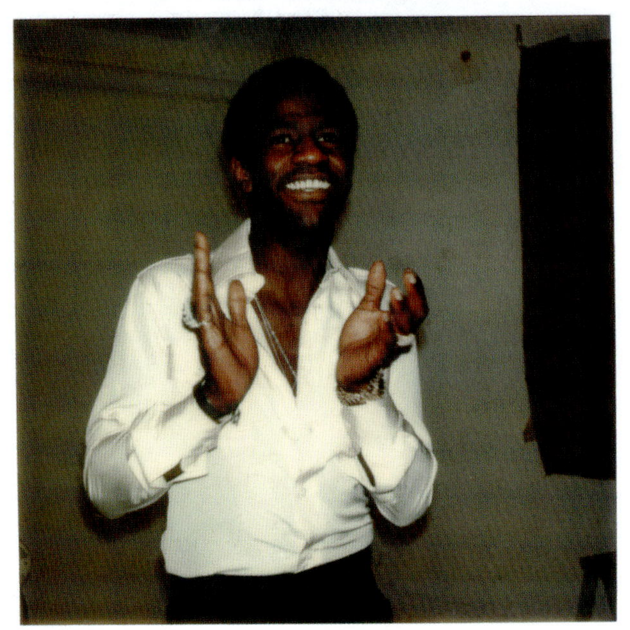

Melissa Manchest

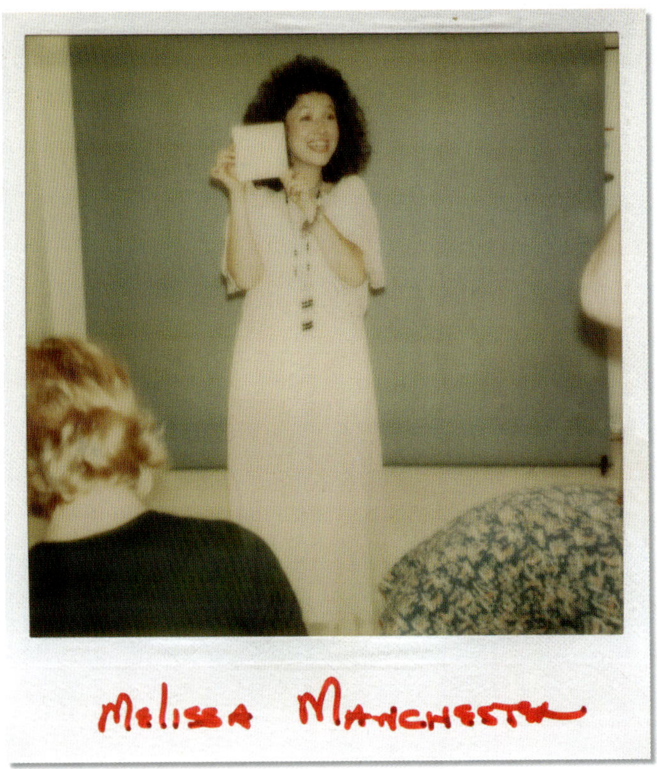

➤➤ *Joni Mitchell with drummer/partner John Guerin*

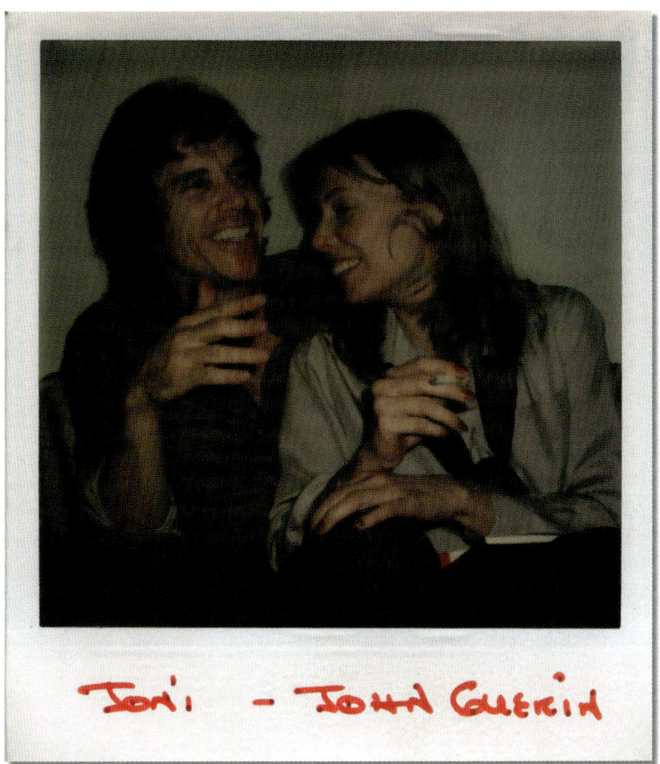

➤➤ *Jodie Foster*

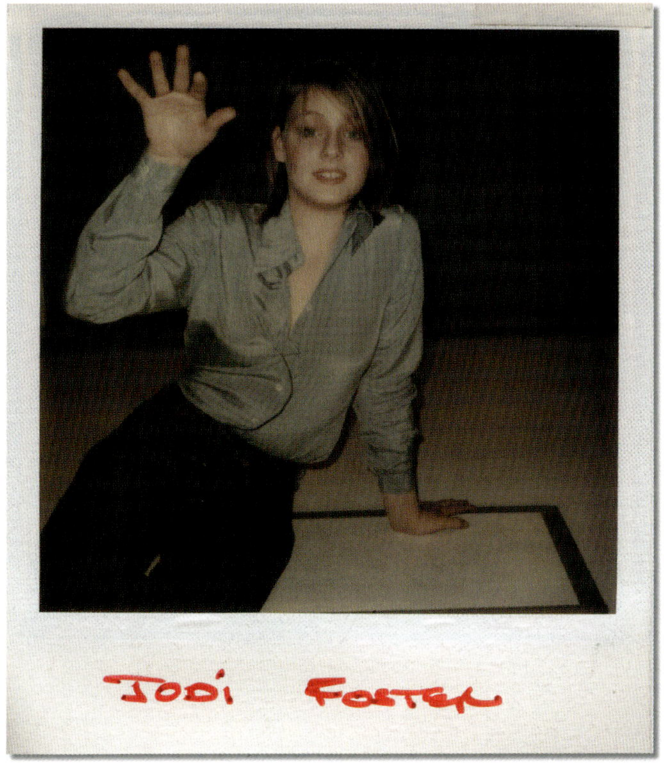

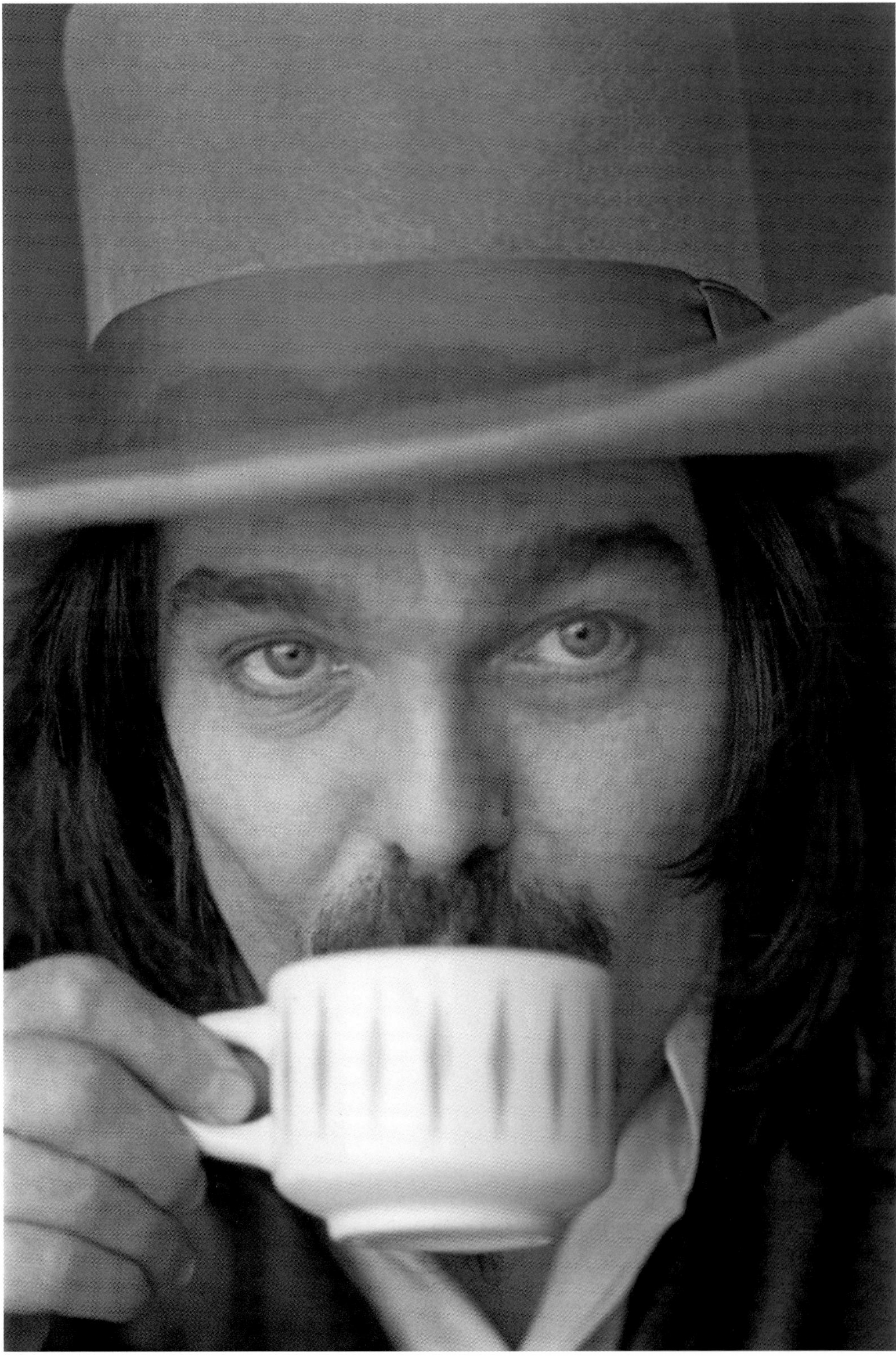

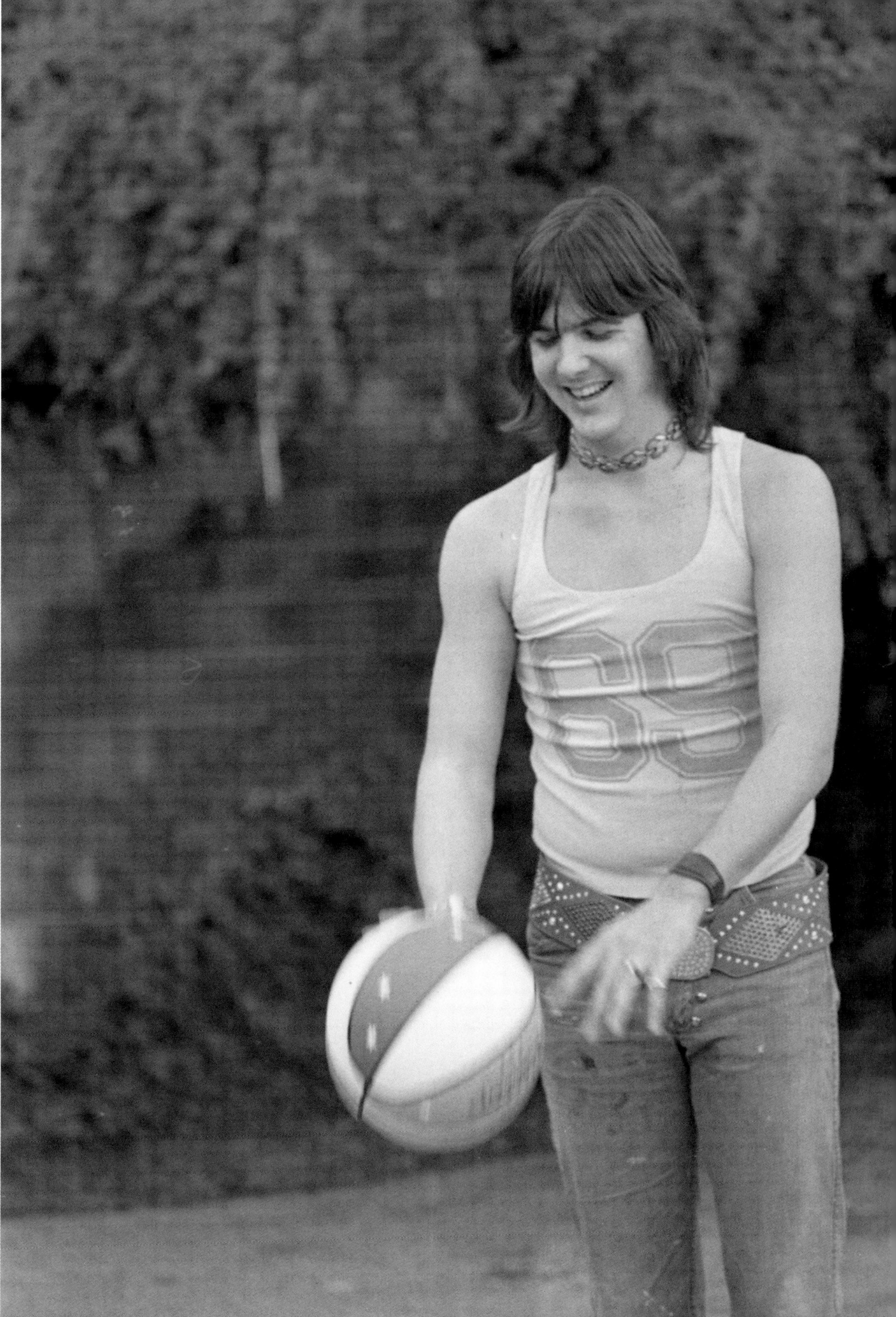

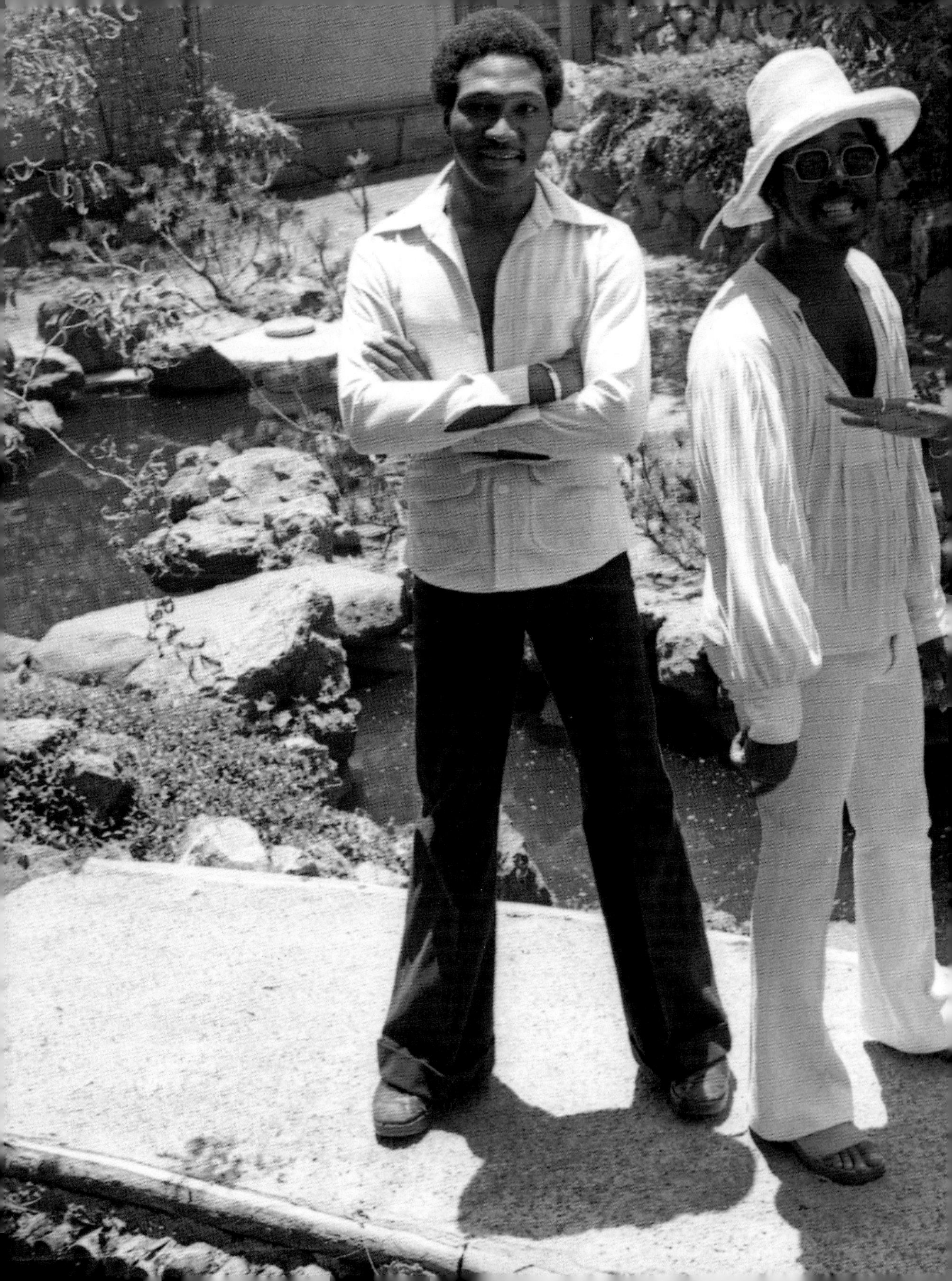

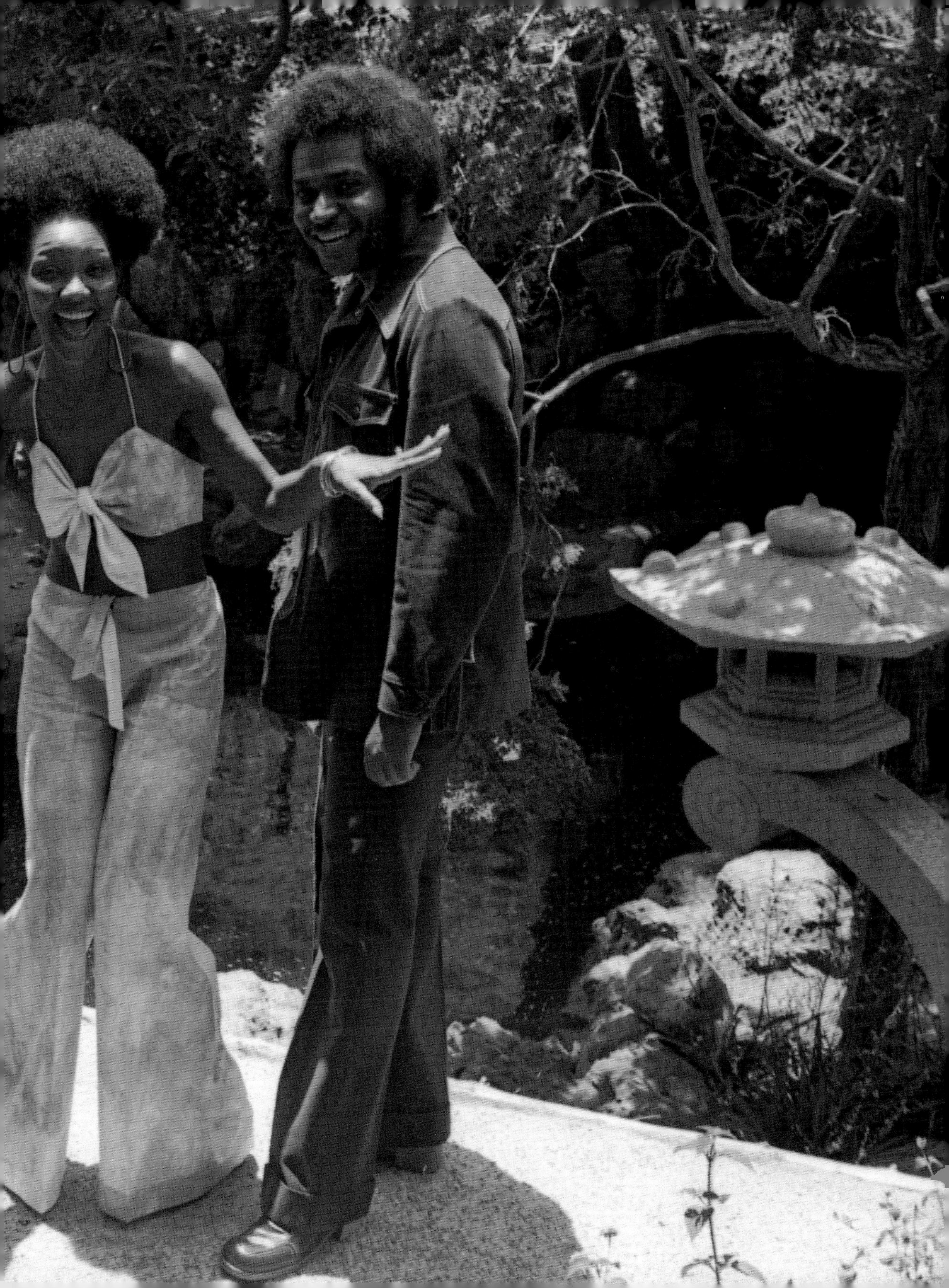

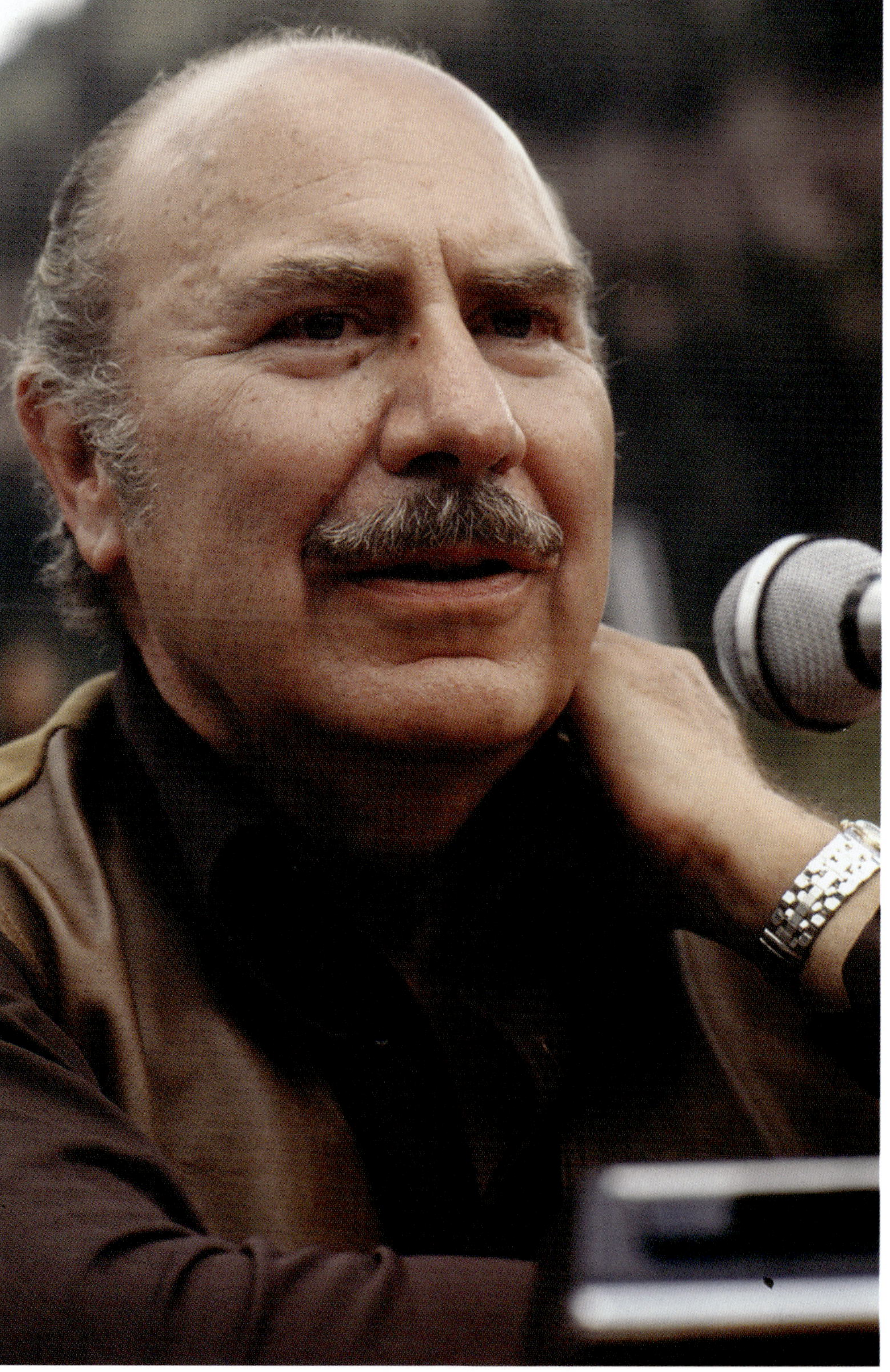

(pg 50)
Captain Beefheart

(pg 51)
Gram Parsons

(pg 52–53)
The Maxayn Group with Emilio Thomas, Andre Lewis, Maxayn Lewis, and Hank Redd. They released 3 albums on Capricorn Records, which were distributed through Warner / Reprise.

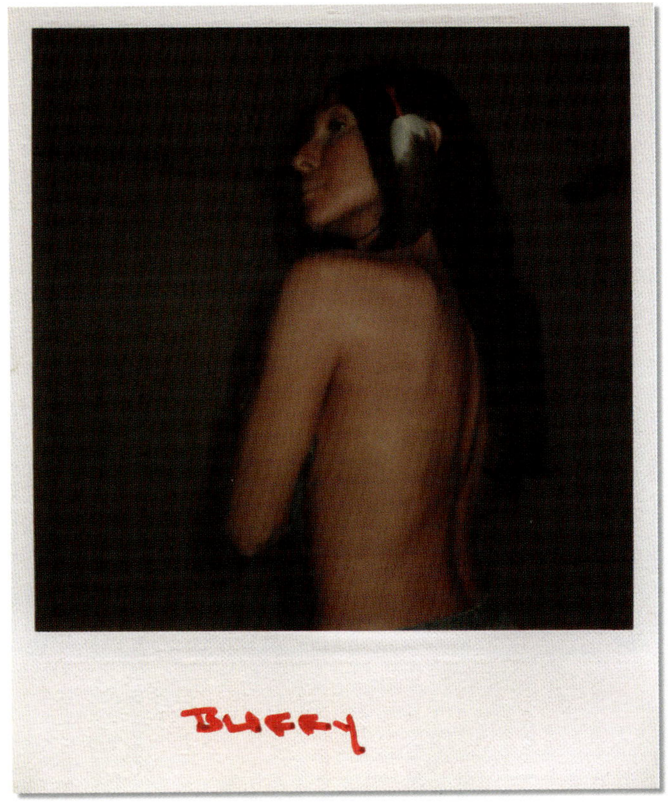

James Card—film preservationist who established the motion picture collection at the George Eastman House in Rochester, NY, a massive archive of moving images.

Buffy St. Marie, Indigenous Canadian singer / songwriter and composer of "Universal Soldier," "Cod'ine," "Until It's Time for You to Go," and many others. A strong performer in her own right, Buffy has had her songs sung by the likes of Donovan and Quicksilver Messenger Service. At one point, she was married to the infamous producer / arranger / musician Jack Nitzsche.

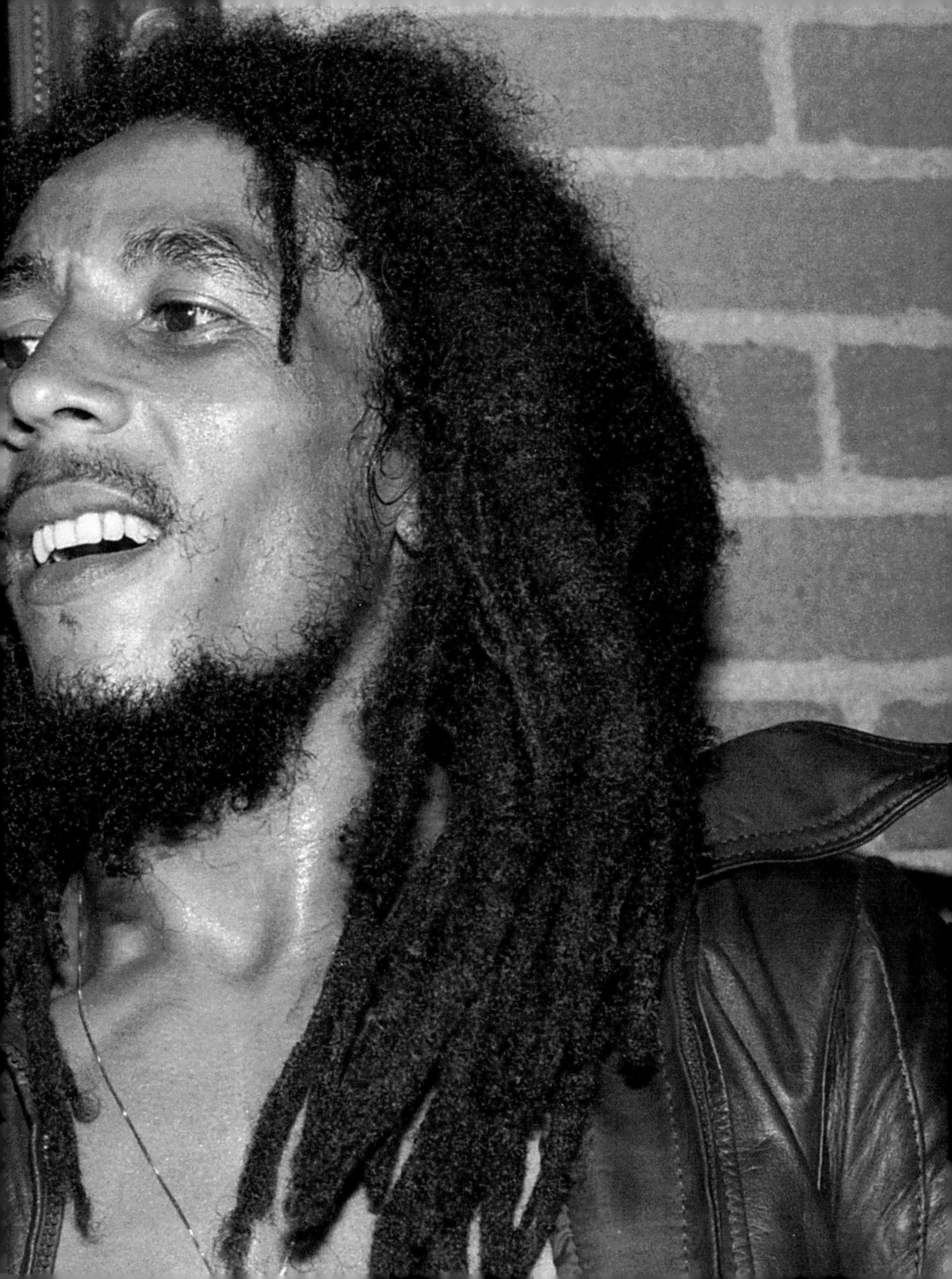

(pg. 56–57) Bob Marley with wife Rita Marley at Rita's birthday party in Beverly Hills

Bob Marley

Ginny Winn on **Bob Marley**

I will always remember that night. I'll always remember Bob Marley saying, "Ginny, do you mind taking this picture? No (to the other photographers), only Ginny." I remember how good that felt, and making that connection. And then to have the little reverberations—you get an email asking for a shot, and you have the shot. The pictures have a life of their own and they end up here and there. You end up broadening the connections with the people you've photographed.

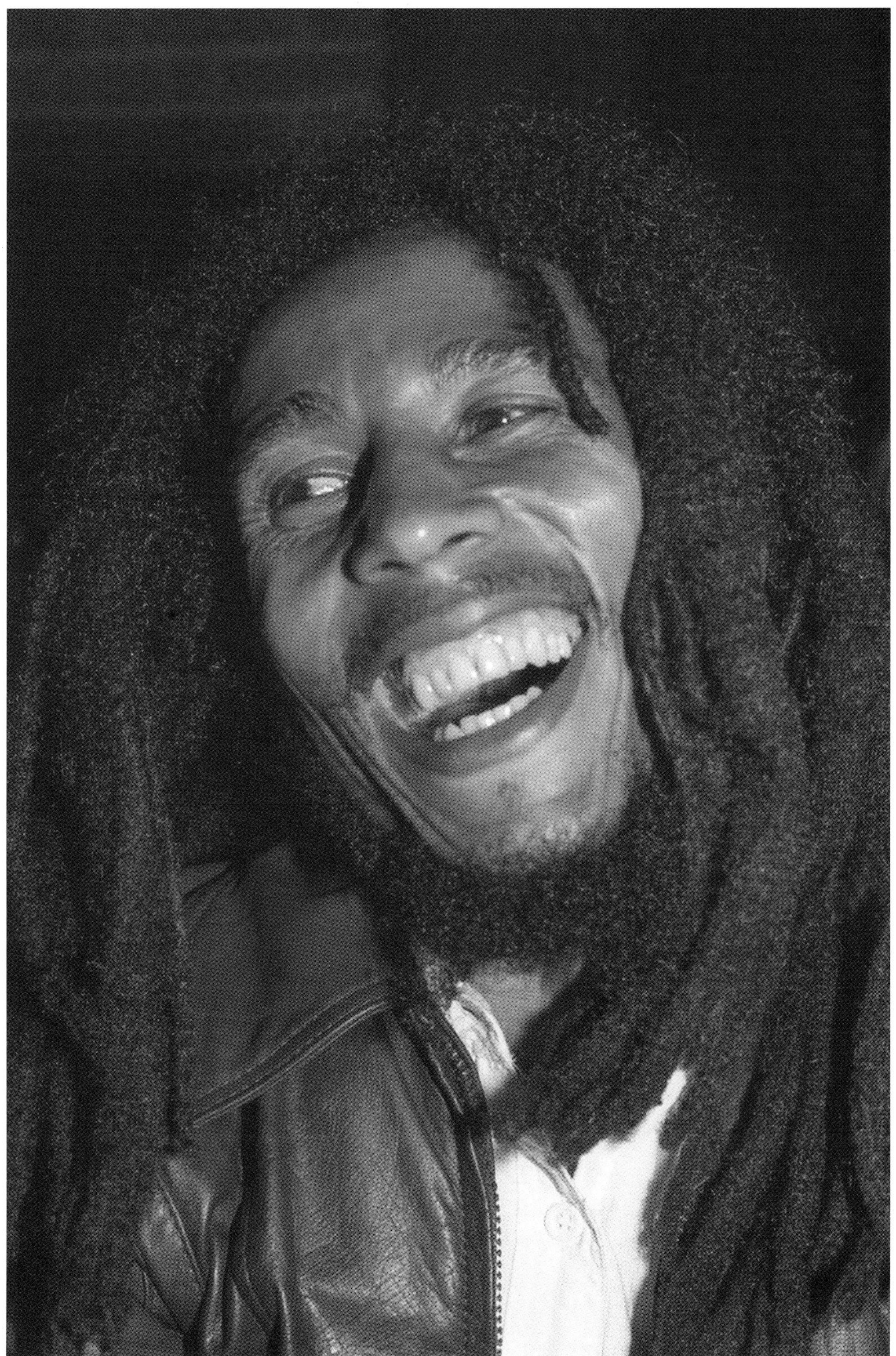

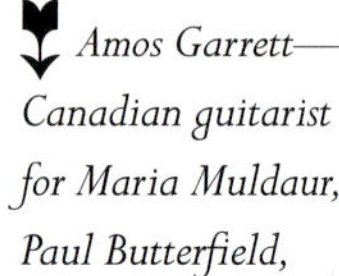

Amos Garrett—Canadian guitarist for Maria Muldaur, Paul Butterfield, Ian & Sylvia Tyson's Great Speckled Bird, Bobby Charles, and many others

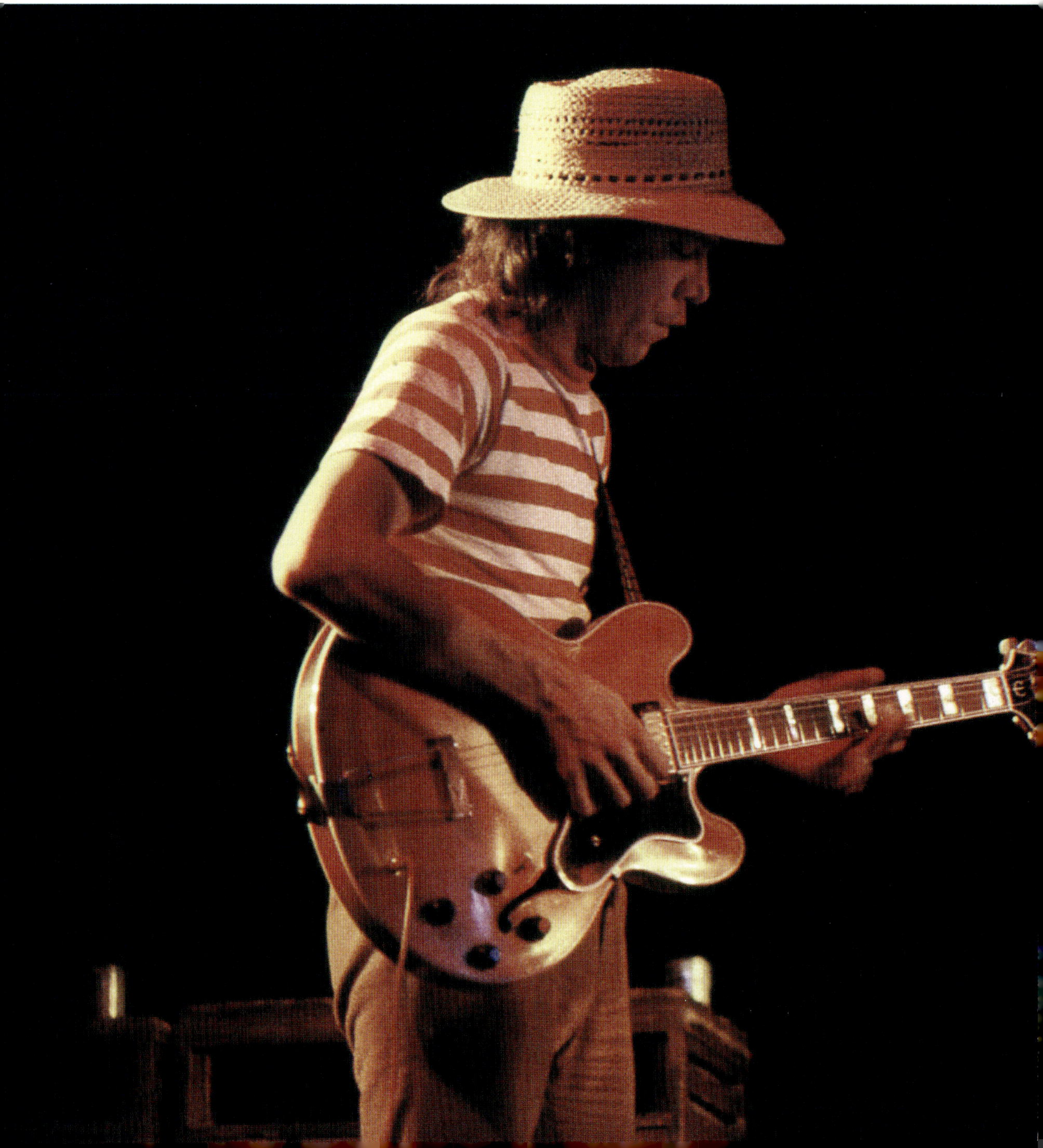

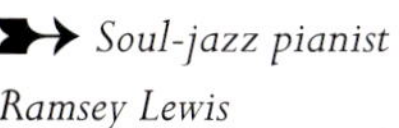

Soul-jazz pianist Ramsey Lewis

Guitarist Leo Kottke

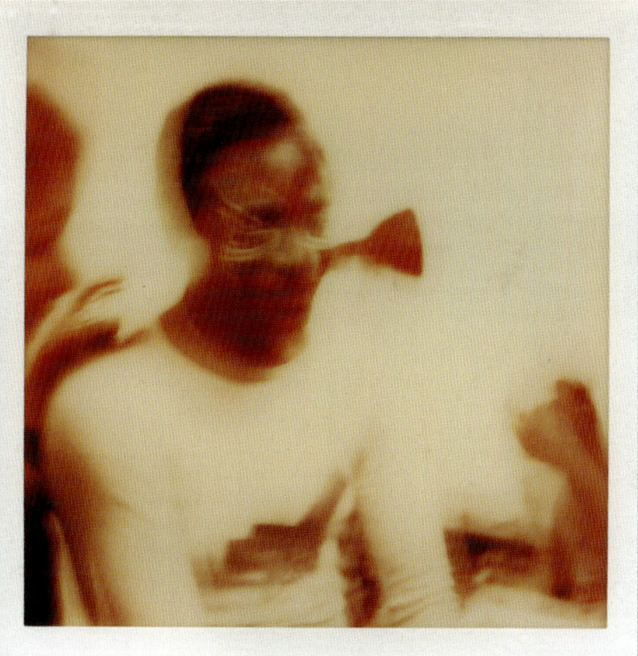

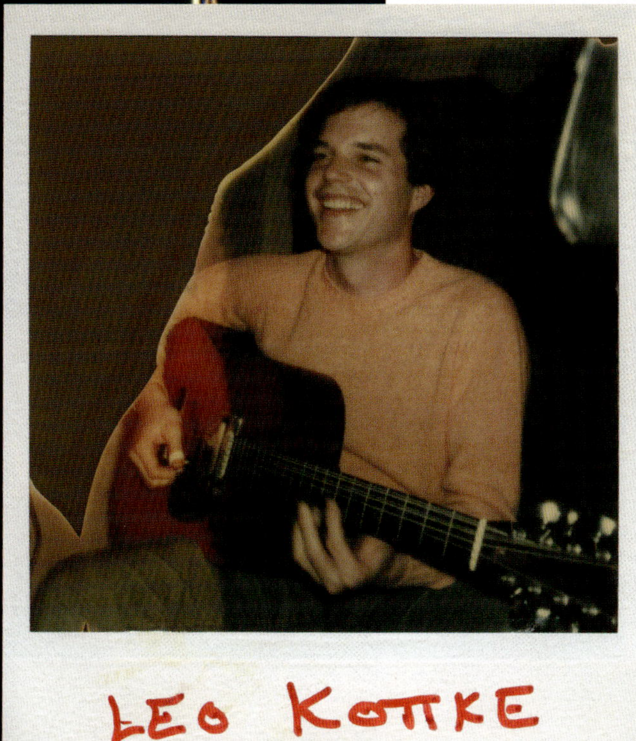

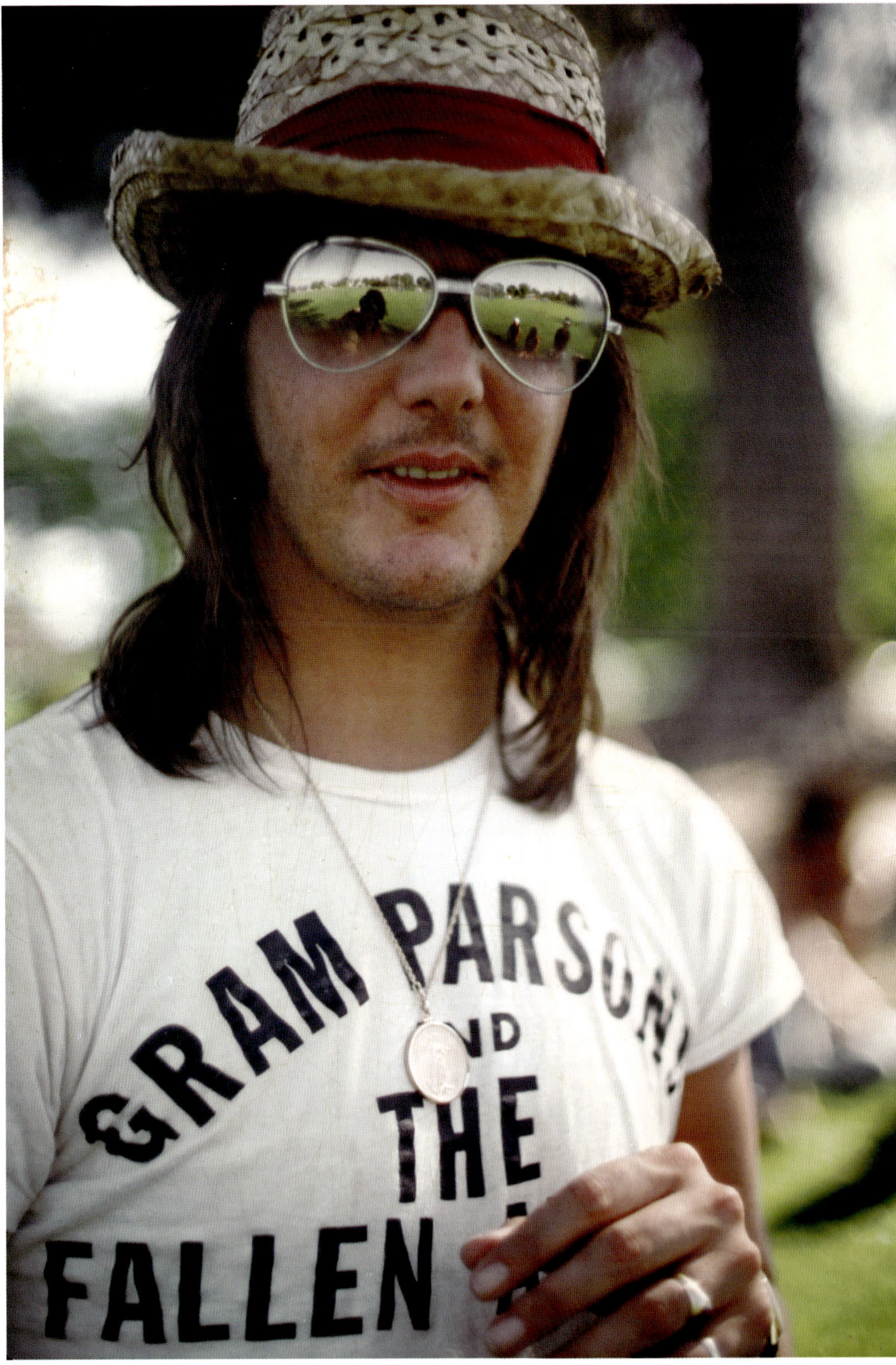
GRAM
THE
FALLEN

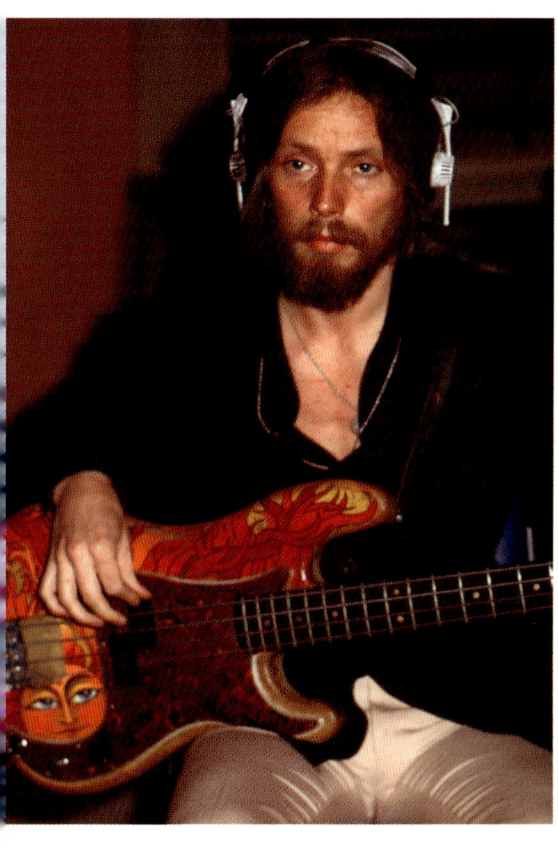

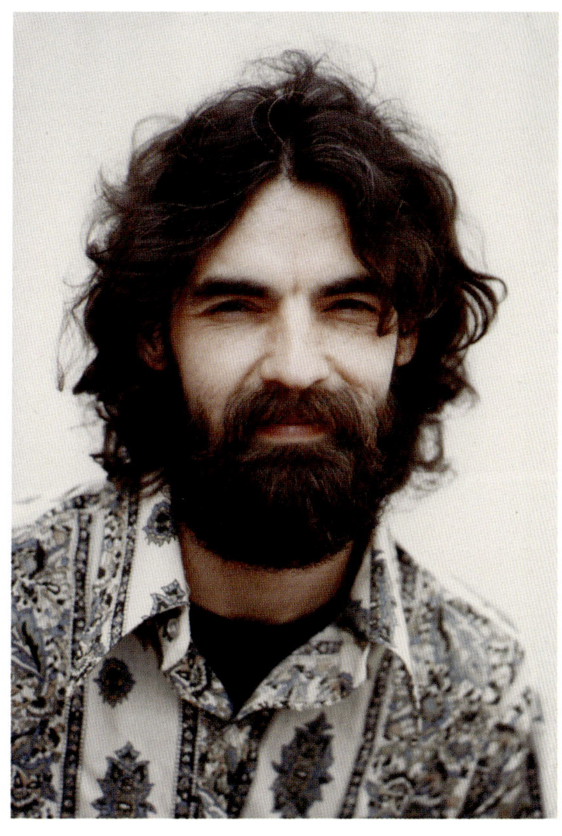

Bassist Klaus Voorman of the Plastic Ono Band and illustrator of the Beatle's Revolver *album cover; that's his fab bass playing on Carly Simon's "You're So Vain" as well.*

Bassist Chris Ethridge of The International Submarine Band and The Flying Burrito Brothers

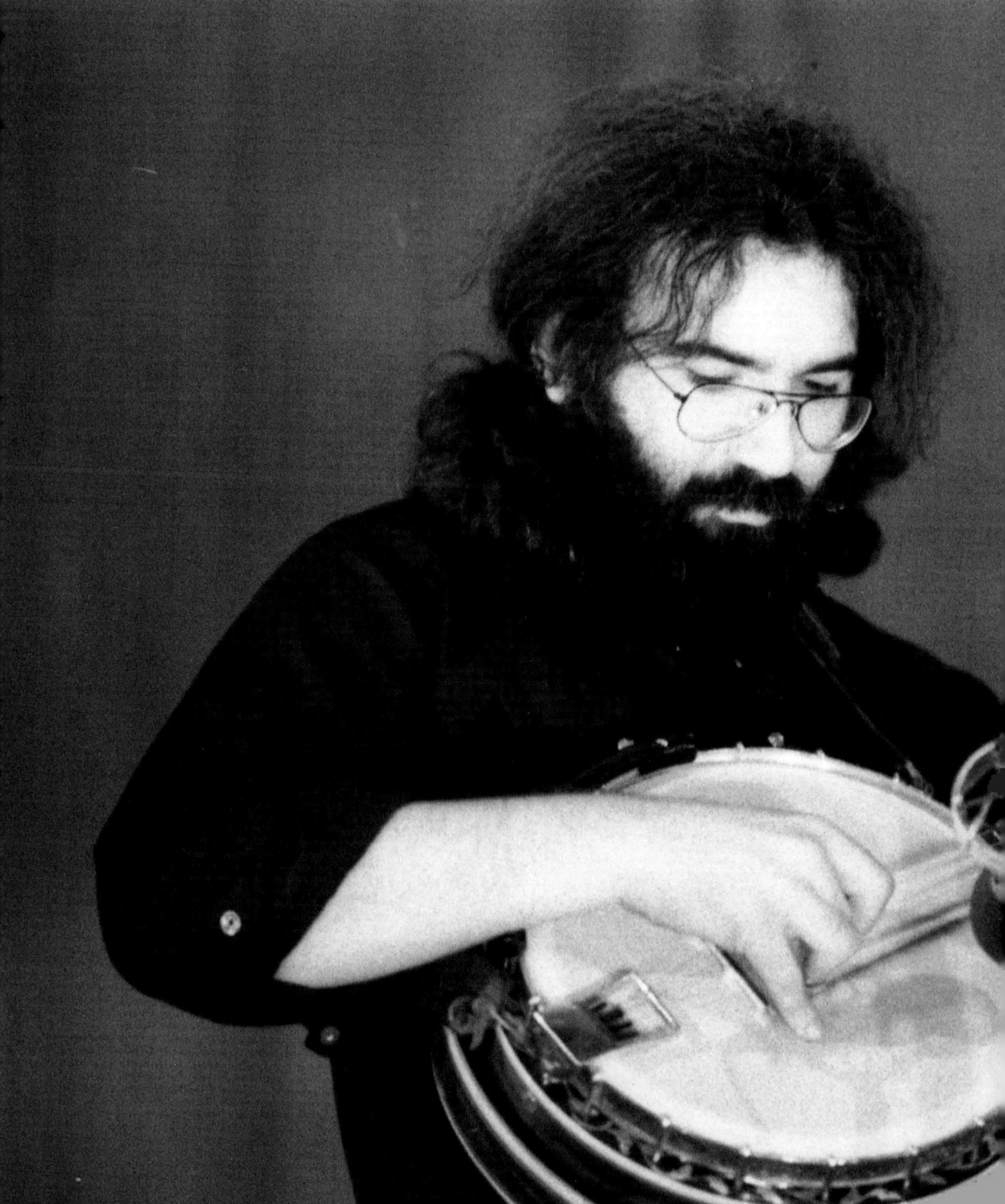

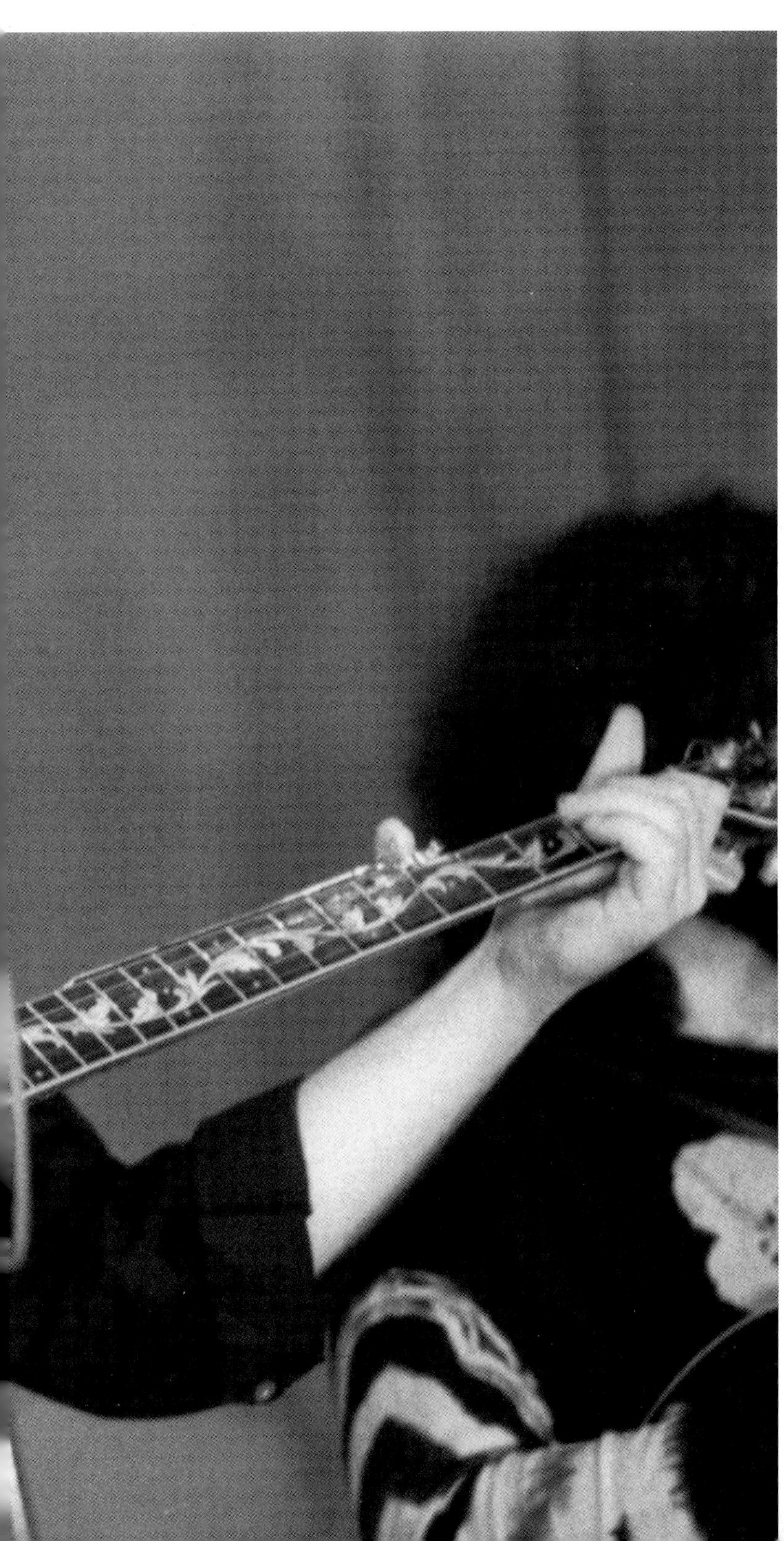

Jerry Garcia

(pg. 66) Soul singer Bobby Sheen

(pg. 67) Singer/songwriter Alan O'Day—composer of Helen Reddy's "Angie Baby"

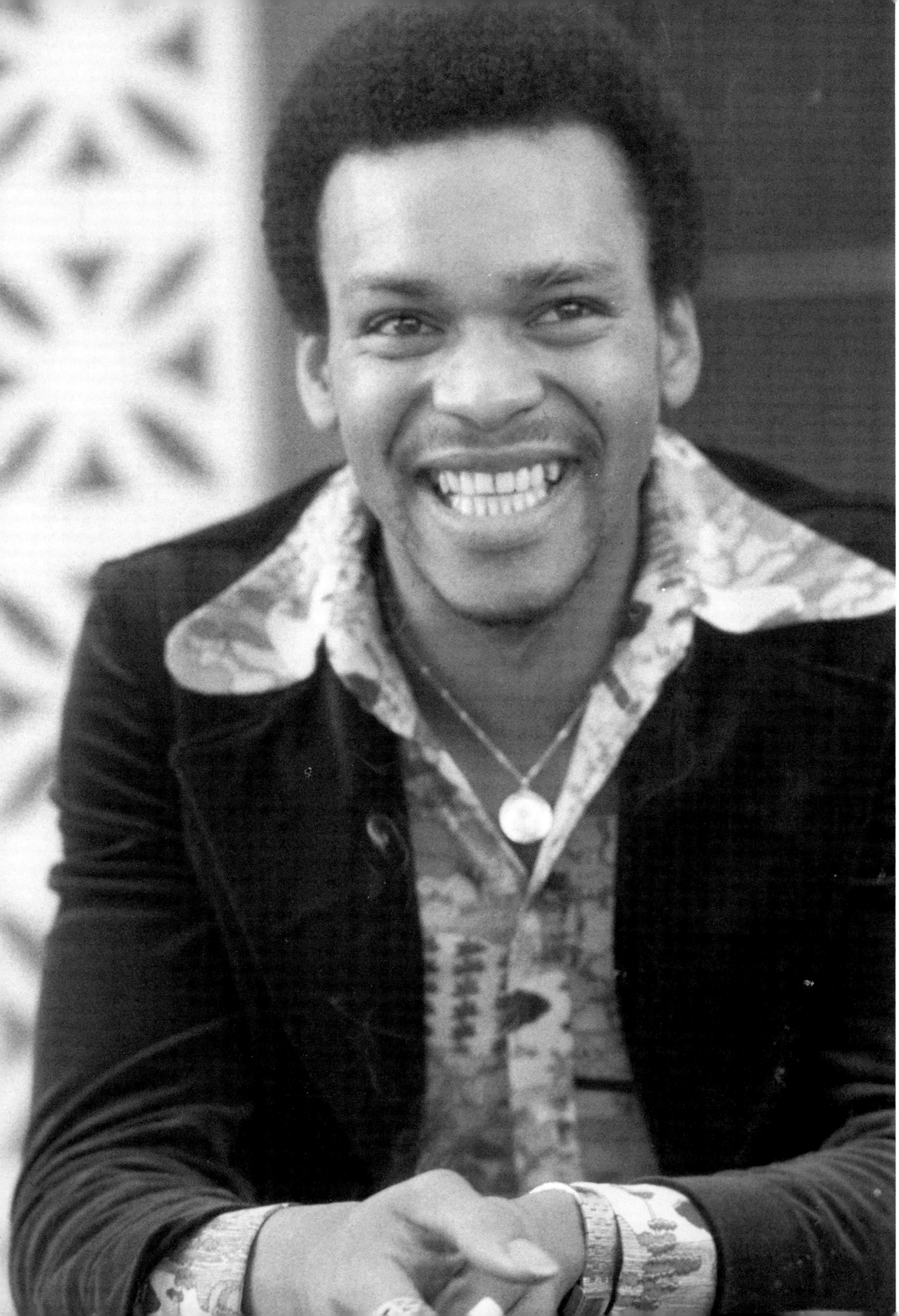

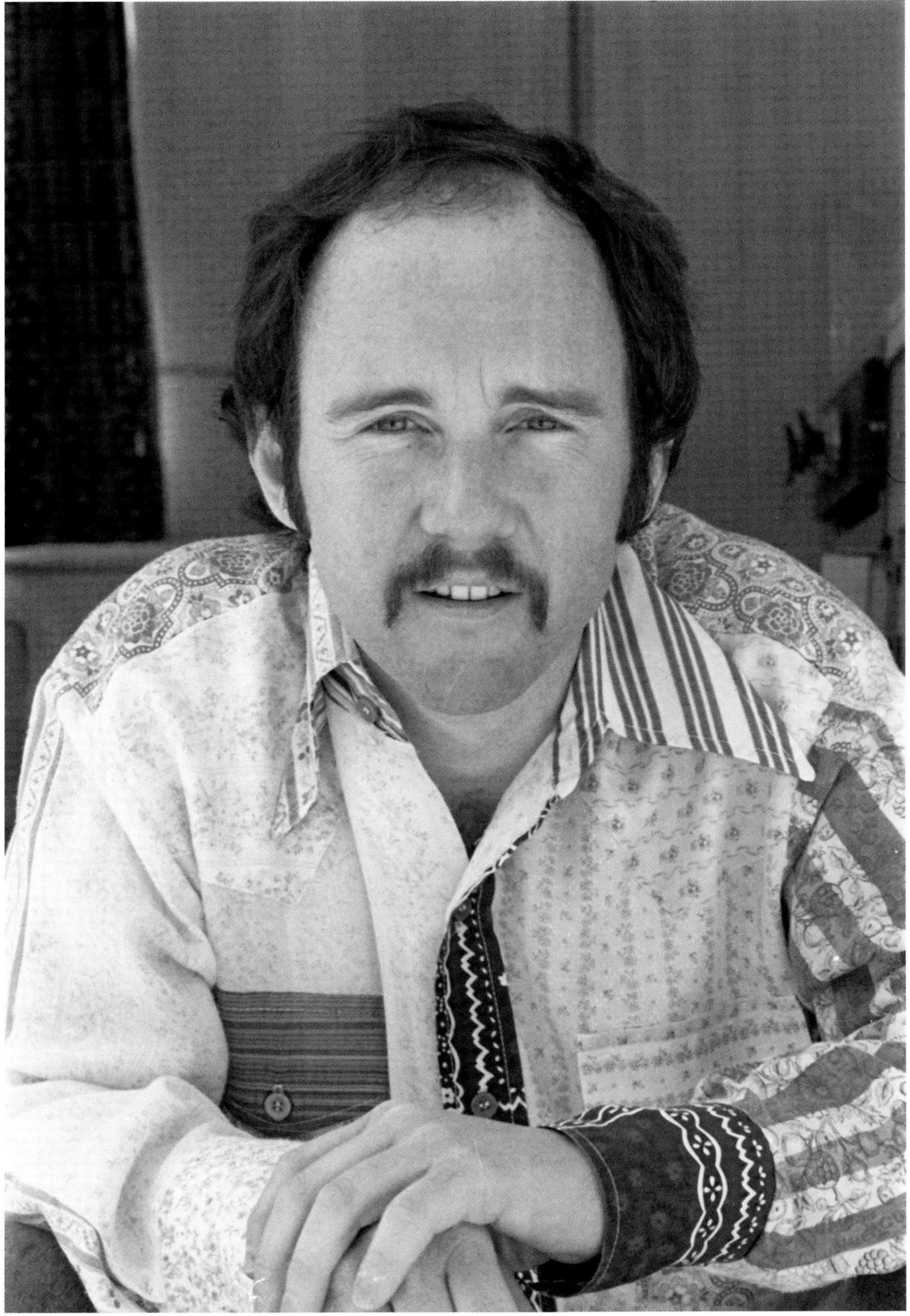

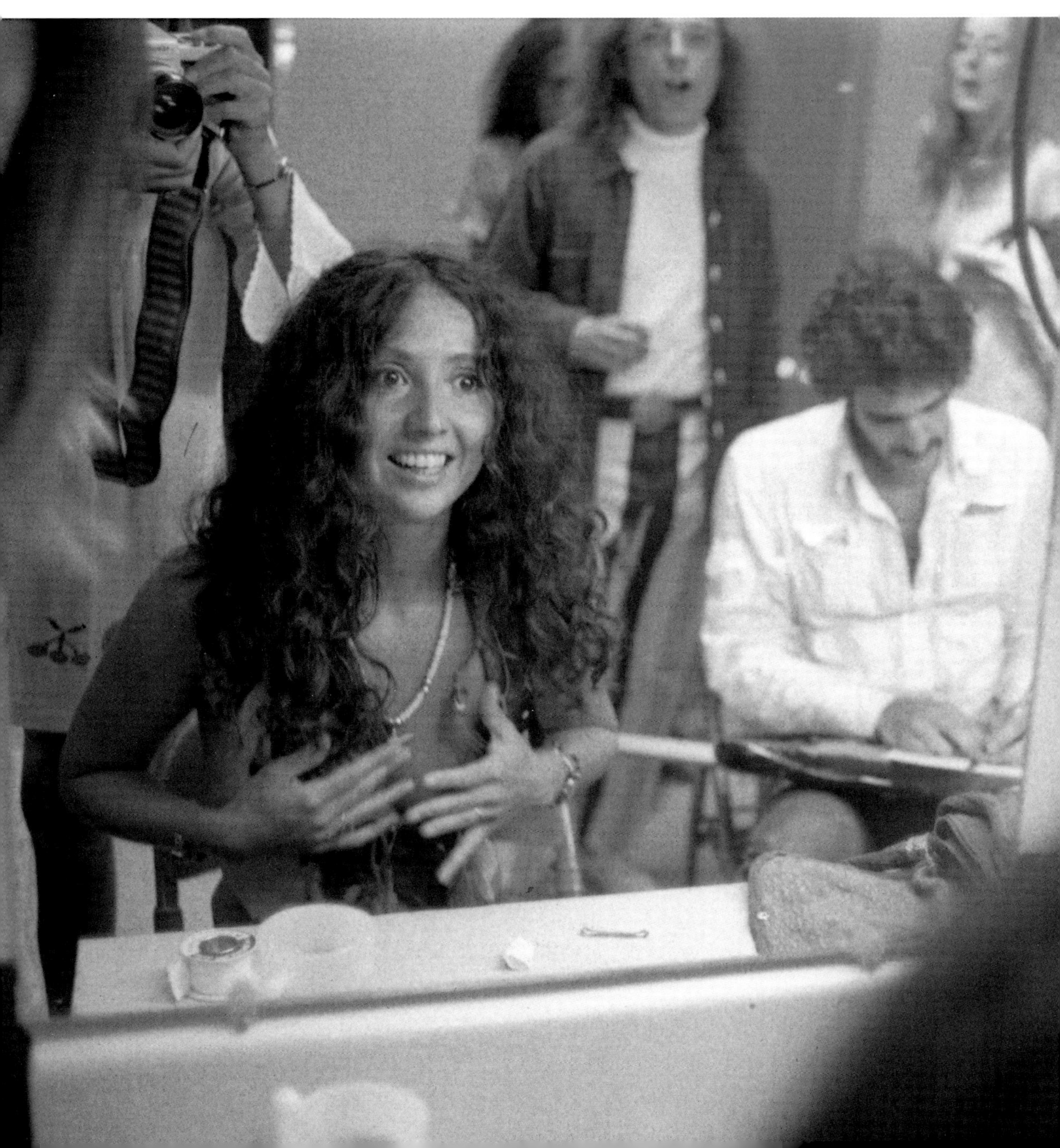

The mercurial guitarist John Fahey

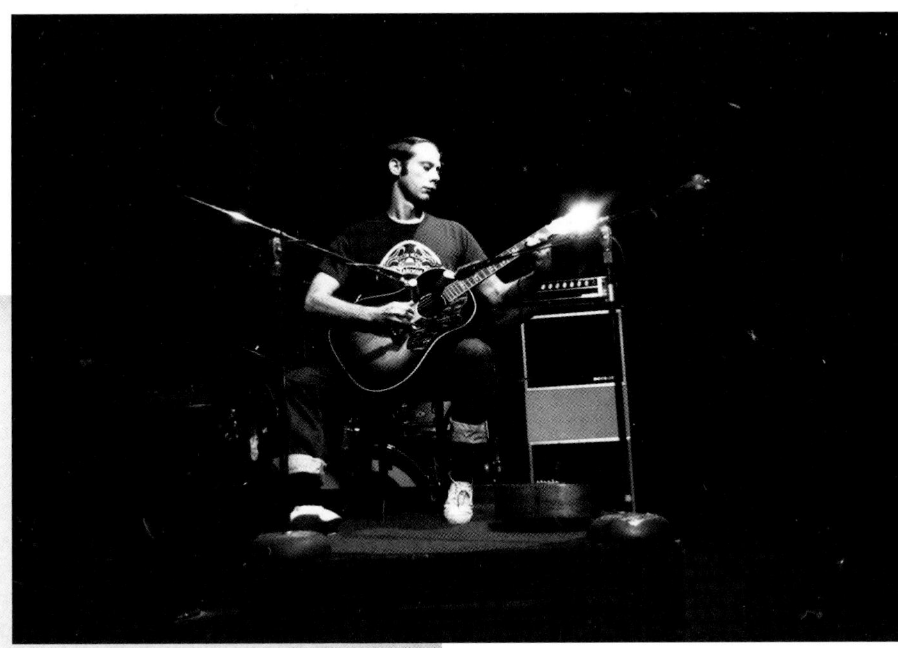

"I'll tell you something that I've been thinking about—a couple years ago somebody interviewed me for something, I forget what it was. They said, 'You know, Maria, you single-handedly invented the genre Americana decades before anyone gave it a name.' And I said, 'What do you mean by that?' And they start citing—they didn't go back as far as these two albums [Geoff & Maria Muldaur's Pottery Pie *and* Sweet Potatoes*], but my first album that had a Jimmie Rodgers song. It had a New Orleans blues—'Don't You Feel My Leg'—it had a Dolly Parton song, and it had several contemporary songwriters, so I realized, listening to this album, that comment came back. And I went, 'Yeah, that's what we were doing.' Americana."*

—Maria Muldaur in conversation with Pat Thomas

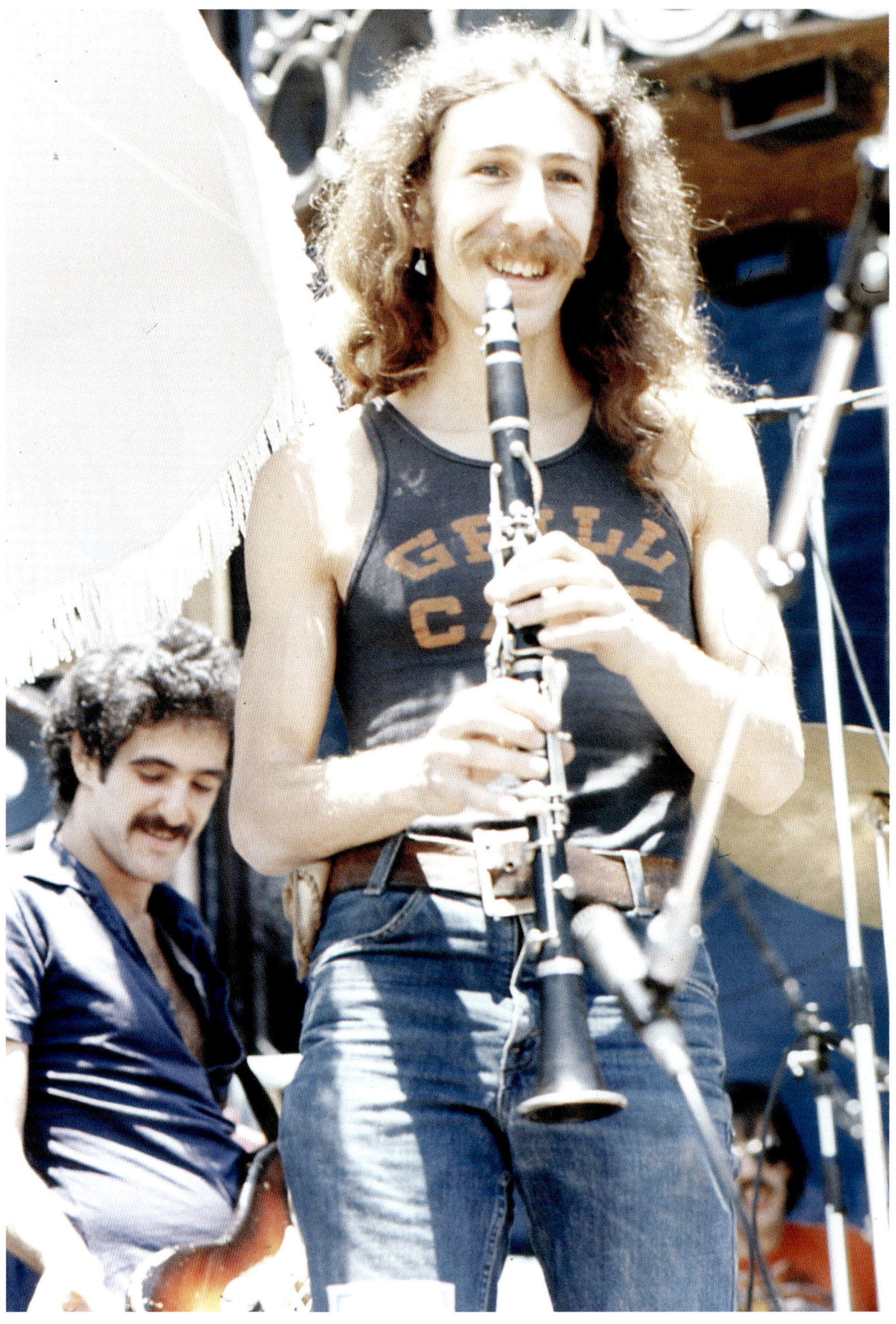

"When I got to Los Angeles, somebody called me and said there was this perfect job for me at Warner Brothers. And it was doing what I was doing, photographer, but it was with the artists and the new releases. And I would shoot whoever I could. And then I started to do videos for the artists too. I went through the halls at Warner Brothers, knocking on the executives' doors, collecting money to do those first films. And if artists were there in the building, they would call me to take their picture. So, in that sense, I was really in such a great spot. And it was like a family too, which I didn't appreciate enough at the time because I was very independent."

Jazz saxophonist Benny Carter

(pg. 71) Clarinetist / multi-instrumentalist Joel Tepp as heard on albums by Iain Matthews of Fairport Convention, Linda Ronstadt, Kate & Anna McGarrigle, Bonnie Raitt, and Crazy Horse

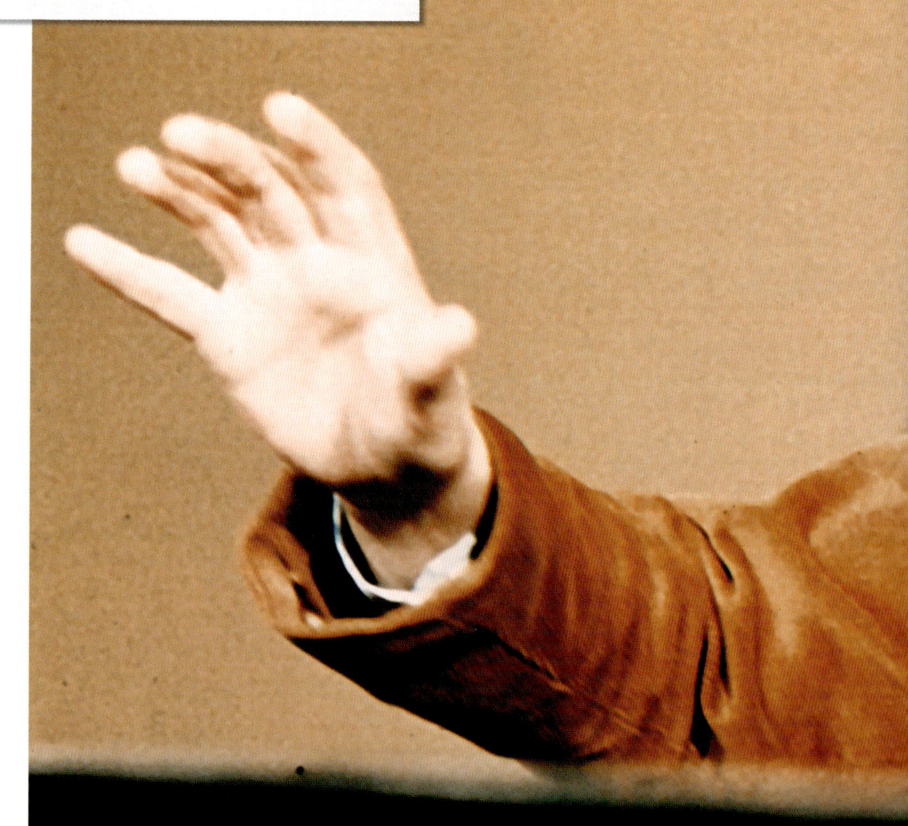

Arlo Guthrie

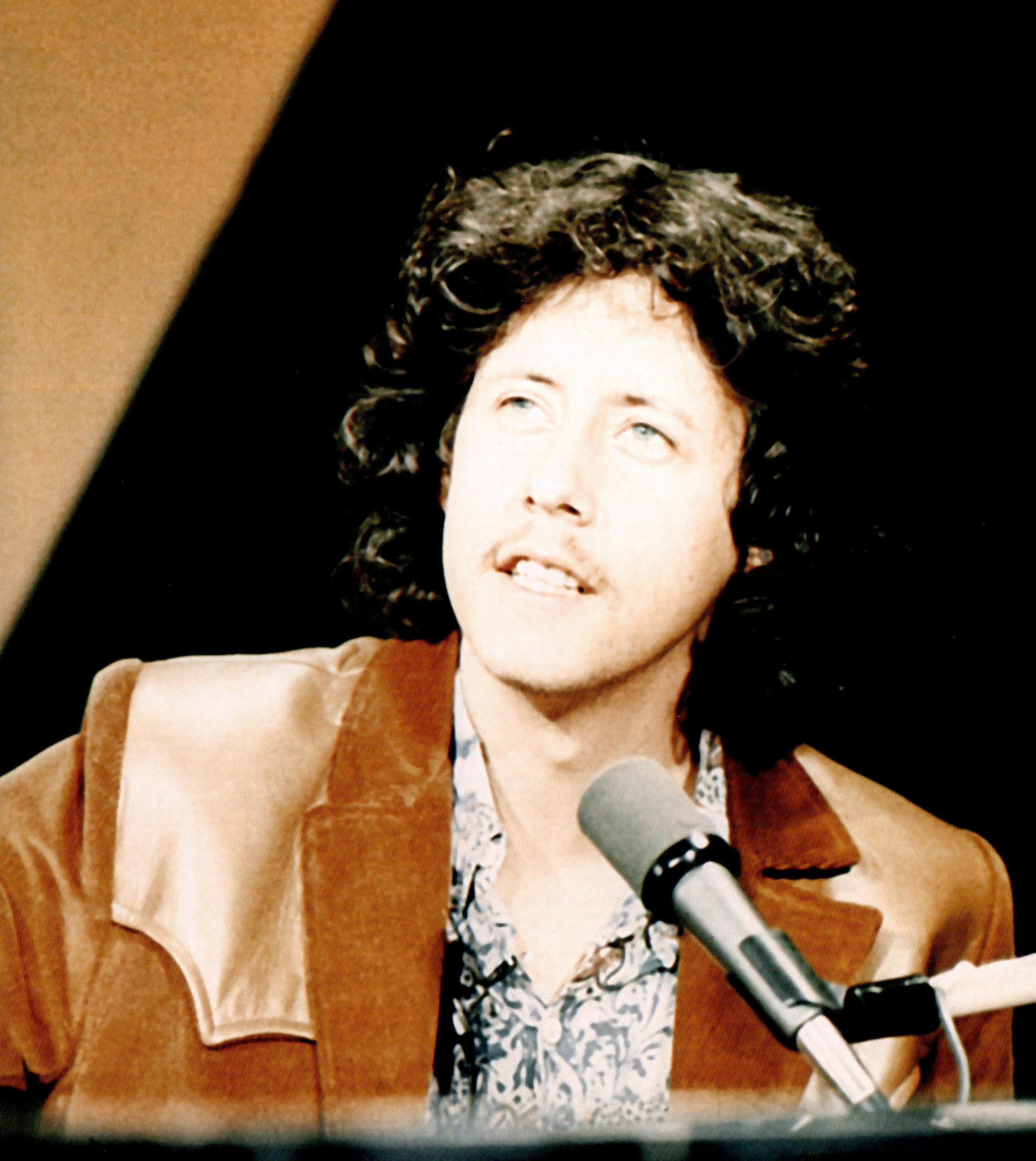

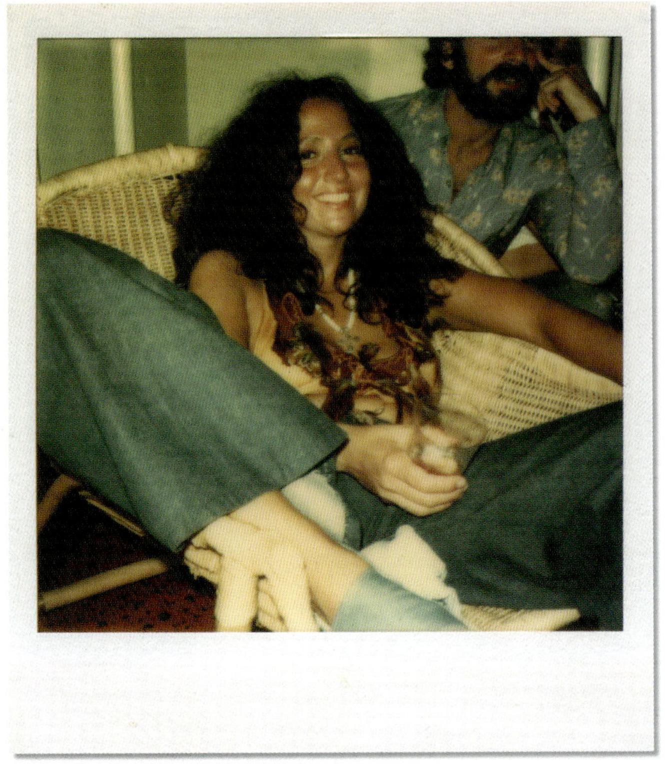

Maria Muldaur

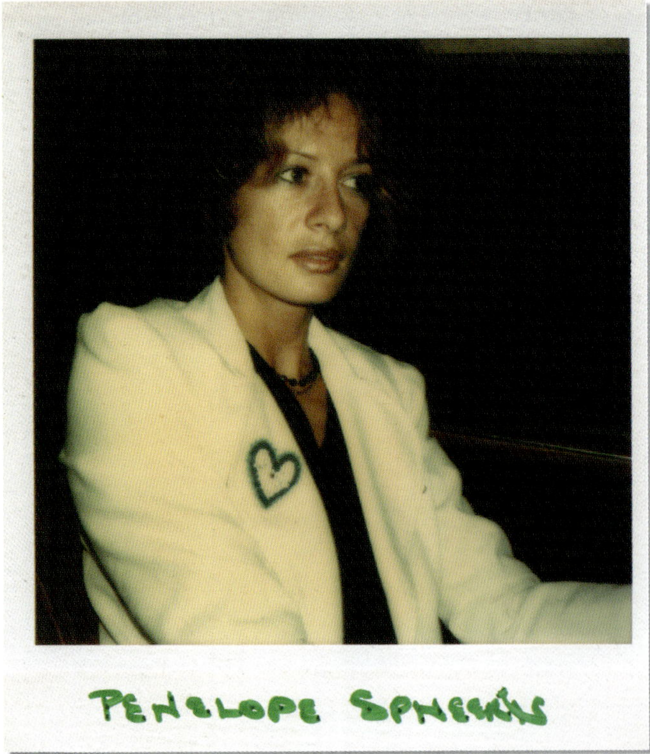

Penelope Spheeris—director of The Decline of Western Civilization *and* Wayne's World

➤➤ *Movie producer Arlene Rothberg*

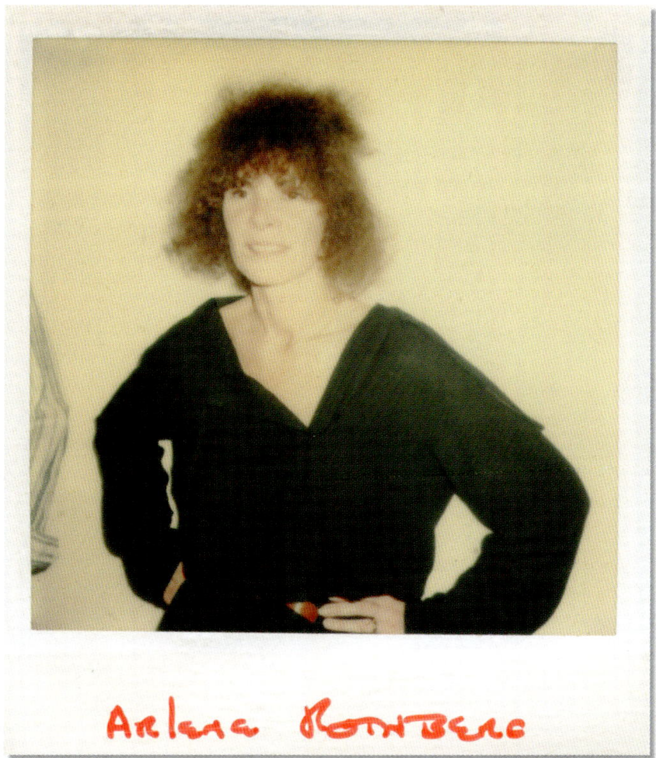

➤➤ *Actress Roz Kelly—"Pinky" Tuscadero on the TV series* Happy Days

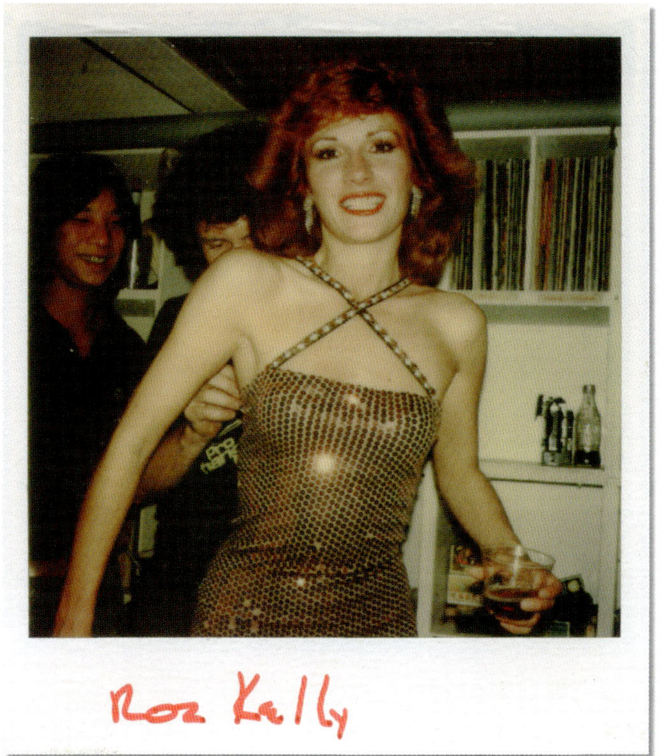

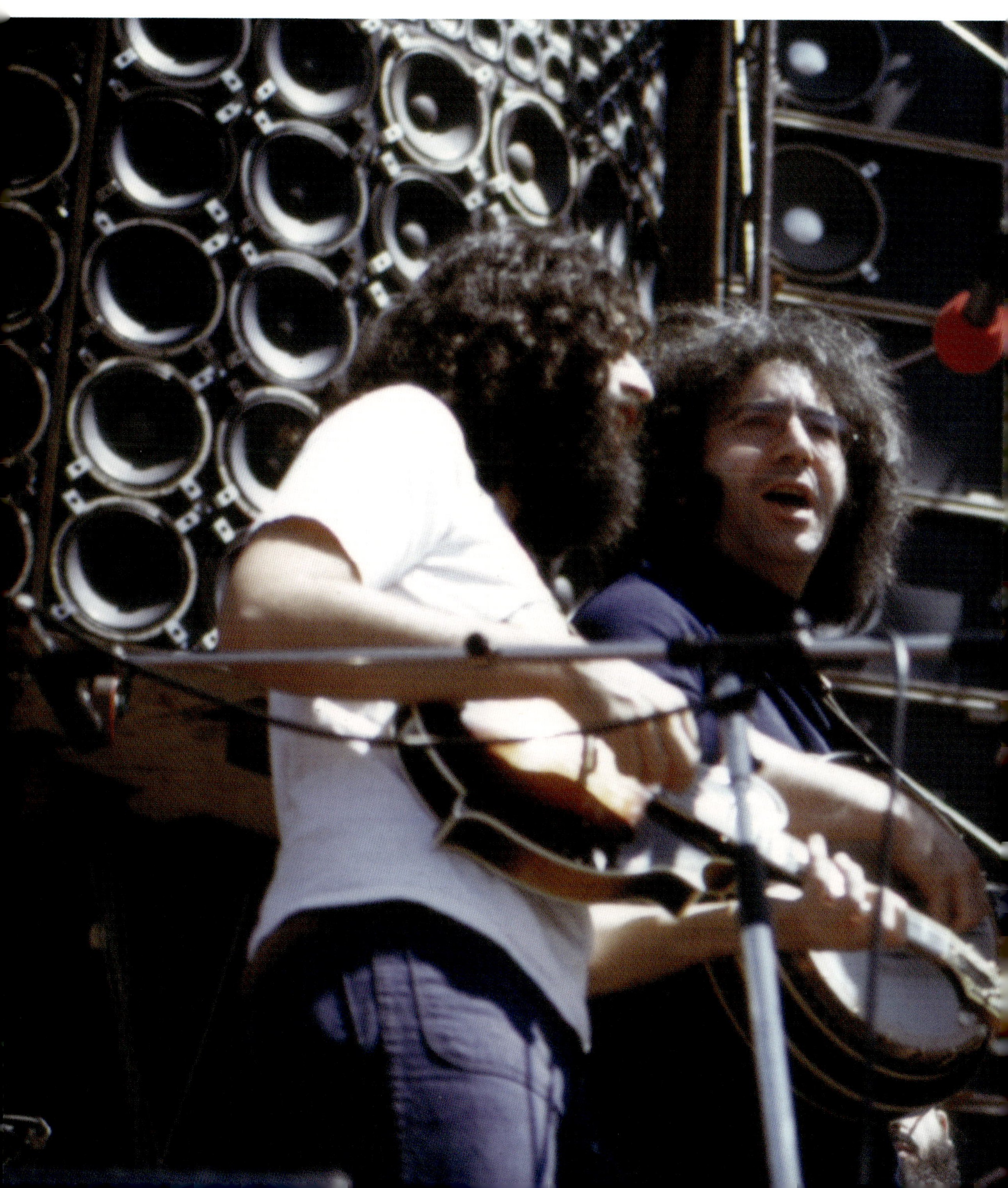

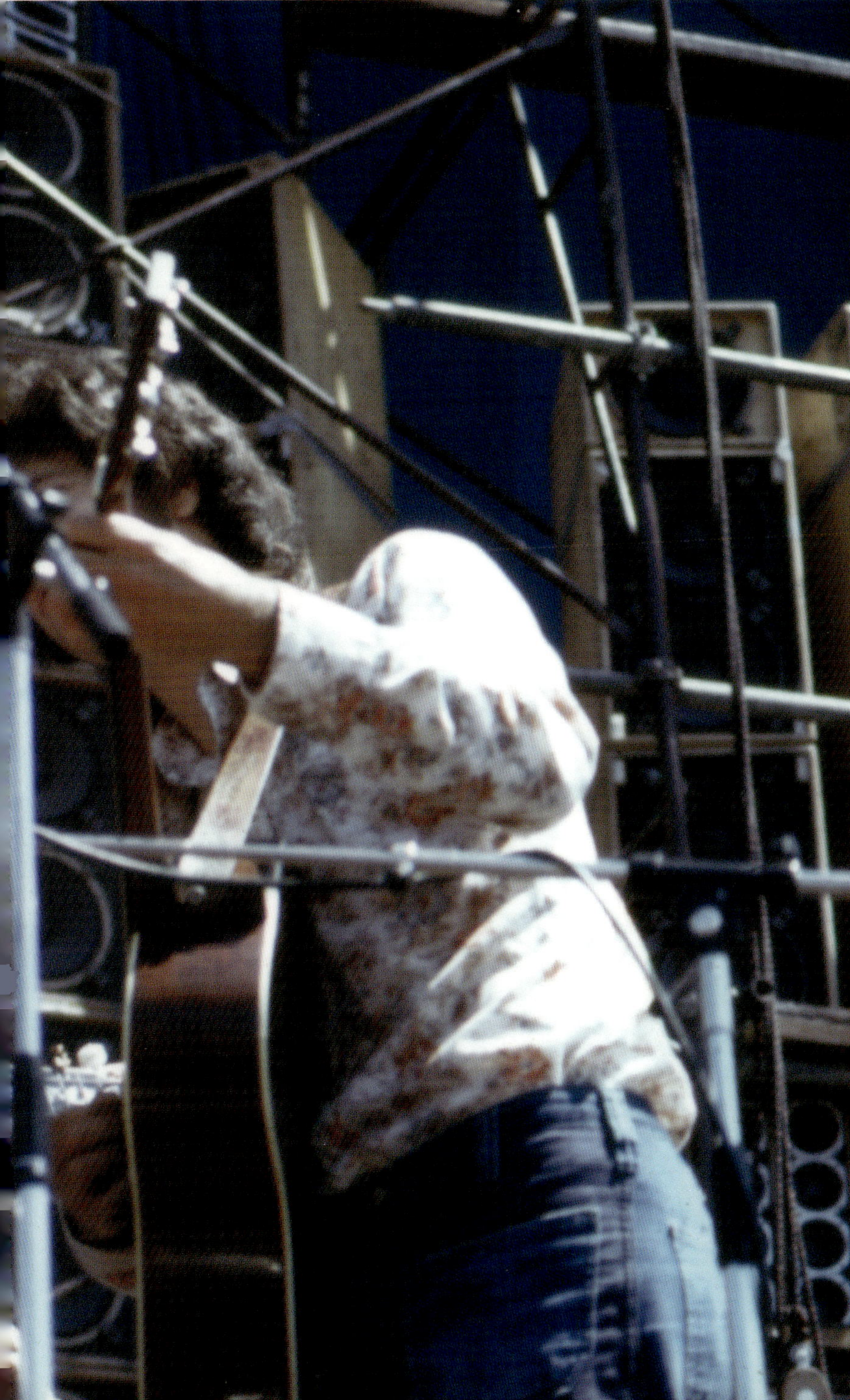

←← *Jerry Garcia with David Grisman (Mandolin) and Peter Rowan (Guitar)*

→→ *(pg 78) Gram Parsons*

→→ *(pg. 78) Bonnie Raitt*

→→ *(pg. 79) Drummer Roger Earl of Foghat*

→→ *(pg. 79) Captain Beefheart*

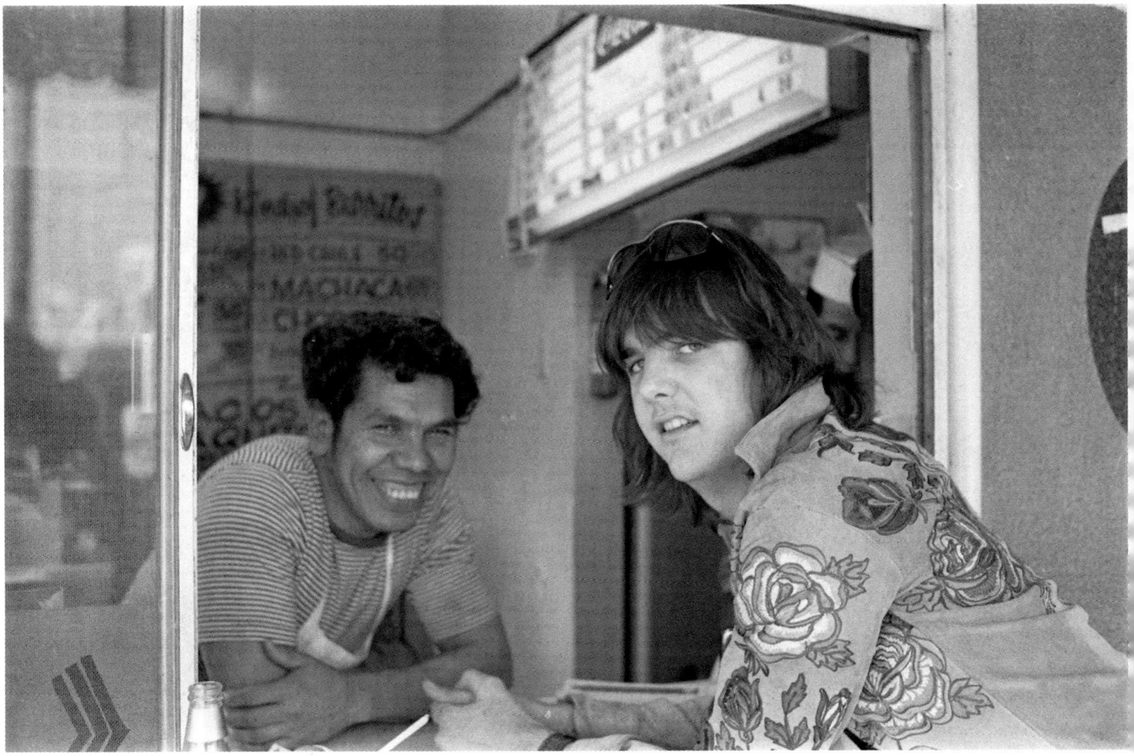

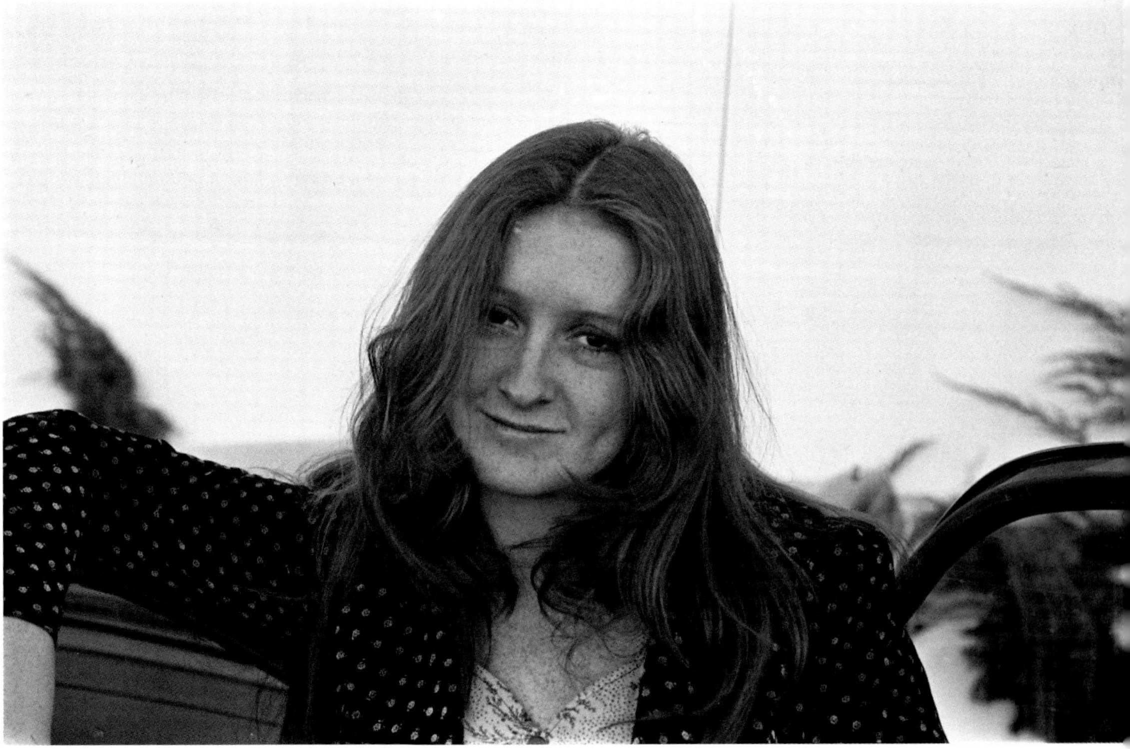

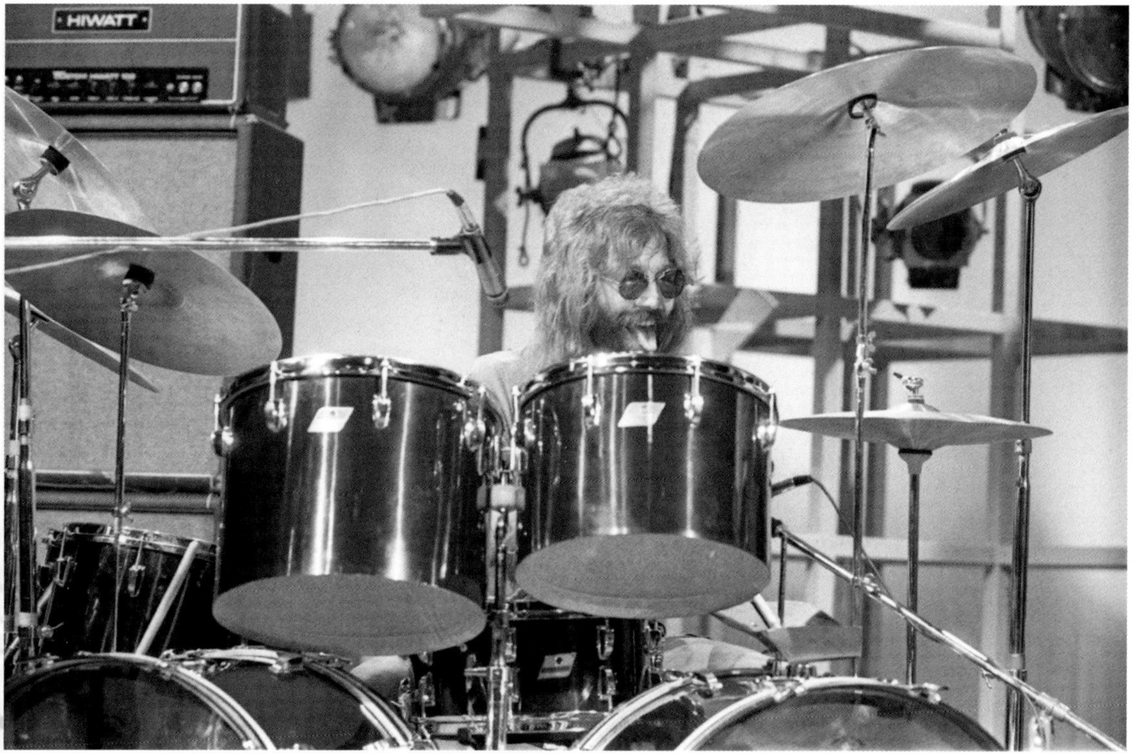

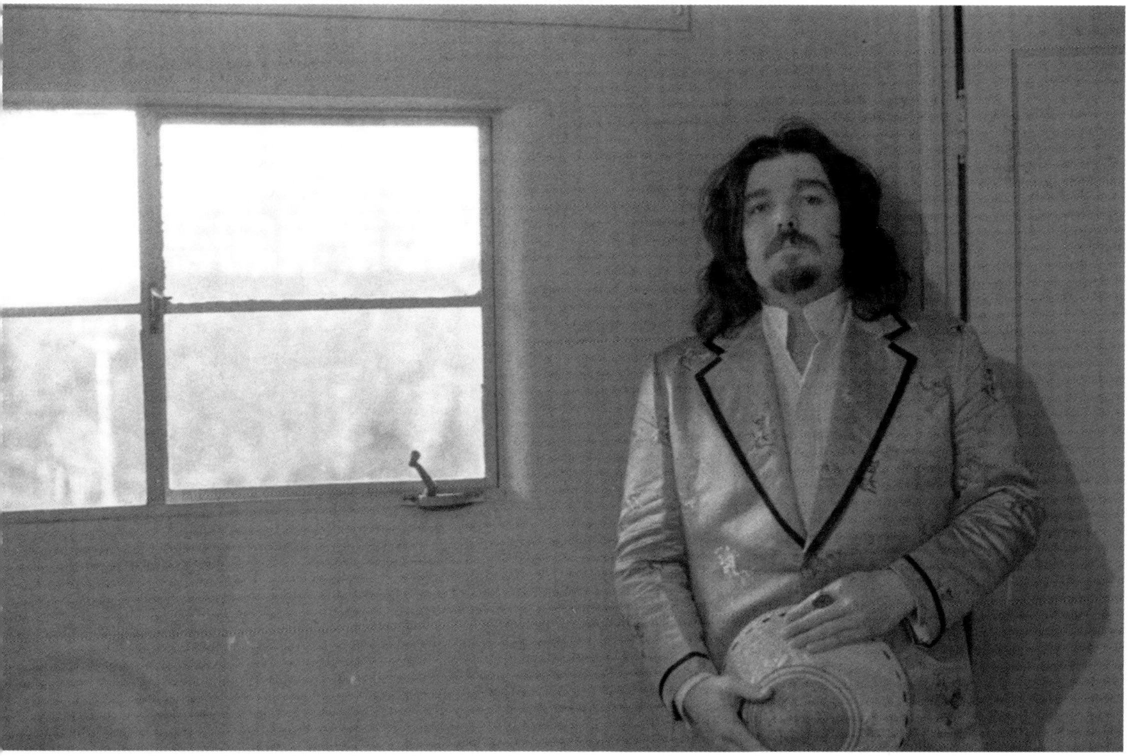

Ginny Winn on
Captain Beefheart

I spent a day with Captain Beefheart. Though a little leery in the beginning, he became a gracious and informative host as we toured the area around Eureka, near where he lived, and different places. I took a lot of pictures of him. The best thing was, at the end of the day, he took me to a little airport there, awaiting a small plane in this 1950s coffee shop. I just took my camera, quietly trying to remain unobtrusive, and looked through the lens right at him. We remained relaxed and he just stared into the camera and let me take the shot. The camera was almost invisible, so it's completely natural. Just like that. That's the kind of thing that is so cool when it happens.

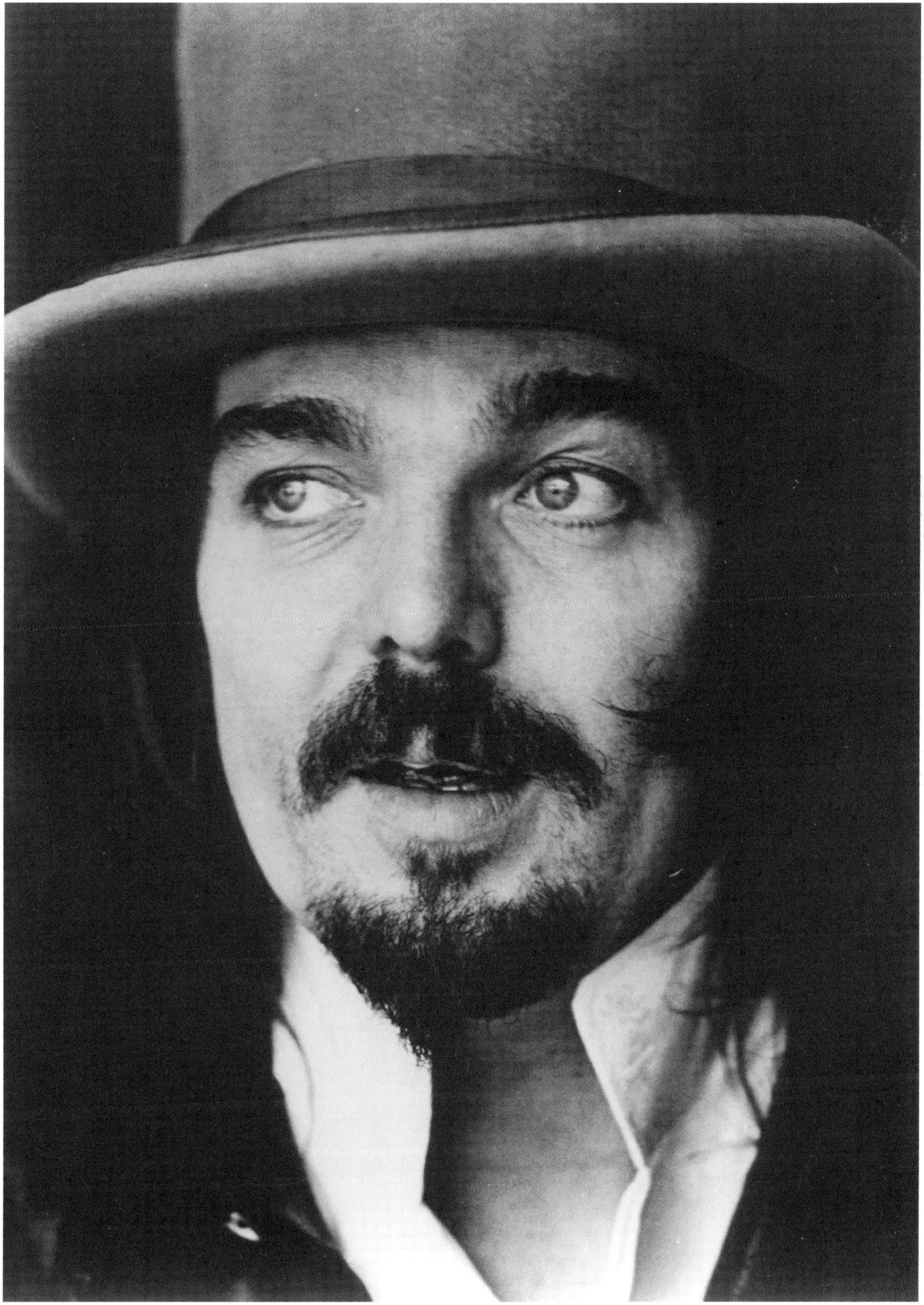

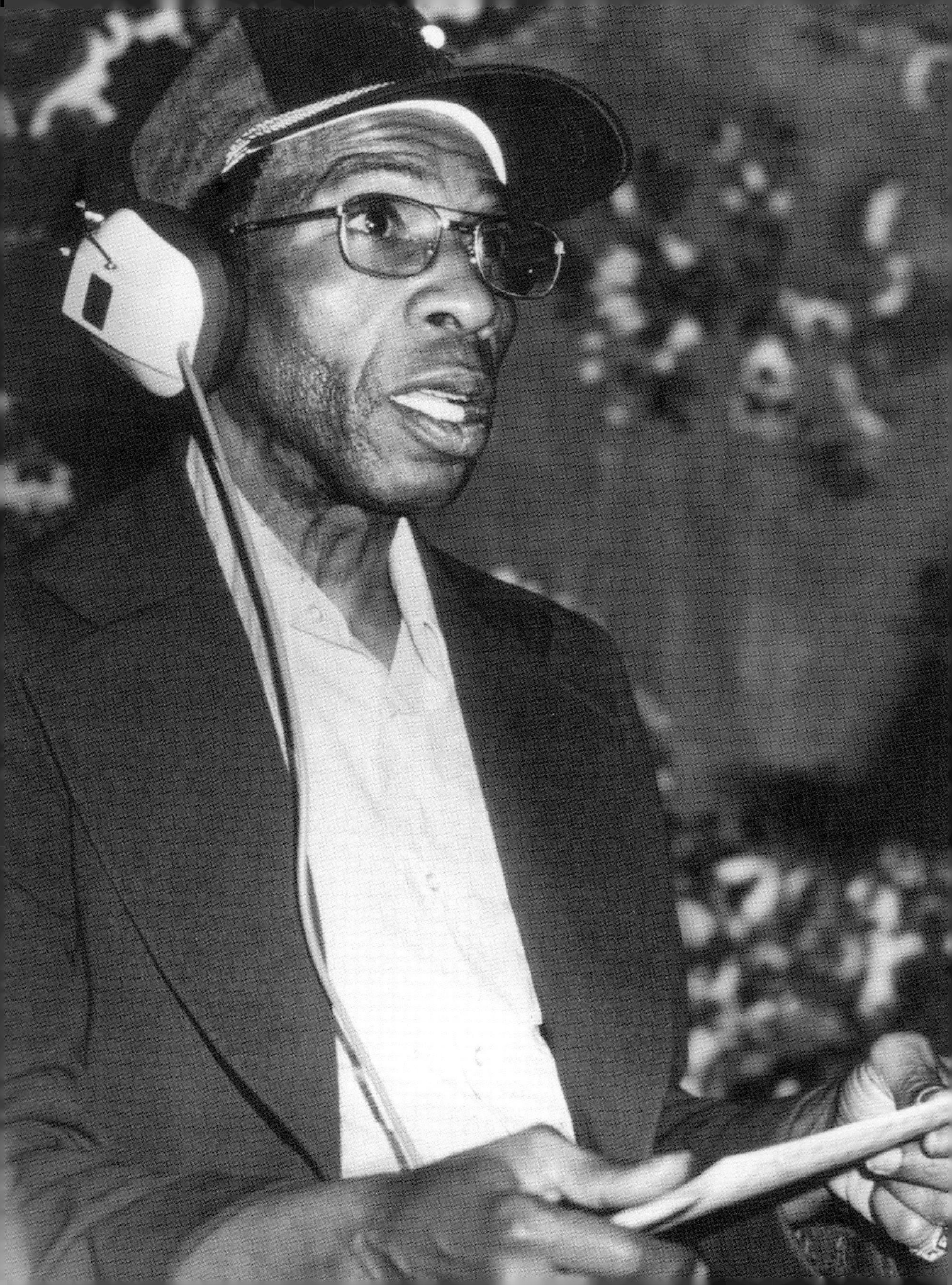

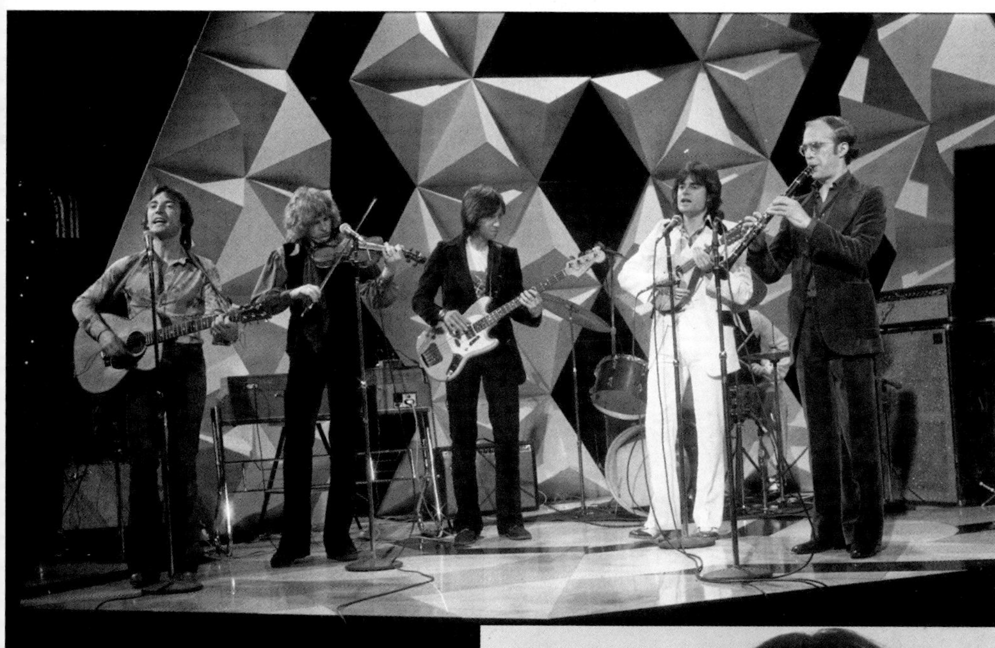

The Incredible String Band were once described as, "music to listen to while sitting in a hot tub in California"—but they were more than just that. An influence on everyone from Robert Plant to Devendra Banhart, they invented their own musical genre which led the psych-folk revolution before that movement had actually been identified as such.

Let's celebrate this lesser known of the two Velvet Underground icons for his superior arrangements, crafted songwriting, and complex production styles over the more commercially successful Lou Reed. Cale has no equal, other musicians would be hard-pressed to duplicate the sound of Fear *or* Paris 1919. *I've heard a thousand bands replicate Lou Reed, never heard anybody sound like John Cale.*

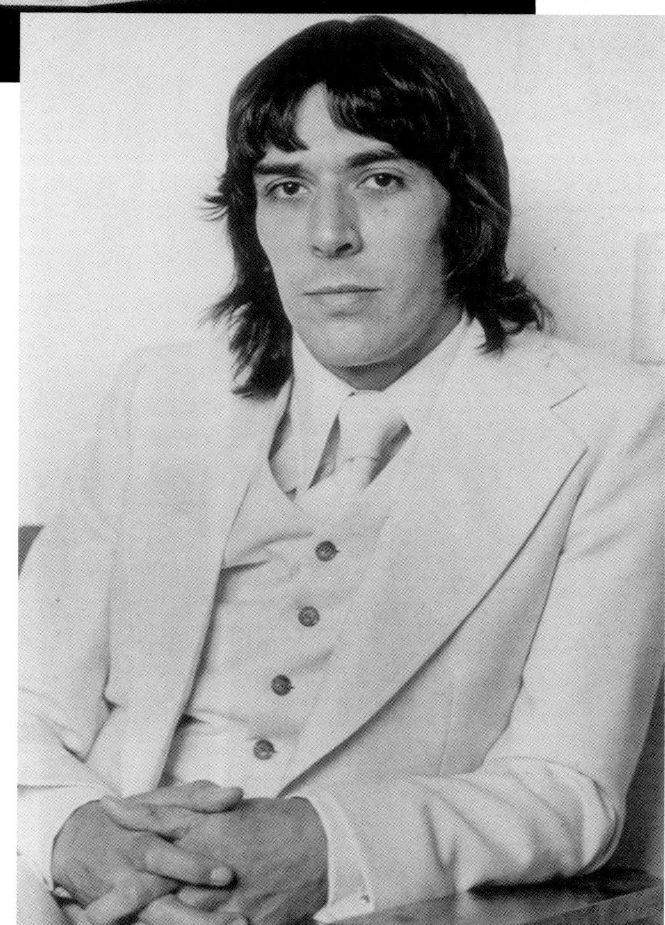

(pg 82) Blues singer/guitarist T-Bone Walker—composer of the classic "Call It Stormy Monday (But Tuesday Is Just as Bad)"

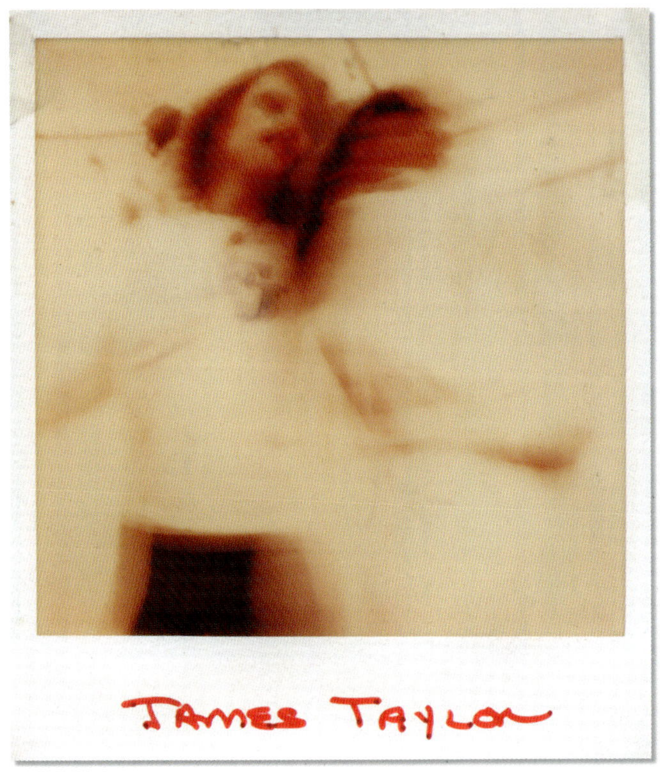

James Taylor

Etta James was inducted into the Rock & Roll Hall of Fame in 1993. Afterwards she pronounced, "They got this shit backwards, it should be the R&B Hall of Fame, where Blacks decide which white rockers deserve to get in."

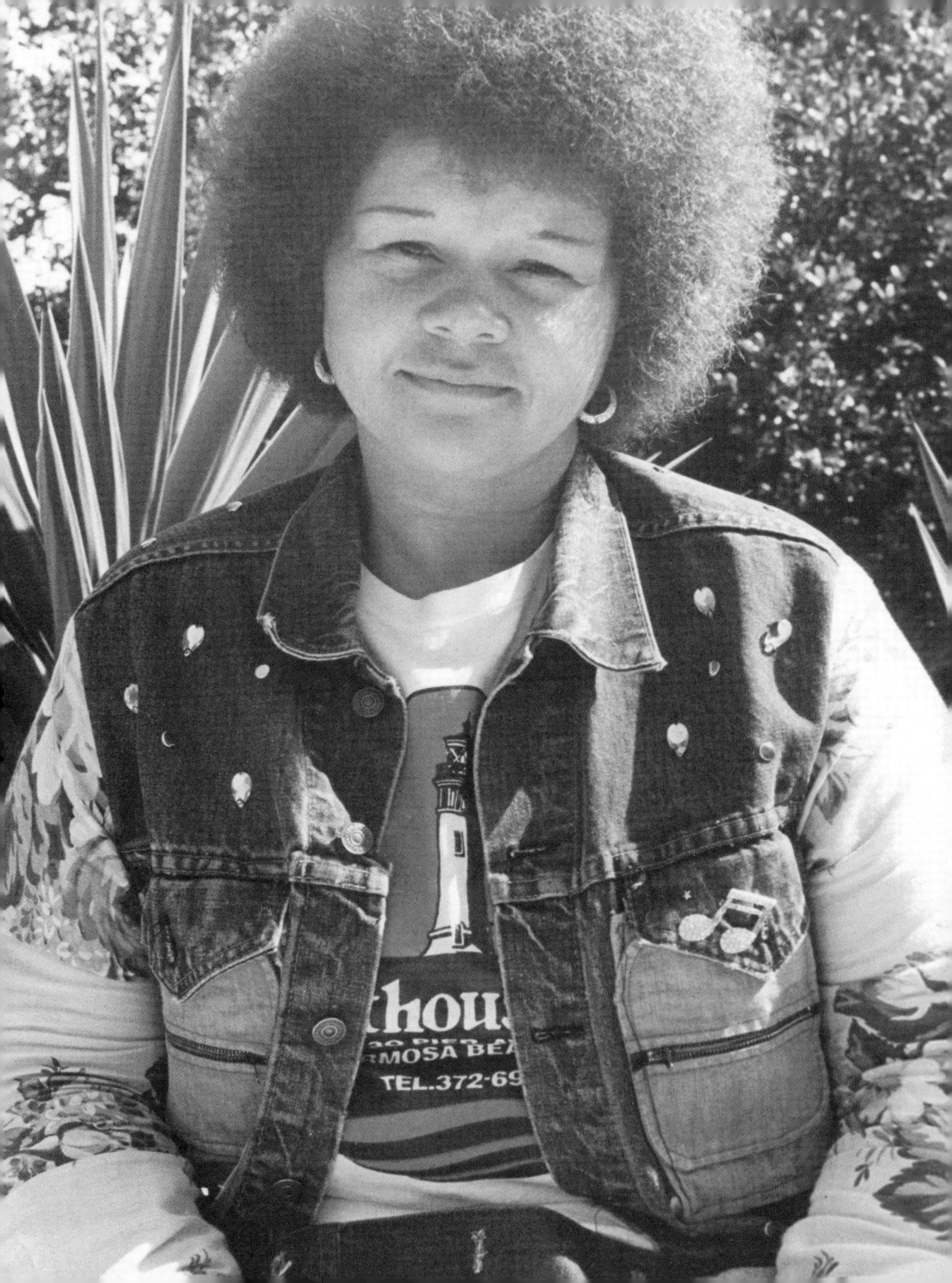
thous
RMOSA BEA
TEL.372-69

Ginny Winn on

Joni Mitchell

I got to be in the studio with Joni Mitchell. I also went to her house with Norman Seeff to film her and we swam in her pool, which was just body temperature. It was heaven. And her house was all the colors and textures that you would imagine Joni Mitchell would have—soft velvet and things like that, hunter green, and a sensual kind of mind, body experience. She is very direct, fun and understated, bright.

➤➝ *Joni Mitchell*

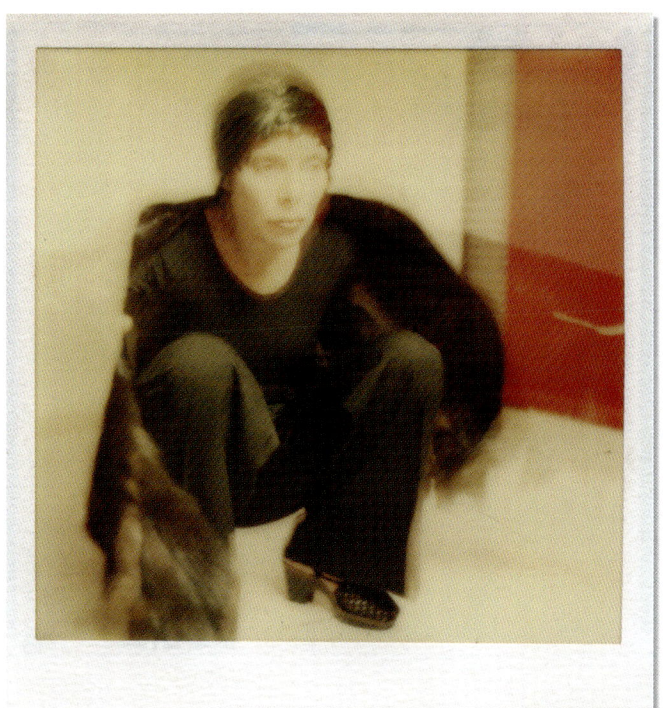

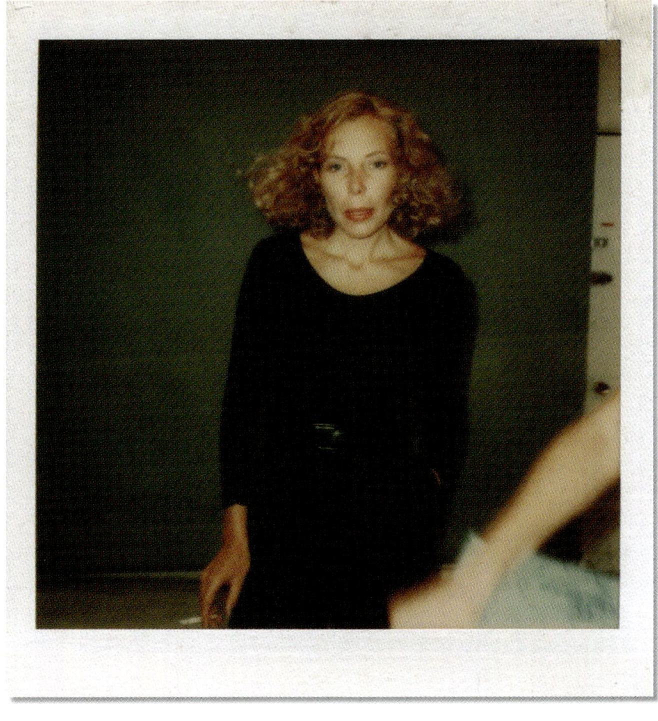

Lesley Gore —vocalist of the 1963 hit, "It's My Party"

Pat's favorite curmudgeon, the ever-inspired Belfast Cowboy, the dynamic Van the Man. One of the most consistent singer/songwriters of his generation—he never went disco or new wave in the 70s, never used the big 80s drum sound and while not every LP is great, there's no misguided turkeys in his catalog. While the Stones sought out Christina Aguilera to perform with, Van hooked up with The Chieftains. He's an incredibly uncompromising artist in the marketplace, more so than even Lou Reed, Neil Young or Bob Dylan. And musically, he's successfully blended both white (Celtic, folk) and black (blues, soul, jazz) influences seamlessly and continuously better than anyone over a 50-year span.

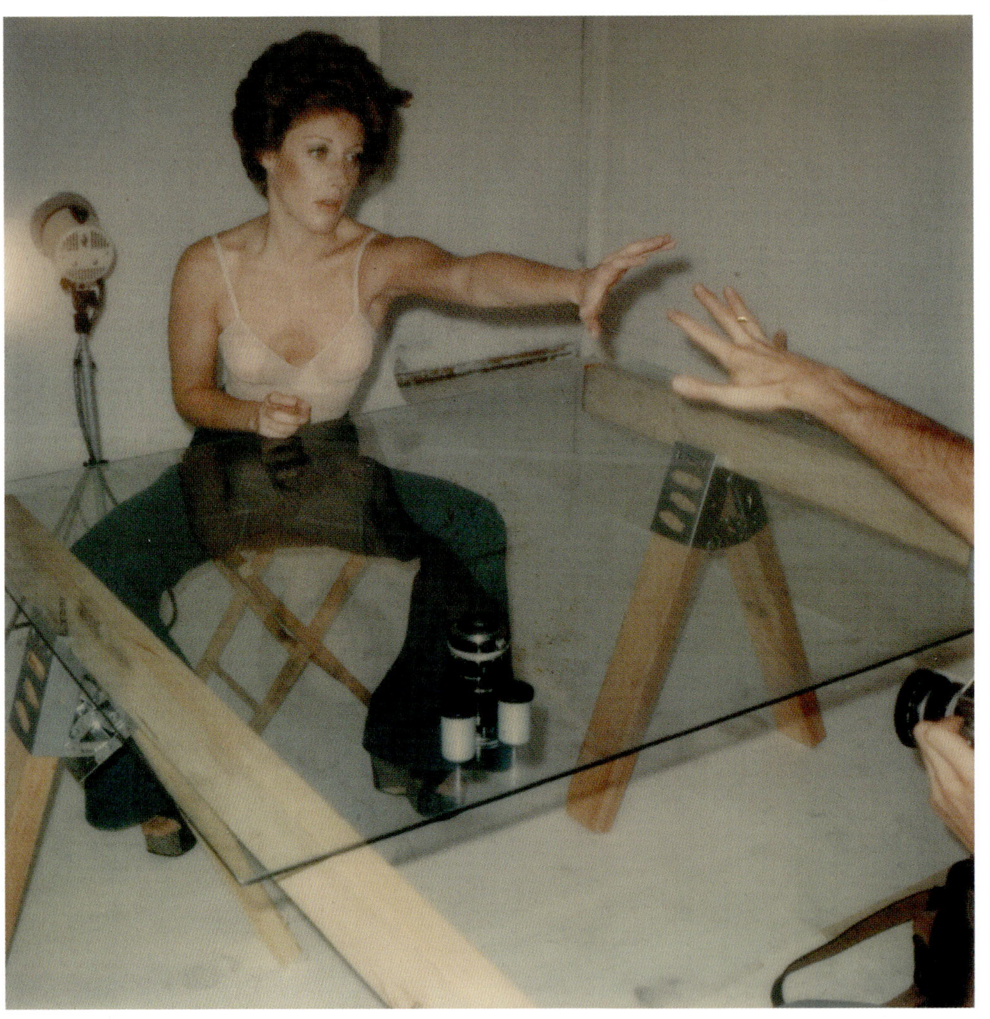

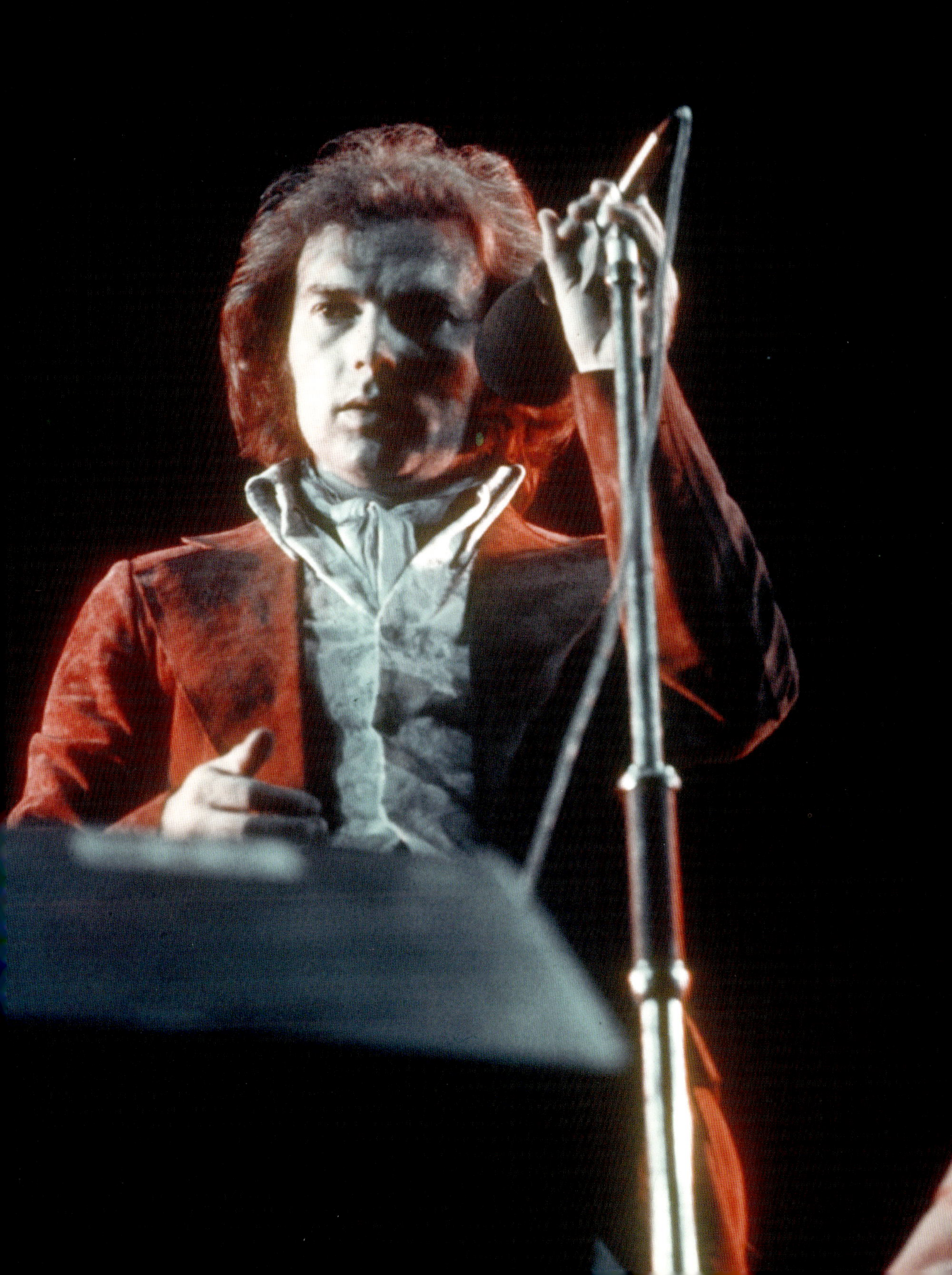

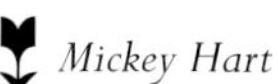
Mickey Hart

Bonnie Bramlett of Delaney & Bonnie and the first white Ikette with Ike & Tina Turner. She co-composed the songs "Groupie (Superstar)" (a hit for The Carpenters), and "Let It Rain" for Eric Clapton.

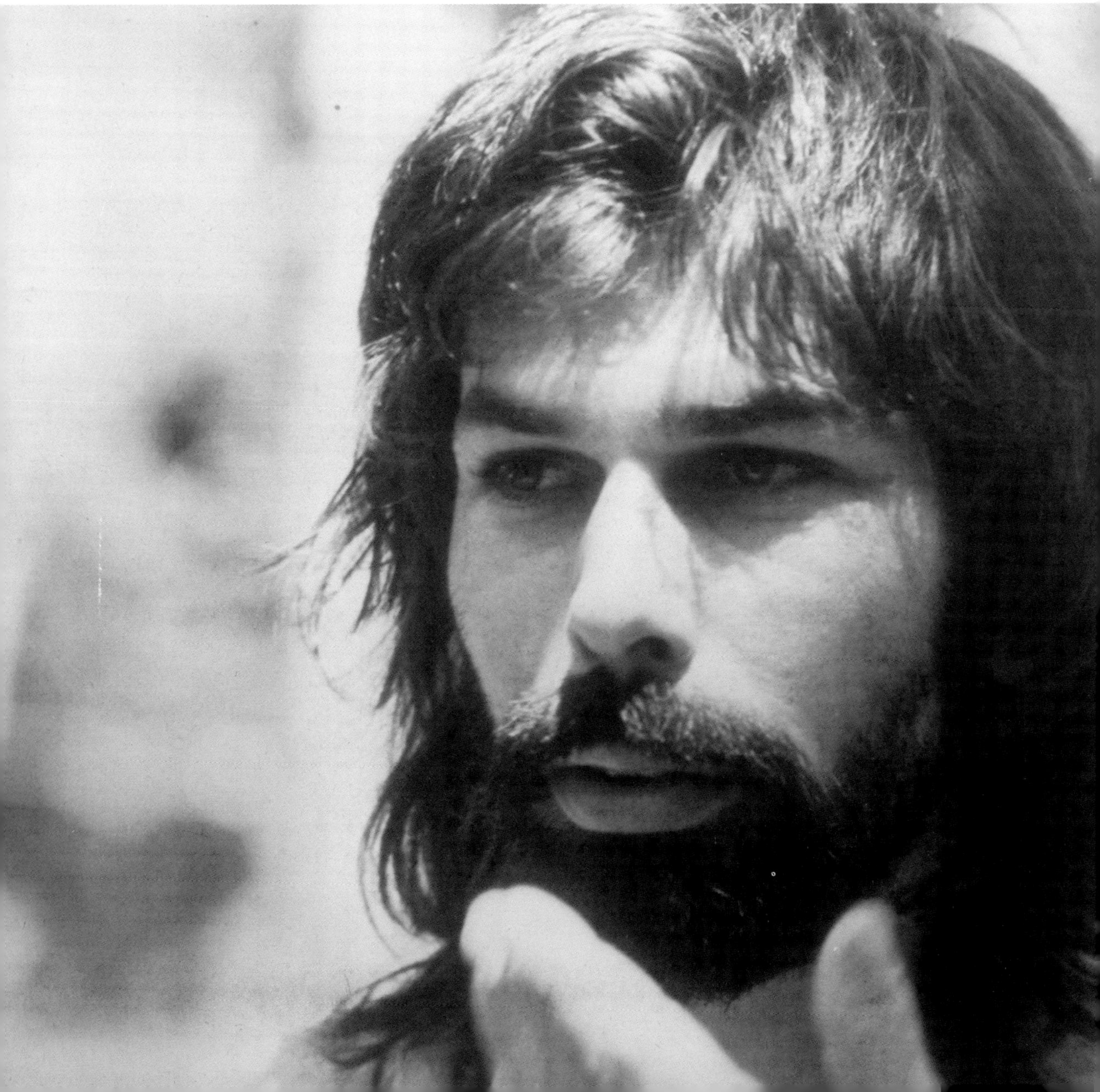

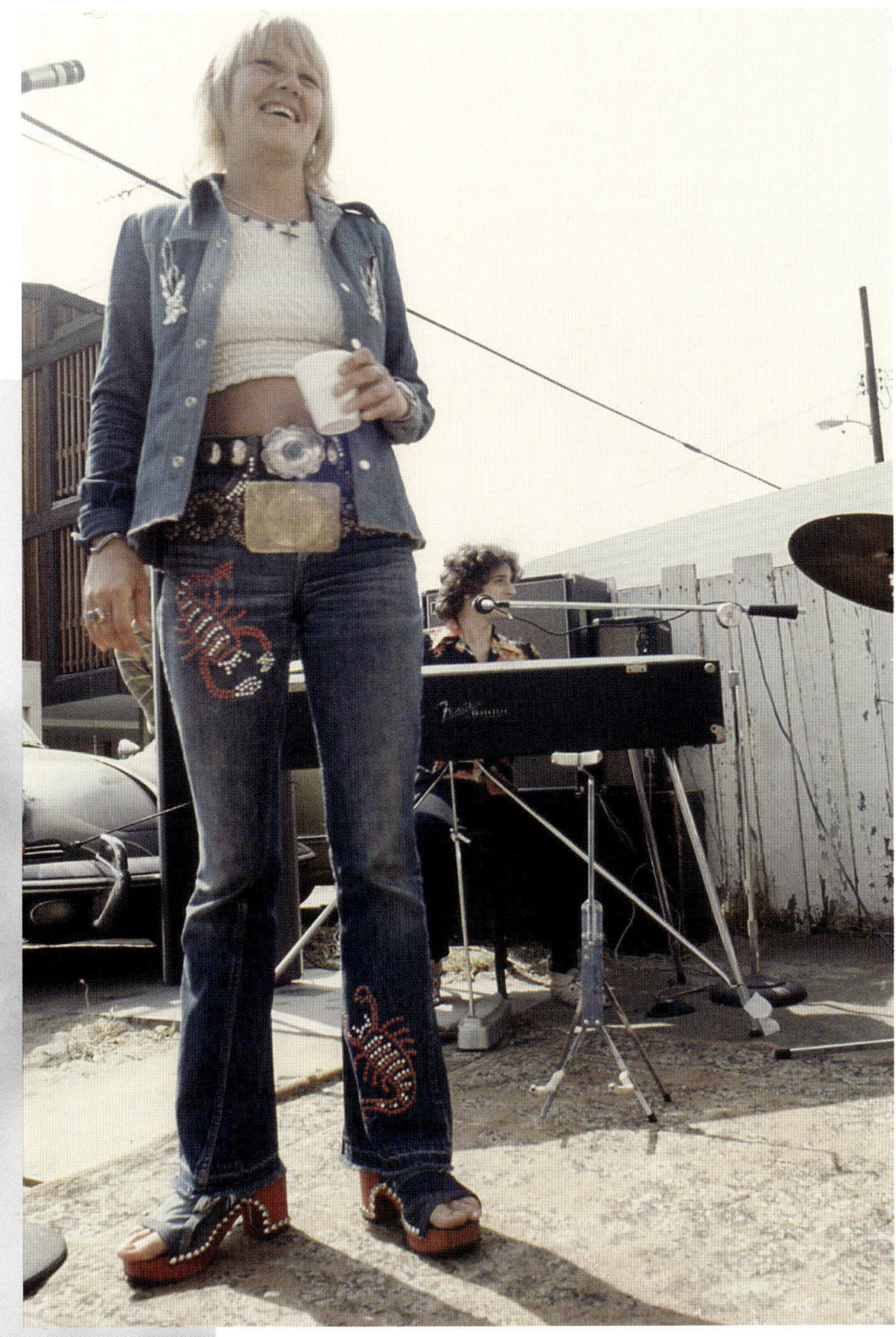

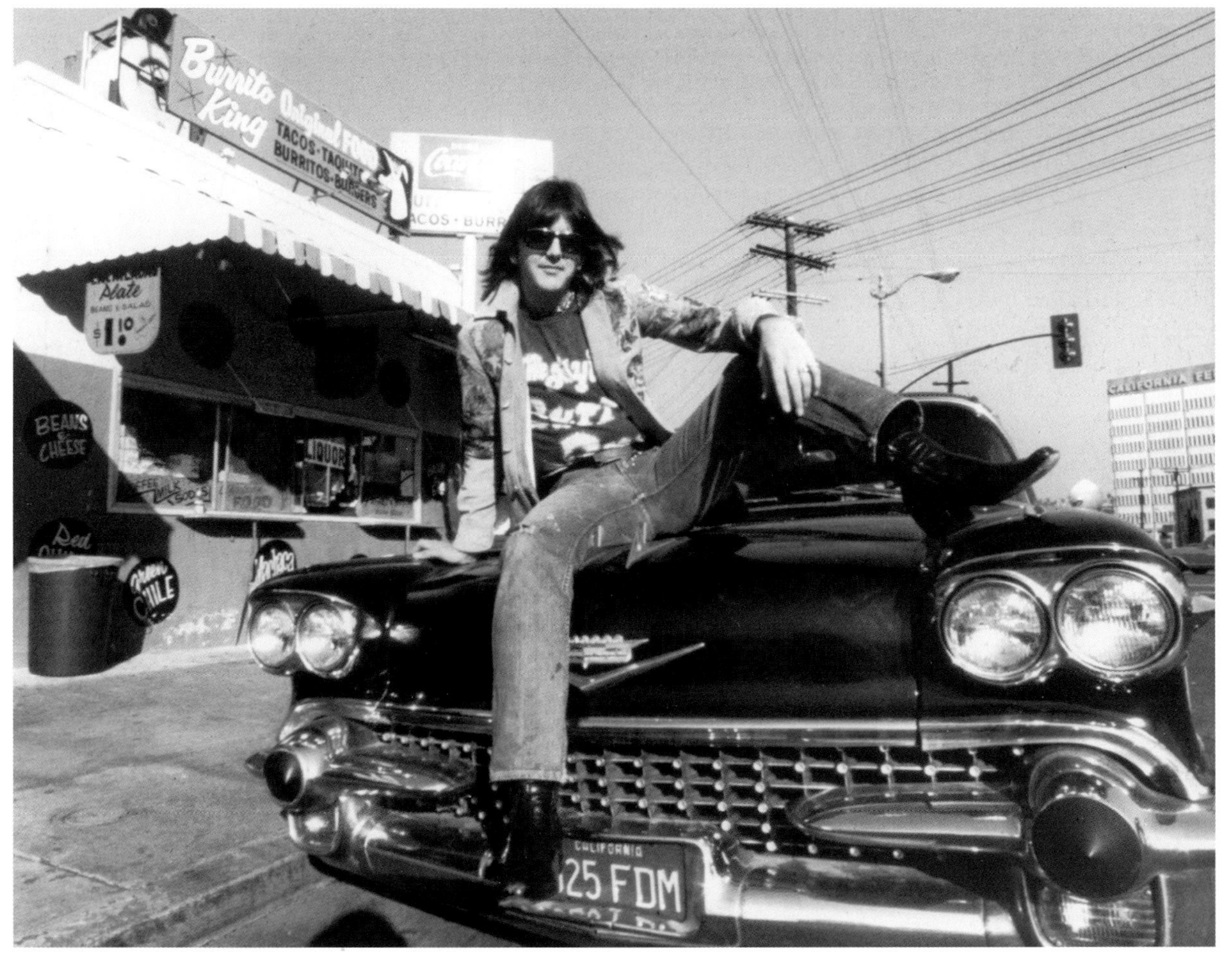
Burrito King
Original FOOD
TACOS · TAQUI
BURRITOS · BURGERS
Plate
$1.10
BEANS & CHEESE
LIQUOR
TACOS · BURR
CALIFORNIA
325 FDM

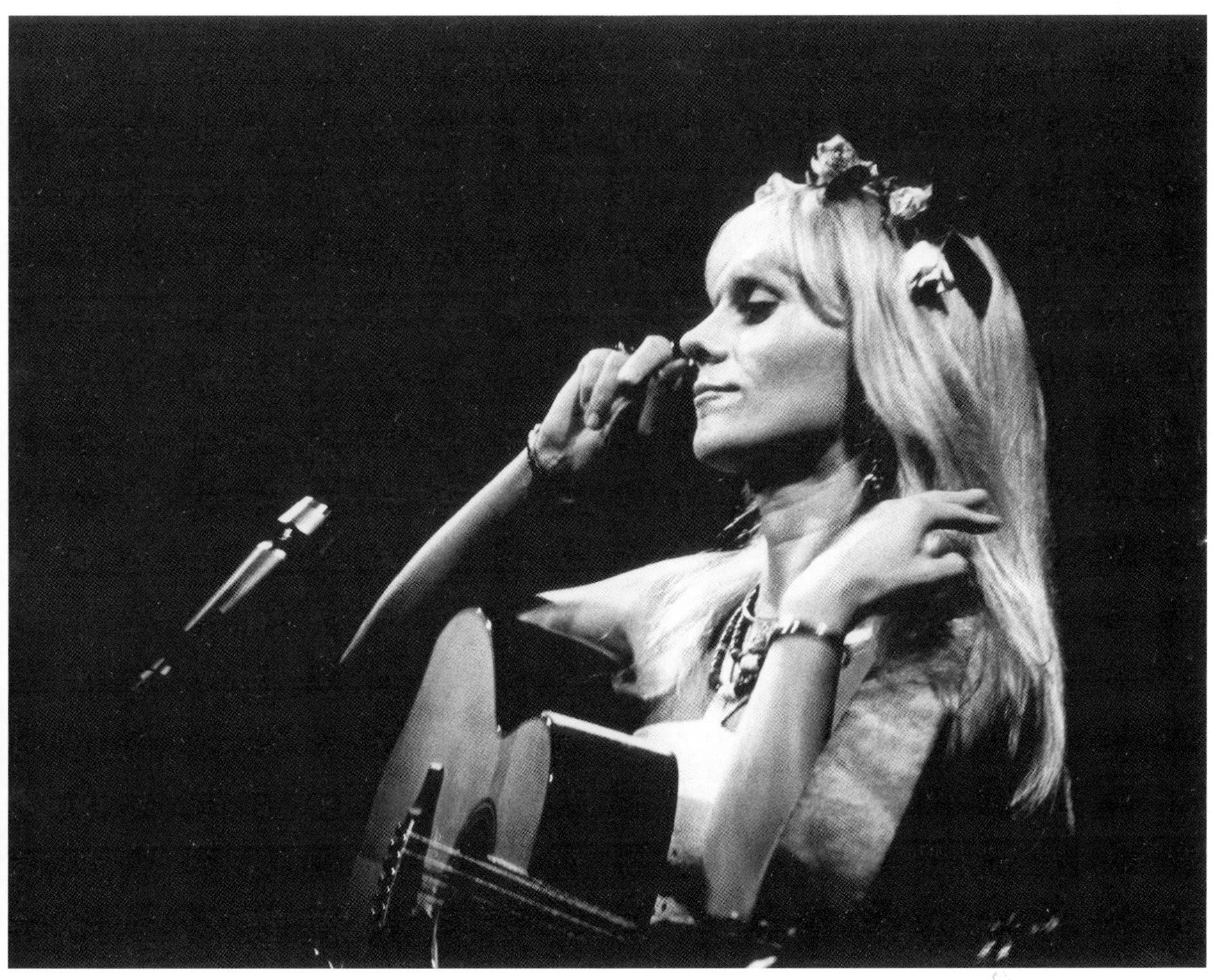

Singer/songwriter Jackie DeShannon, who wrote so many great songs, including 1969's uplifting "Put a Little Love in Your Heart." In the 1970s, she collaborated with Van Morrison on several recordings including his album Hard Nose the Highway *and four songs that Van Morrison and Jackie DeShannon recorded together in 1973 for Atlantic Records: "Sweet Sixteen," "Flamingos Fly," "Santa Fe," and "The Wonder of You"—all four written by Van, except "Santa Fe" which Jackie co-wrote and which was later re-recorded for Van's own* Wavelength *album.*

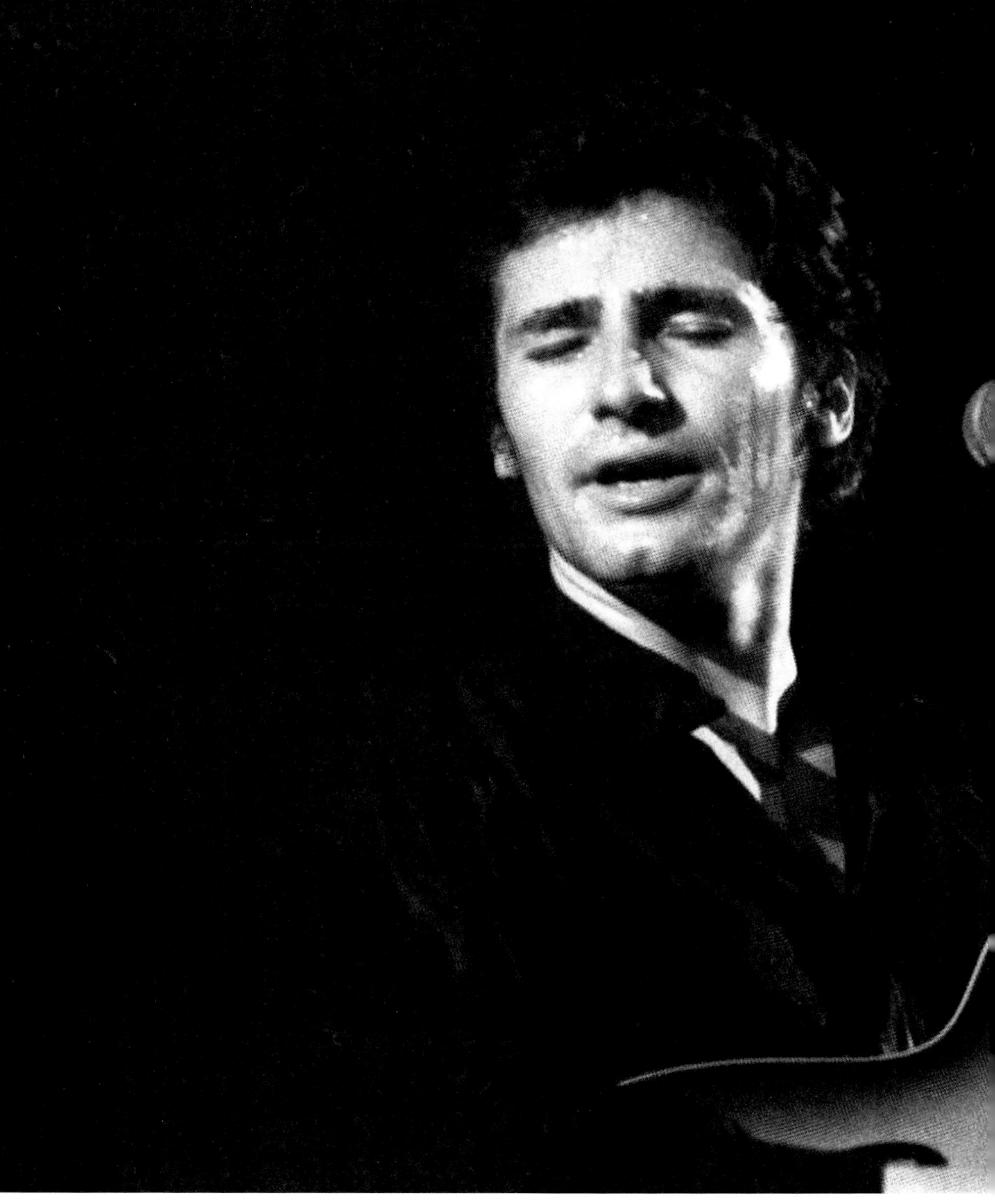

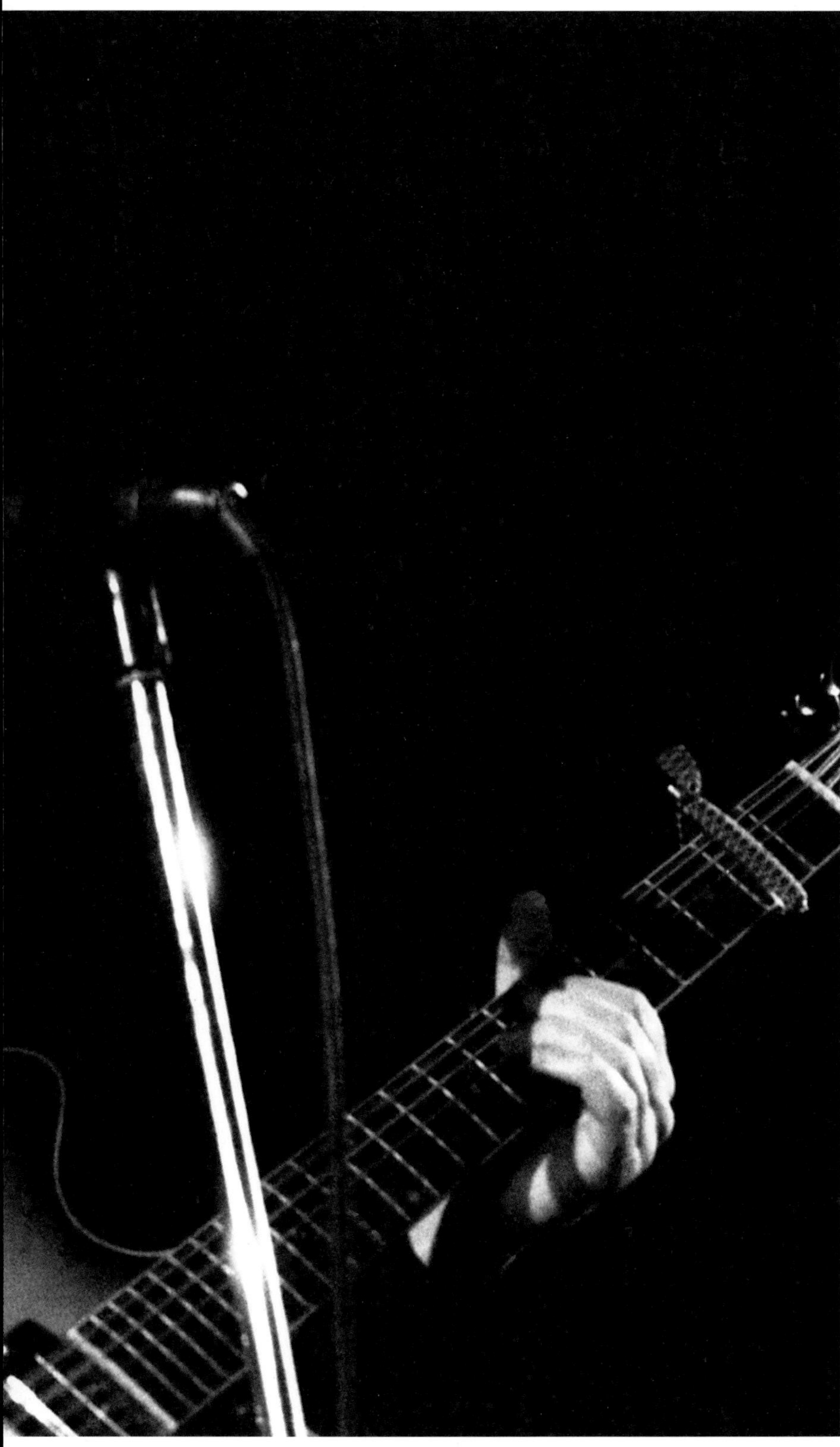

Singer/ songwriter Tim Buckley, father of Jeff, known for his own incredible folk-rock albums such as Goodbye and Hello, *the jazz-folk* Happy Sad, *and the avant-garde masterwork* StarSailor

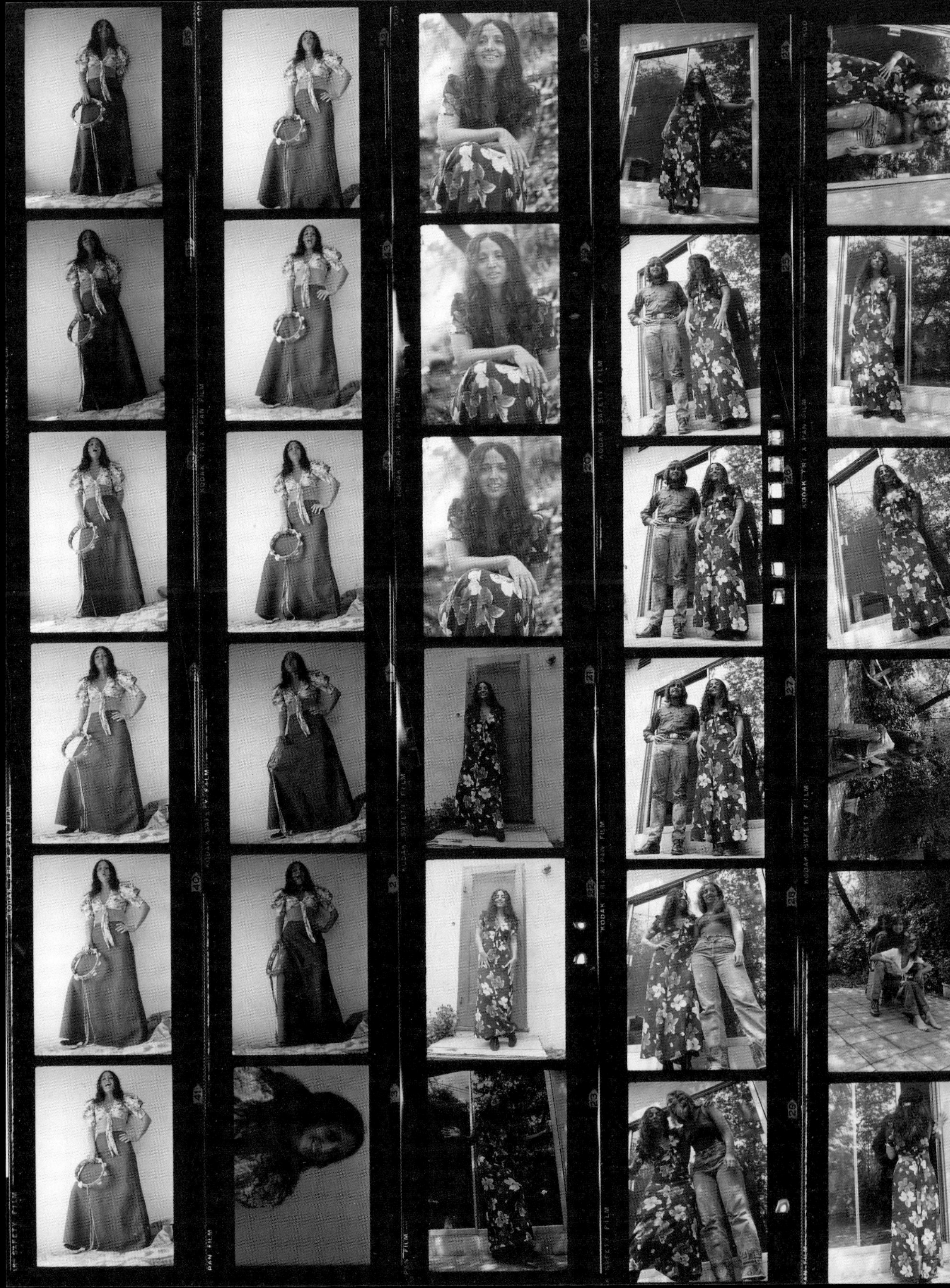

Maria Muldaur

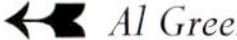

Al Green

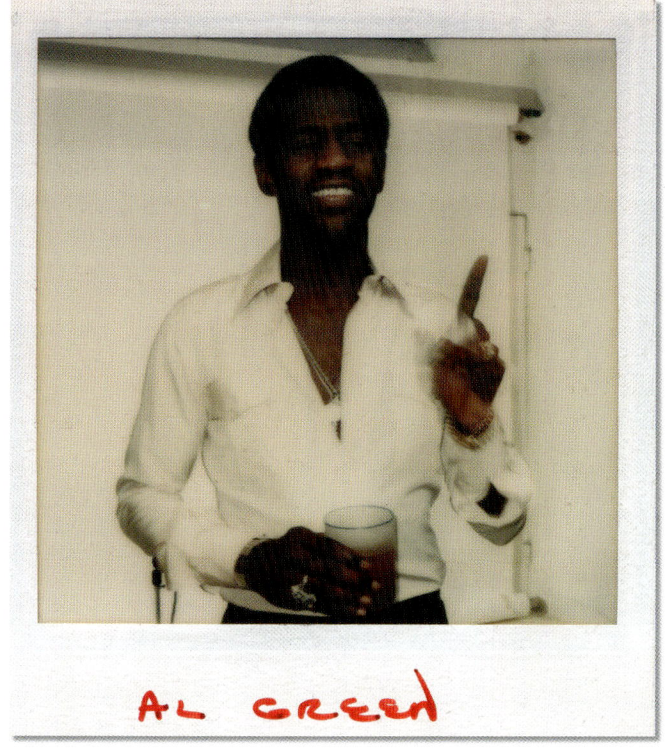

Carly Simon with her child Sarah Taylor

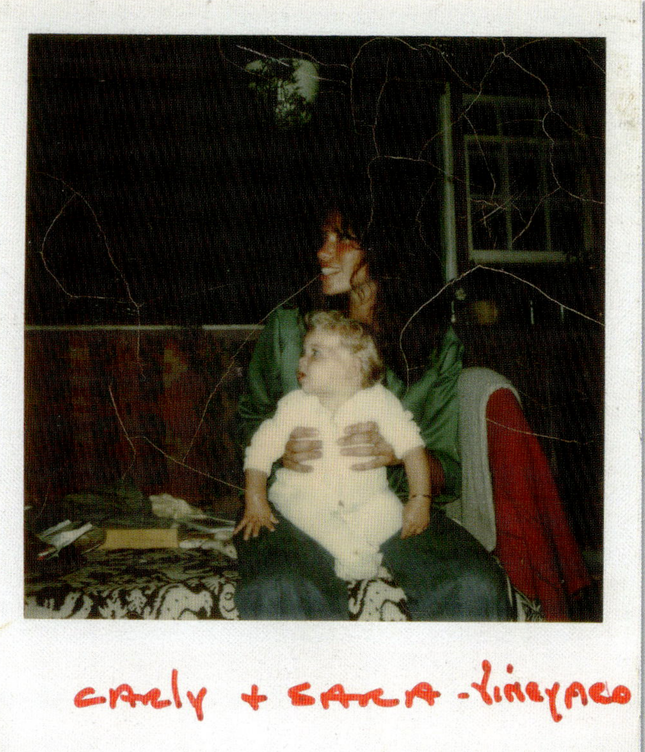

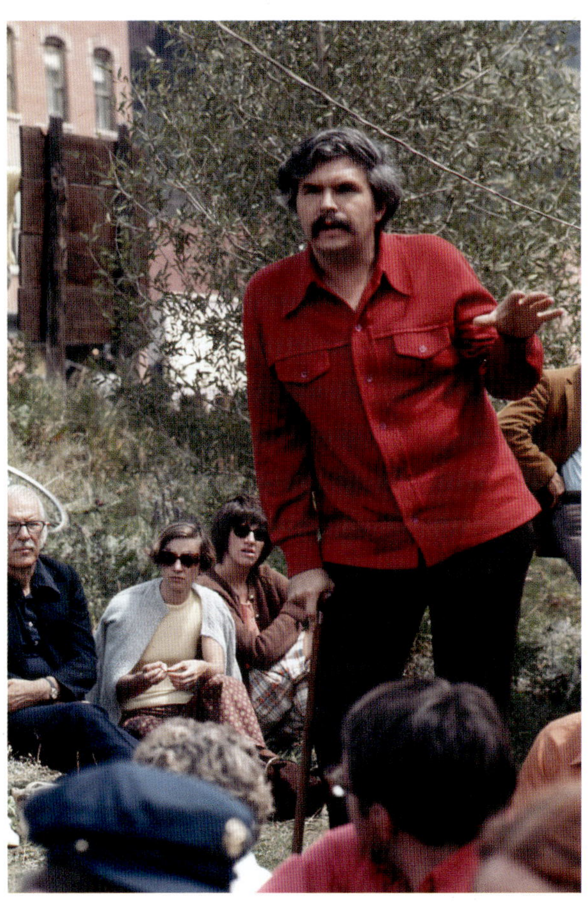

Stan Brakhage at the Telluride Festival—experimental filmmaker who painted directly onto celluloid, did in-camera editing, scratching on film, and played with multiple exposures. His interest in mythology, music, poetry, and visual phenomena fueled his work exploring the universal themes of birth, mortality, sexuality, and innocence; however, his films tended to be silent (without audio).

➔ *Bob Marley*

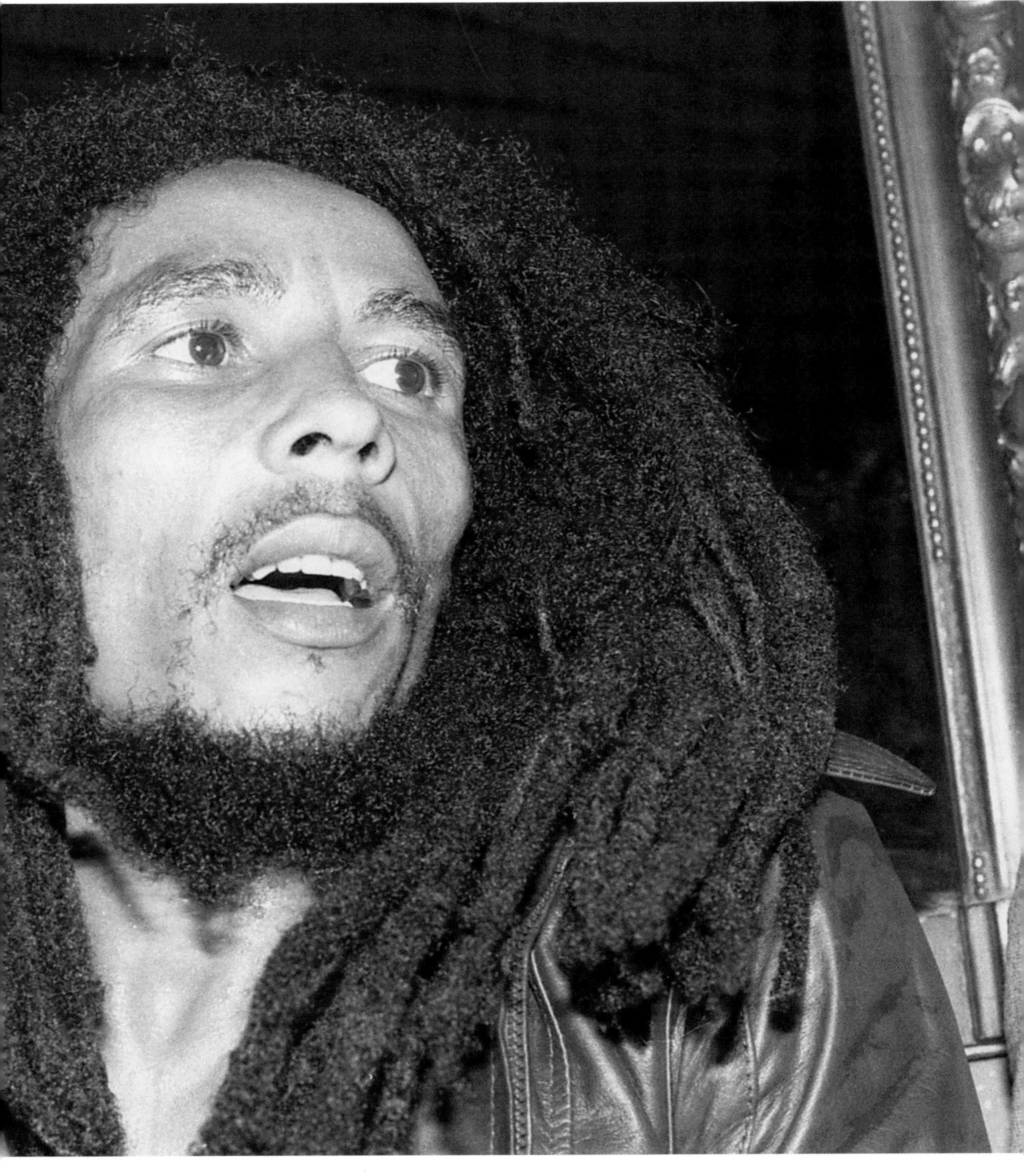

Ginny Winn on
Dr. John

Dr. John, I shot in the studio, but I met him a few times before. I loved his music. I did a lot of shots in the studio with him. People weren't usually allowed in there, but they were great to me about coming in the studio because I was careful about not stepping on any cords. I was good at getting around in the studio. I think it came into play that I had been a dancer and I'm an athlete so I can do the moves to not touch anything while focusing to get good pictures.

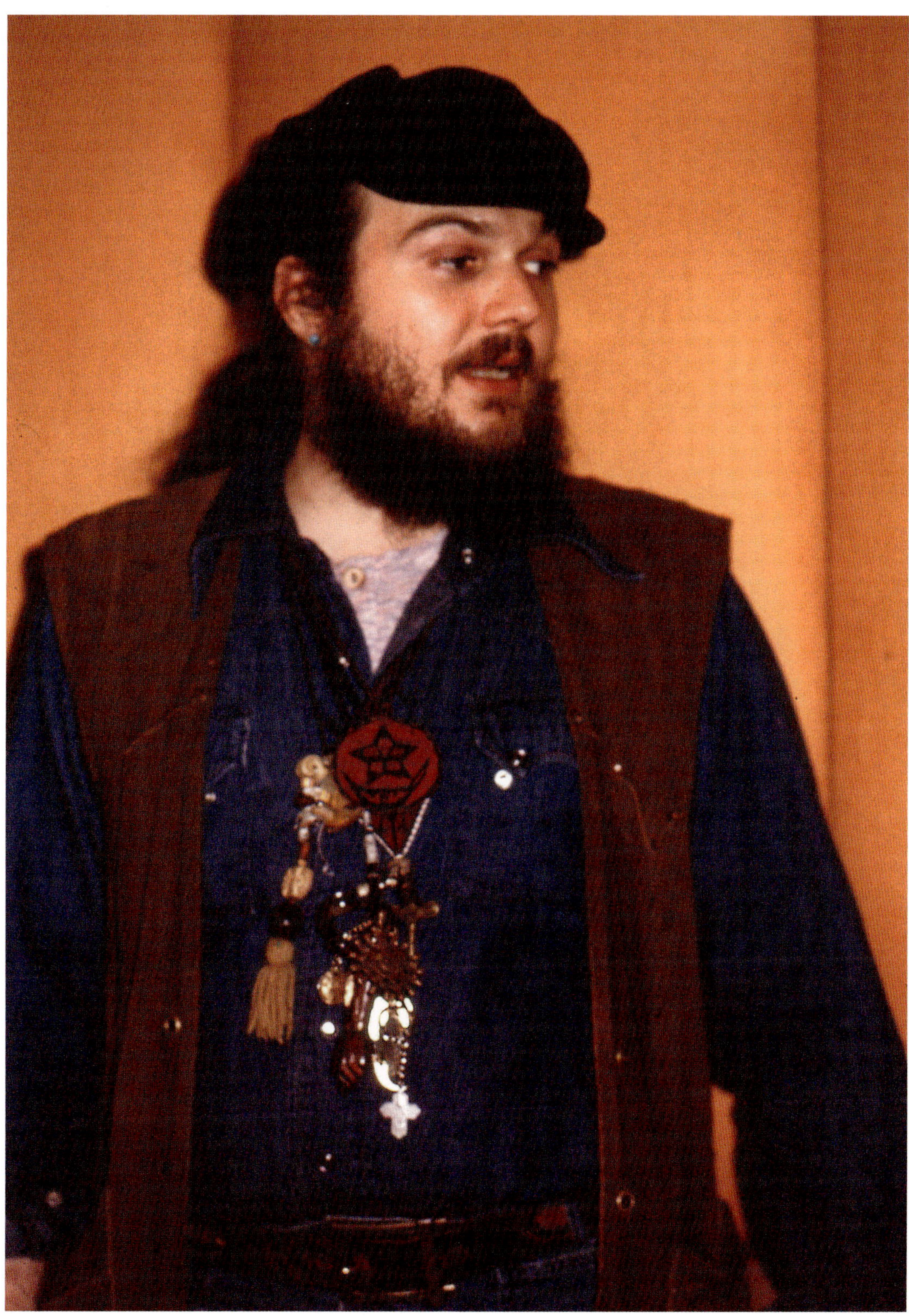

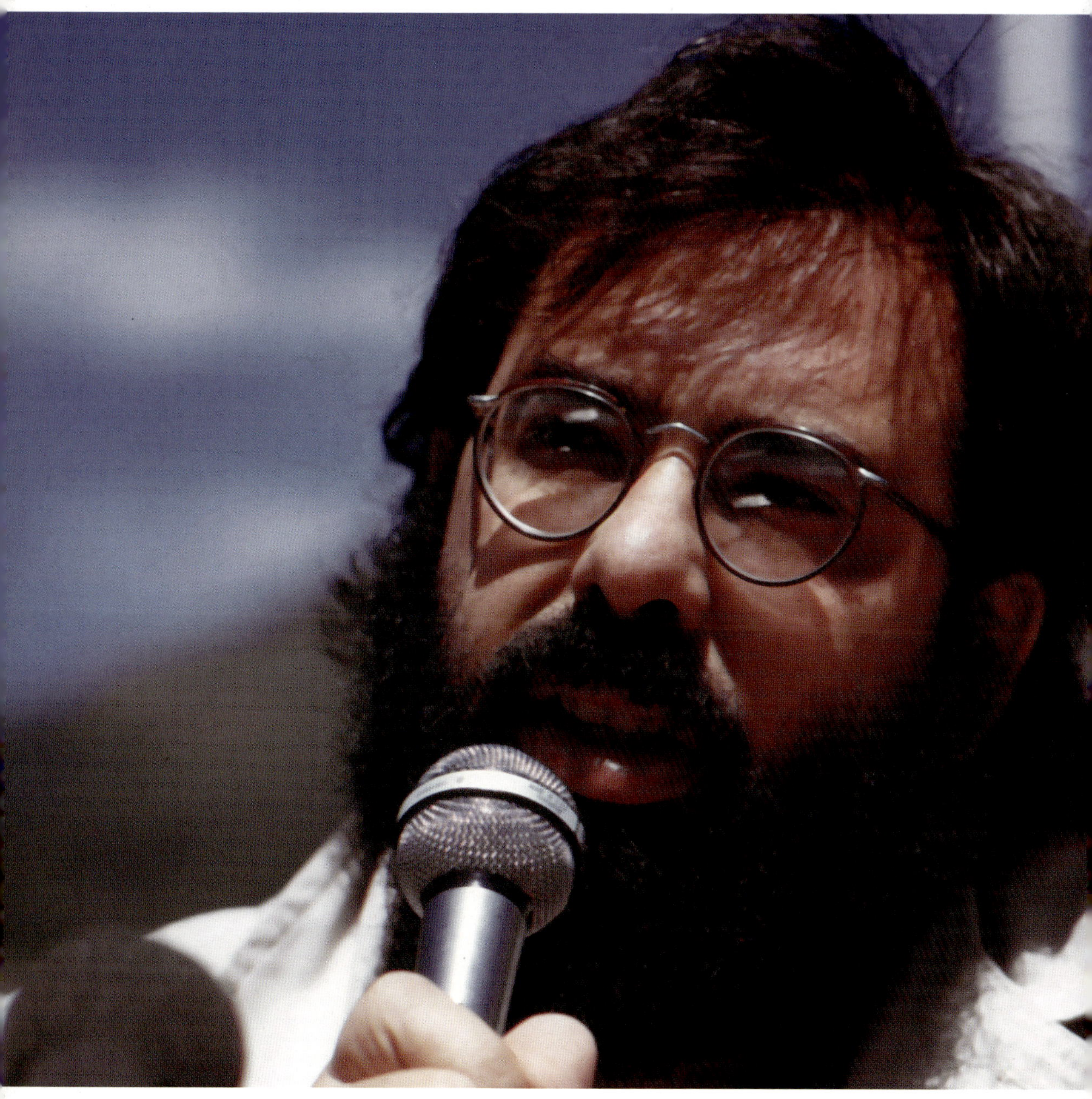

Francis Ford Coppola—Director of The Godfather

Tim Buckley

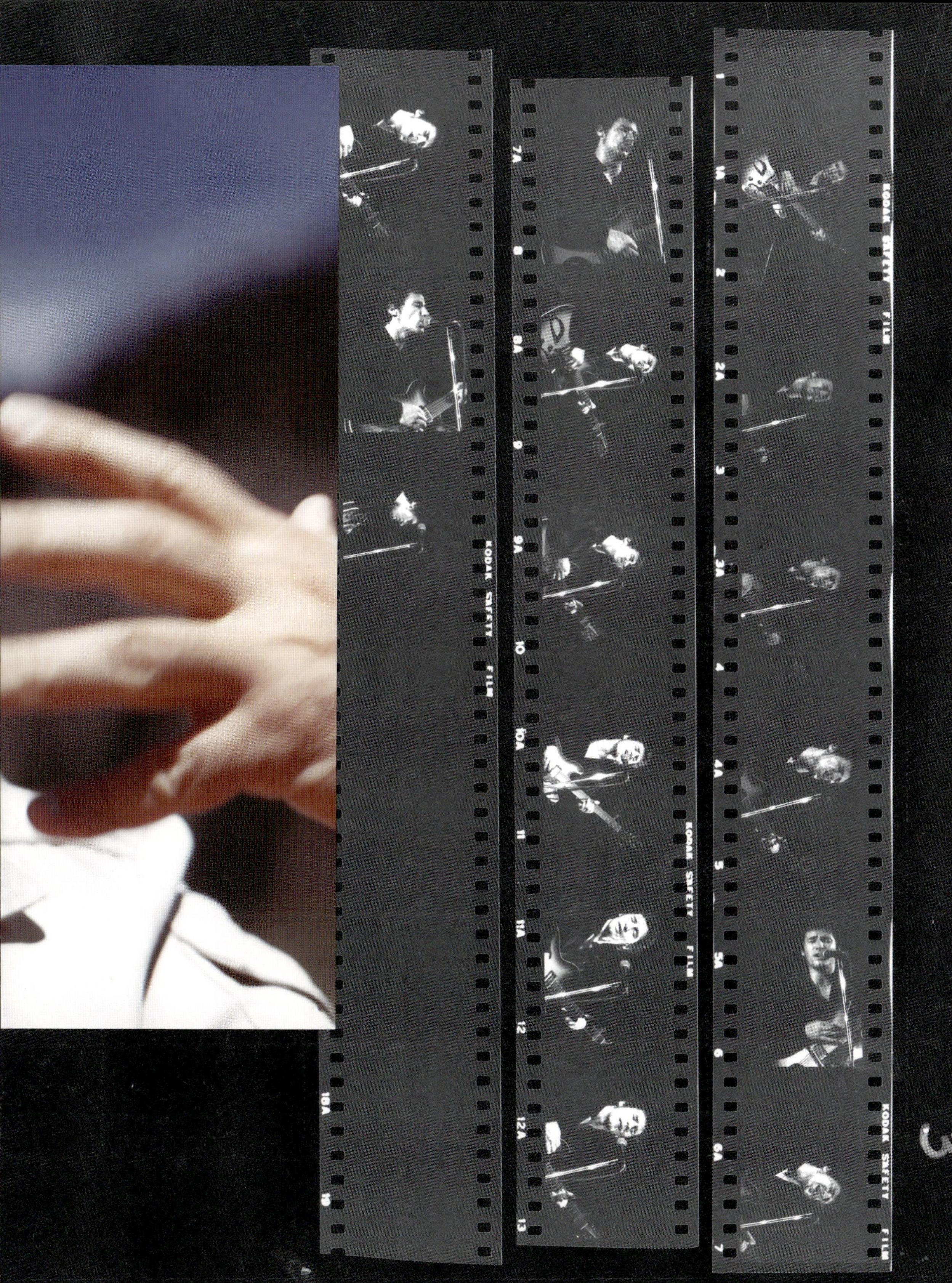
KODAK SAFETY FILM

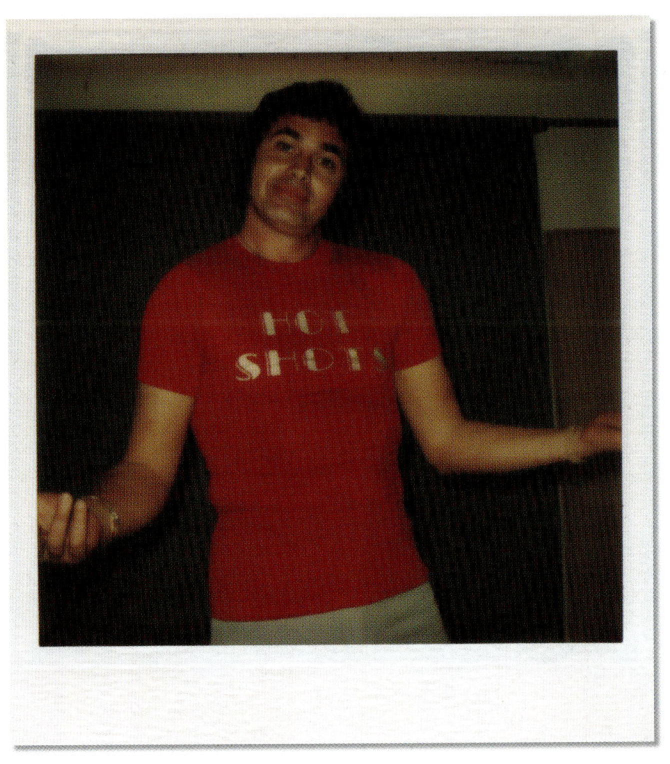

↑ *Engelbert Humperdinck—King of Easy Listening Vocals*

→→ *Jimmy Webb —composer of several of your favorite Glen Campbell hits*

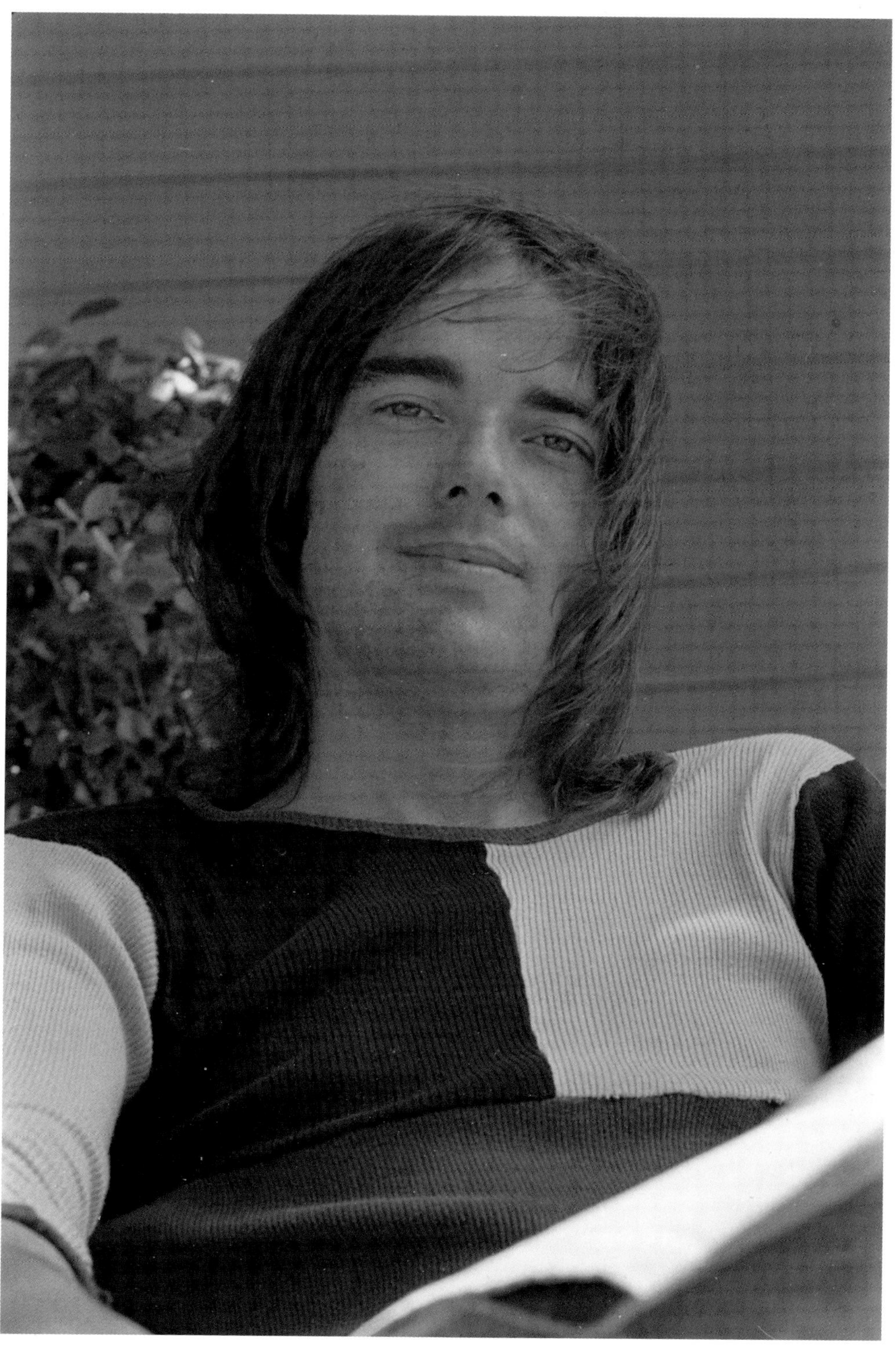

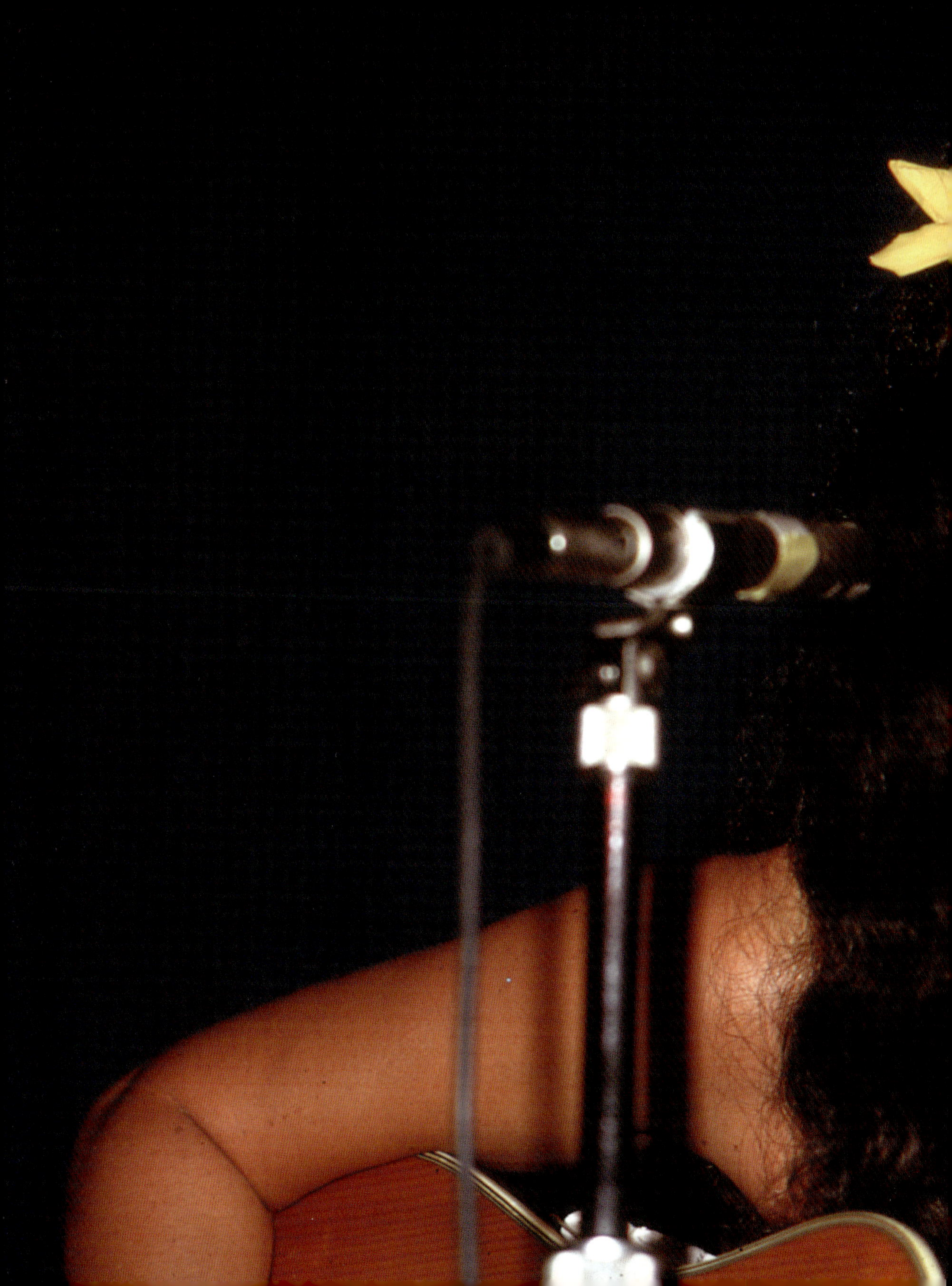

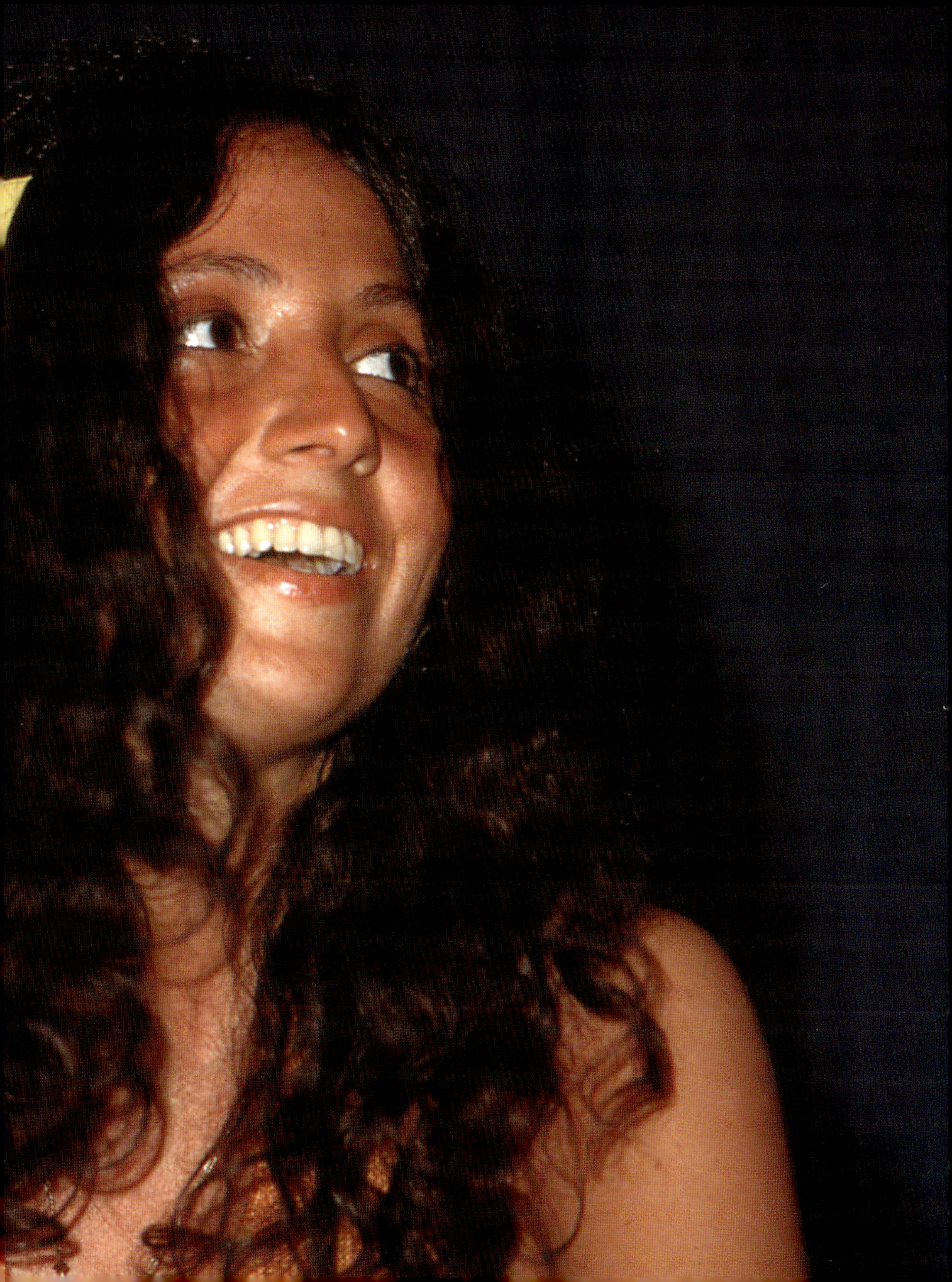

Ginny Winn on
Maria Muldaur

(pg 106–107) Maria Muldaur

Maria Muldaur

Before I even knew Maria, I remember listening to the Kweskin Jug Band and falling in love with her voice. Years later, she came down to L.A. for her first solo album and we connected through Warner Brothers. She ended up renting a house on my street and we became best friends. Our daughters became best friends, too. When my house burned down and I was out of town, she was the one on the phone saying, "Don't worry I'll take care of your kids, cat and dog—they're with me."

Warner/Reprise knew we worked well together, so they'd send me to meet her or go on the road with her. We would hold hands and skip down the street kind of thing, and talk about men and everything under the sun. I shot so many images of her, including that cover for her magical "Midnight at the Oasis." I shot video of Maria and Linda Ronstadt doing "I'm a Woman"—one of the first music videos ever.

Maria's so strong, a true trooper. Her energy is boundless. To this day, she still gives 100% per performance. Plus, she really knows her roots—the music and the musicians. She went on a personal quest to meet the musicians and see how they lived. Her performances are filled with history and humor, always joking, and relating personally to the audience. Her friends might sit up close and get a personal nod, but the whole audience feels that nod.

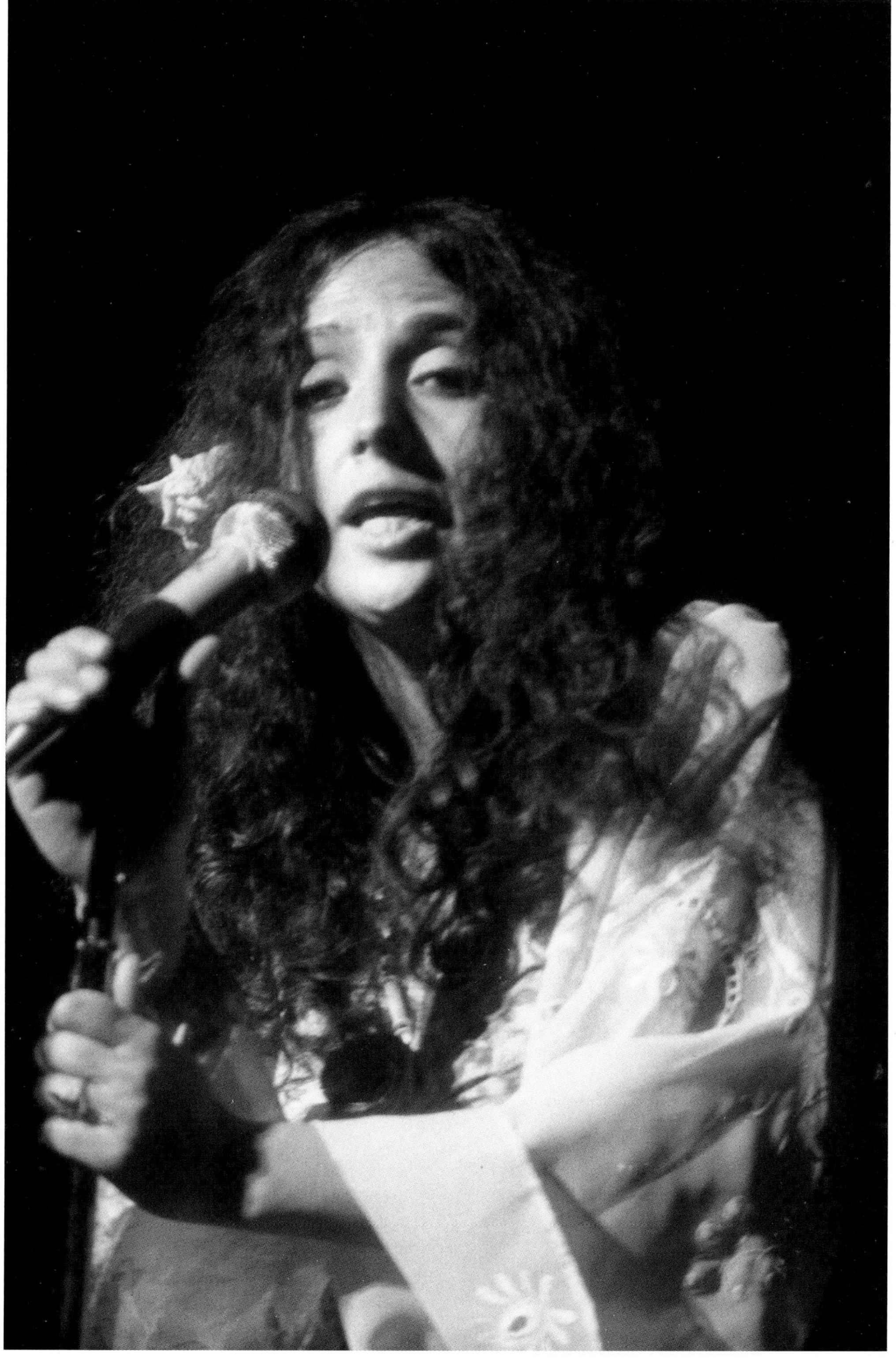

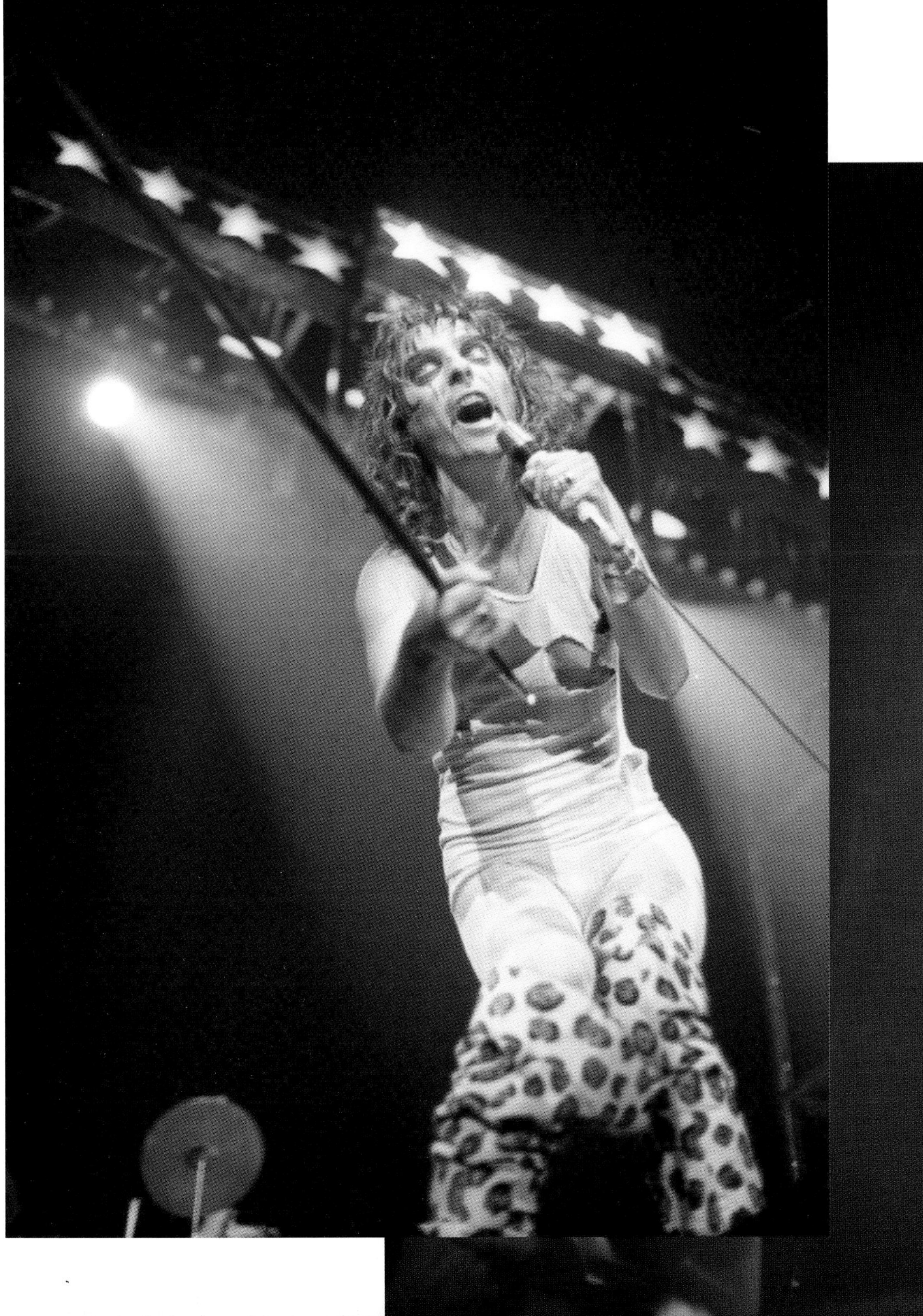

← *Alice Cooper*

↓ *Dennis Dunaway of the Alice Cooper Band*

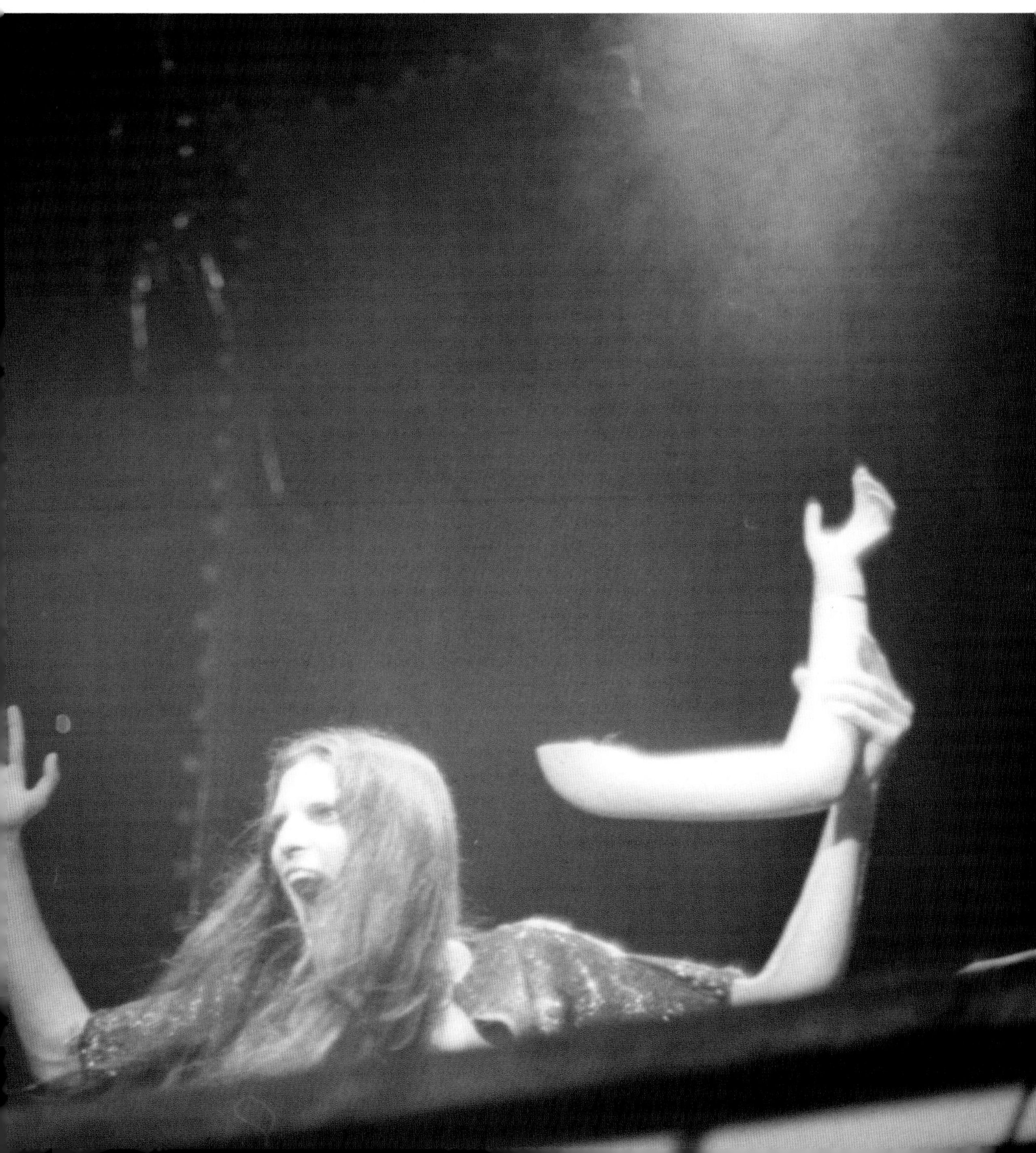

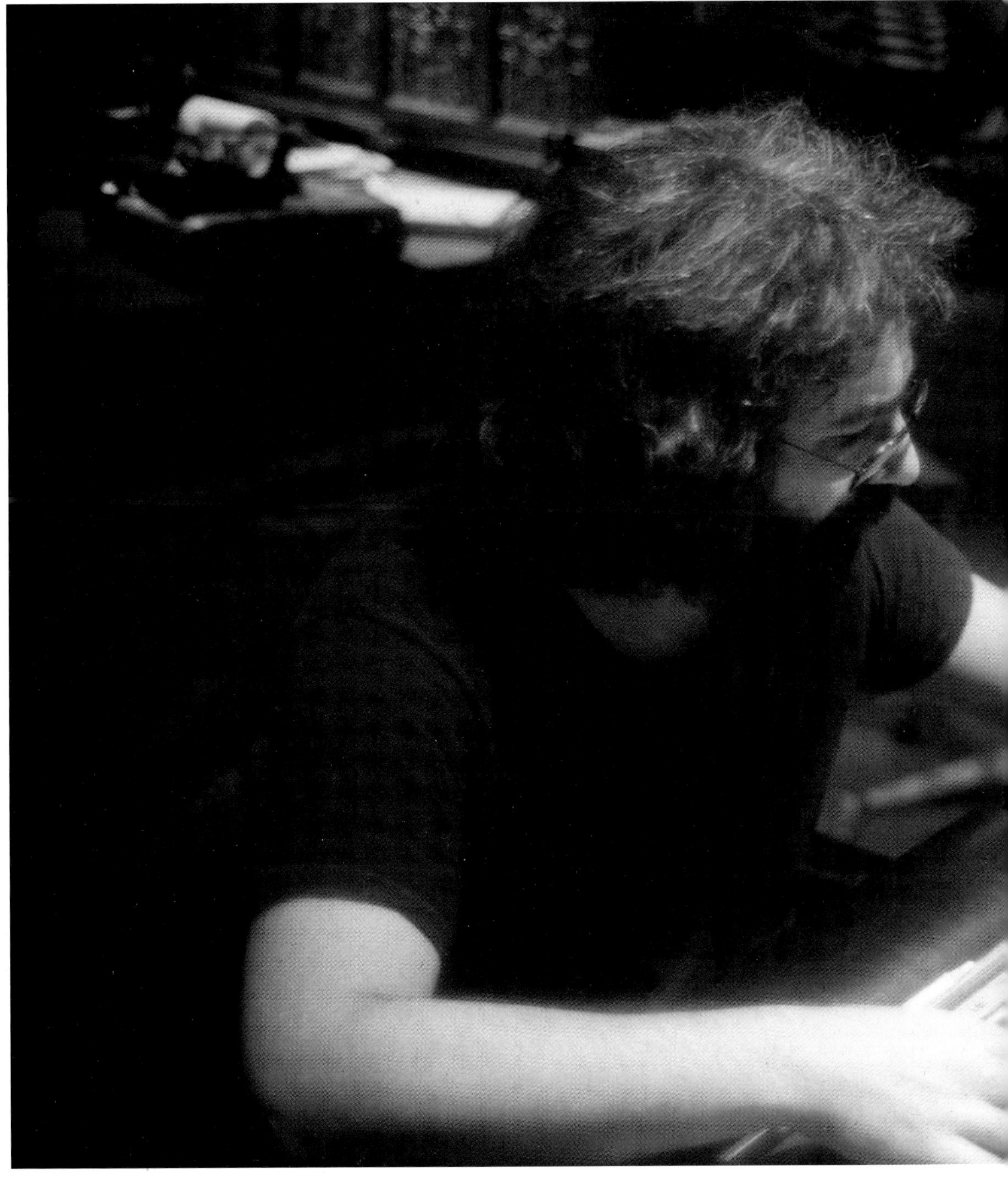

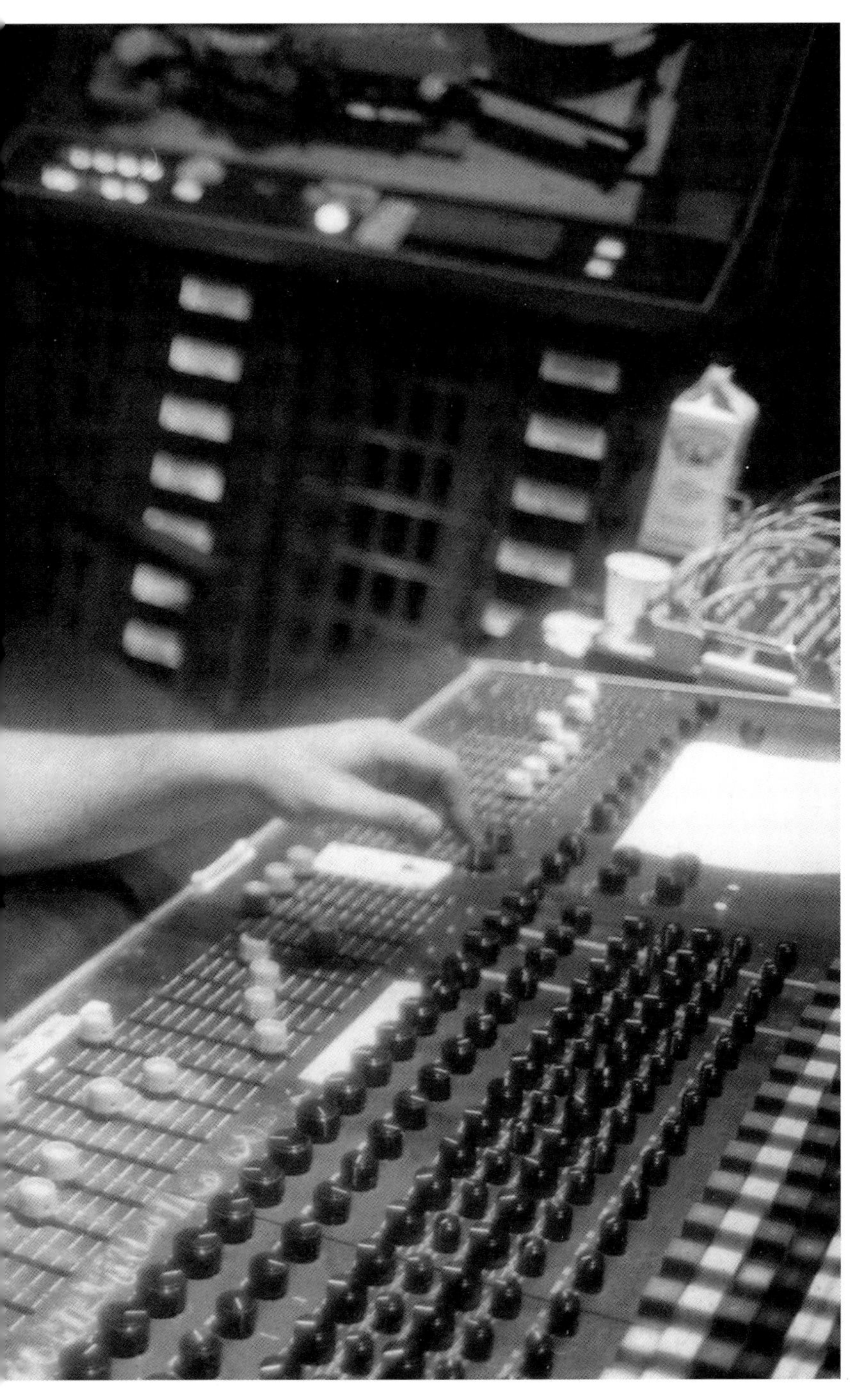

Jerry Garcia

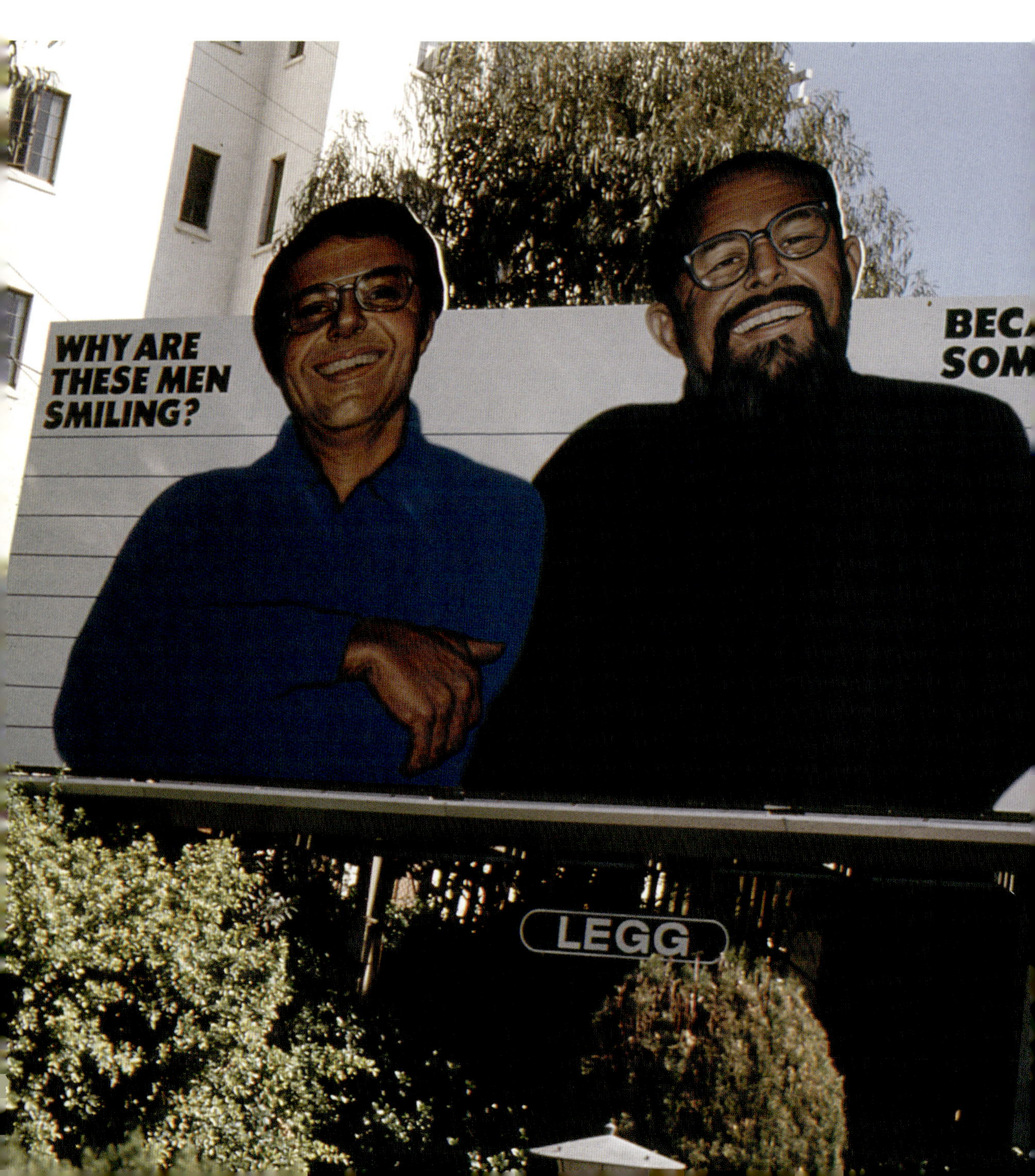
WHY ARE
THESE MEN
SMILING?
BECA
SOM
LEGG

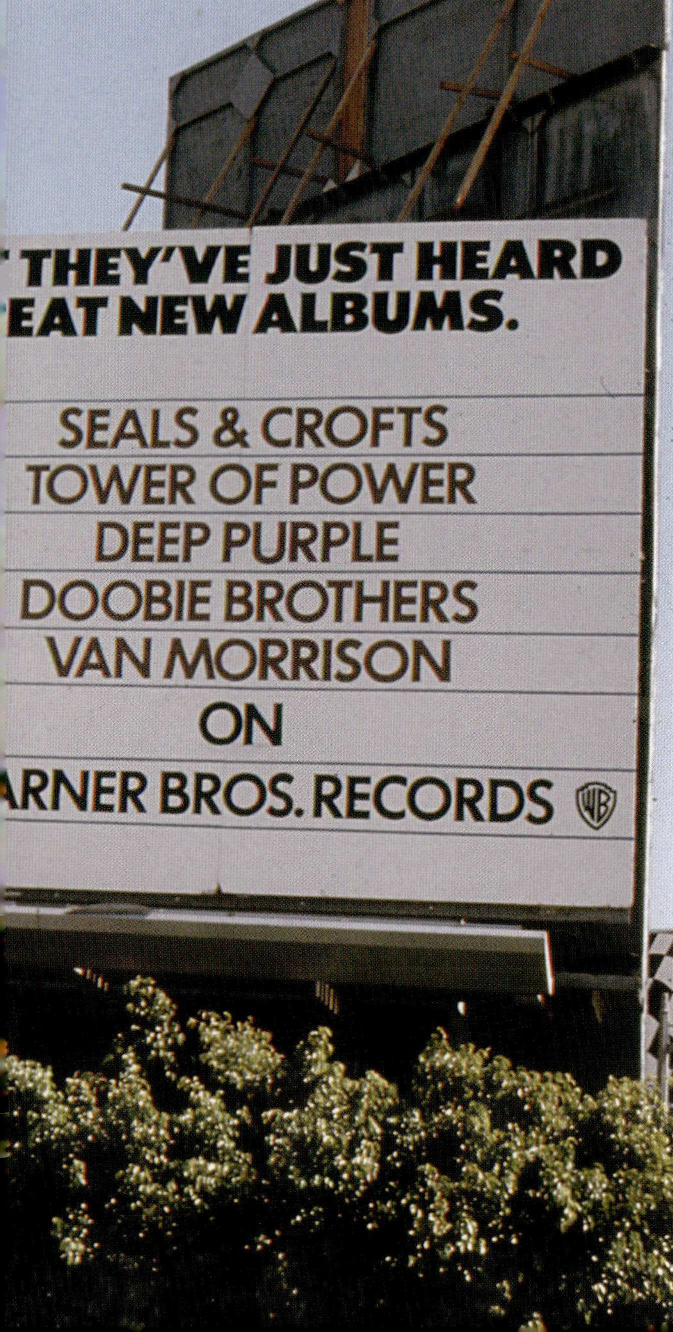

"Bonnie Raitt, Randy Newman, Ry Cooder, Arlo Guthrie, Gordon Lightfoot. It was a sort of artsy non-commercial—you could almost call it Americana now, forty years in hindsight—corner of the label, and there was no pressure to make hit records at all. It was not about having hit singles. If you happened to have one, well, that was great. "Midnight at the Oasis" was a complete accident, a very lucky and blessed one. But that wasn't the point, it was they literally were patrons of the arts and of the artists and the development.

In other words, it helped develop and connect the right artist with the right material and sort of gave them the room to grow, and the wherewithal to do it. So those were golden years, it was a very special thing.

The way I even became a solo artist for Warner Brothers was like, Mo Ostin just had an idea; it's amazing to me, and it would never happen in this day and age the same way. We were very blessed that there were people like Mo—in the same vein as Jerry Wexler, and other greats like that—who were all about the music first, and the commercial success way second."

– Maria Muldaur in conversation with Pat Thomas about the golden era of the Warner / Reprise label

"And so, in the couple years that ensued after we [Geoff and Maria] actually settled into Woodstock, and then started attempting to put songs together for our next album, we must have gone through every bass player east of the Mississippi. And nobody was good enough for Geoffrey. Until Paul Butterfield said, 'Listen, I know a guy.' We heard from so-and-so, and Geoffrey would go, 'No, he's not the right feel!' And so… and we just wanted to have some gigs. The rest of us just wanted to go out and play some gigs somewhere, in Albany or wherever. And so, Butterfield told us, 'There's this young bass player. He's really good and he's really soulful and he's a really accomplished musician. He did some sessions with Bloomfield and Al Kooper, you know, those Super Sessions at the Fillmore. And his name is John Kahn.'

He had John come, we got in touch with him, he said, 'Sure, I'll come East and do an album!' The poor guy, born and raised in Beverly Hills, shows up in the dead of winter, with a light jacket, the kind of jacket you'd wear in L.A. in the fall. It's freezing, a blizzard out. He gets on the train—flies into New York and takes the train up, there's a dreadful blizzard. I wasn't even there—things had gotten kind of tense there, so I had taken a little trip with my daughter to Boston, and I was staying with David Grisman and his wife and kids.

Anyway, so poor John Kahn finds himself snowed in with Geoff Muldaur and it gets to be there's nothing in the house—they're down to nothing to eat in the house, and they can't get out. And our neighbor was Garth Hudson, and Geoffrey drank a lot of Bacardi and tonic in those days; he and Amos [Garrett], that was their drink. Bacardi and tonic with lime. So finally, Garth plows himself out of his driveway and down to our driveway, and says, 'I'm going to town for provisions, you want me to get anything?' And poor John thought, 'Oh thank God, we're gonna have some soup or something.' All Geoffrey asked him to get was more Bacardi and tonic and limes.

So, anyway, he spent the week drilling—playing obscure Fletcher Henderson records or Duke Ellington records or whatever, stuff from that era, and then drilling John like, 'OK, who's playing the alto solo on this one?' And John would always surprise him with the right answer. So, after this sort of trial by fire—or ice, as the case may be—he was approved and hired to be the bass player and hired on those sessions. And so that's how—that's one of the things that created the holdup, there was no bass player east of the Mississippi, or even east of the Rockies that was worthy, until we found John Kahn."

– Maria Muldaur in conversation with Pat Thomas about bassist John Kahn

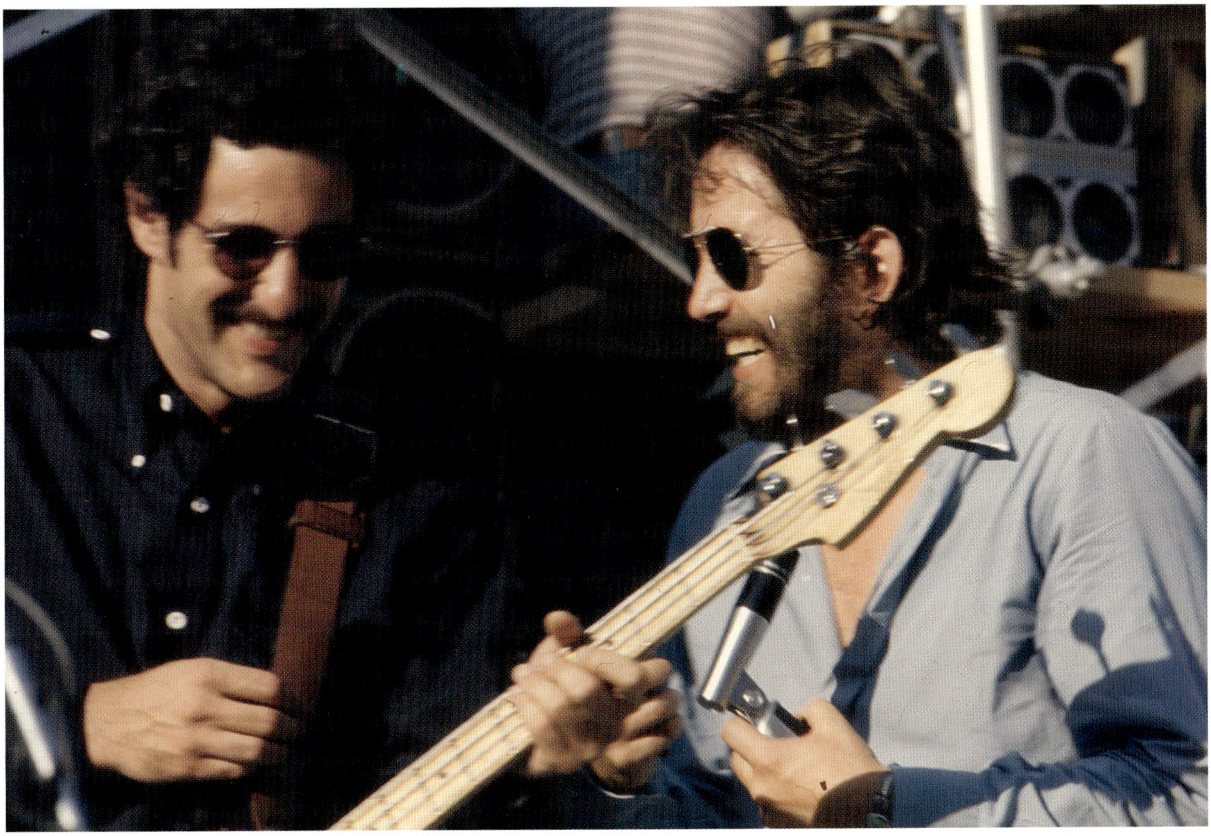

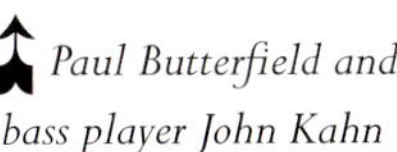

Paul Butterfield and bass player John Kahn

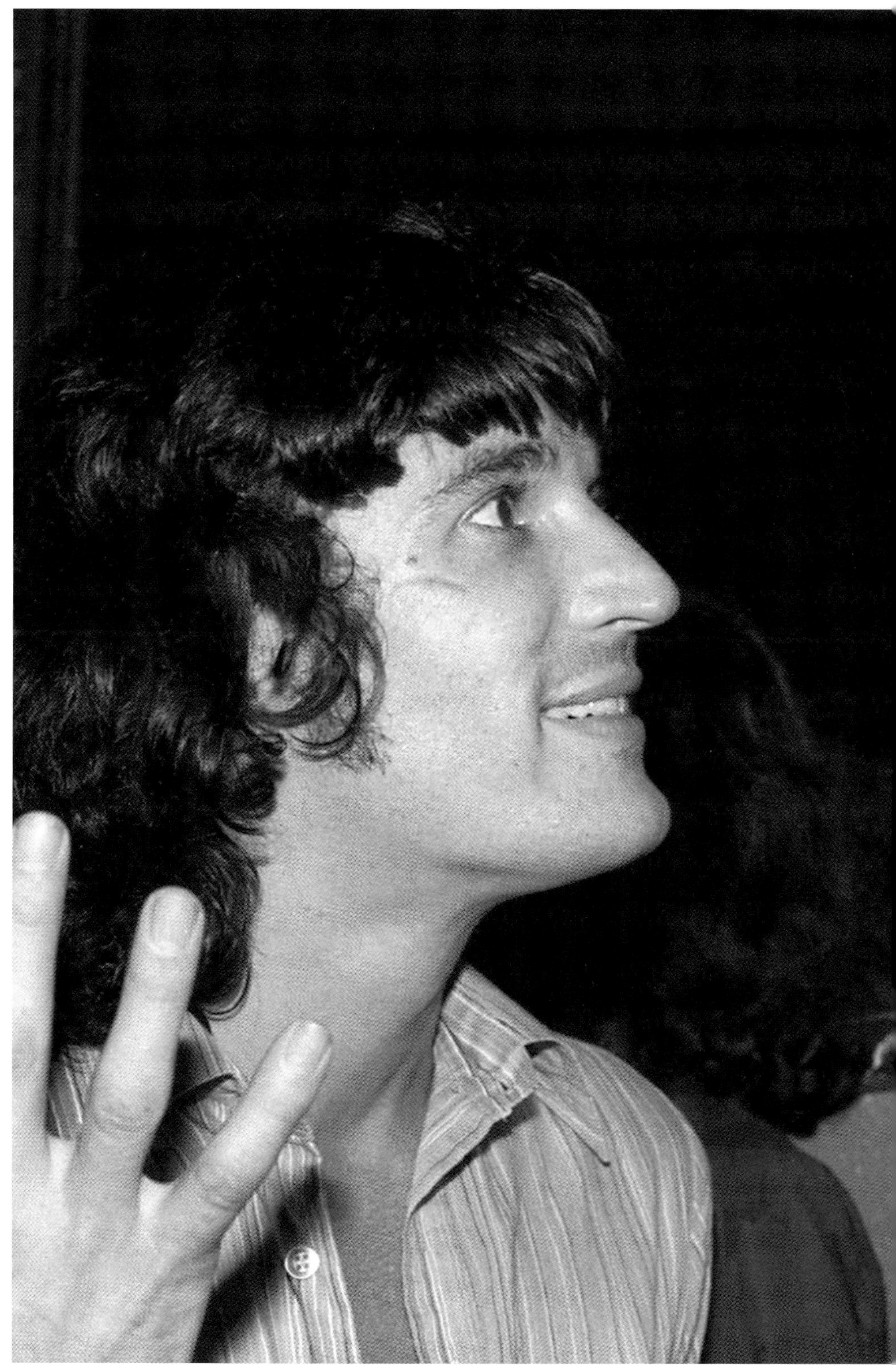

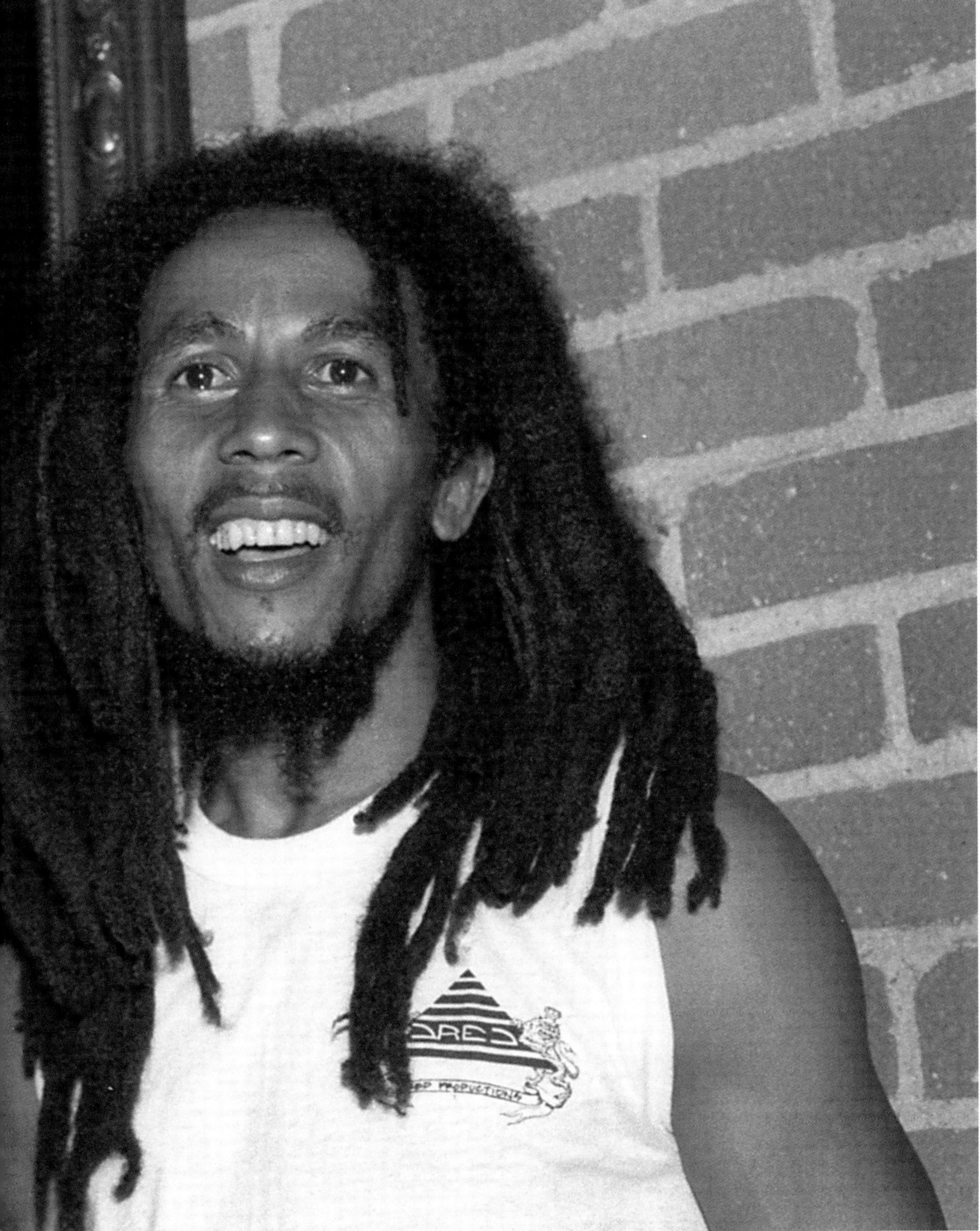

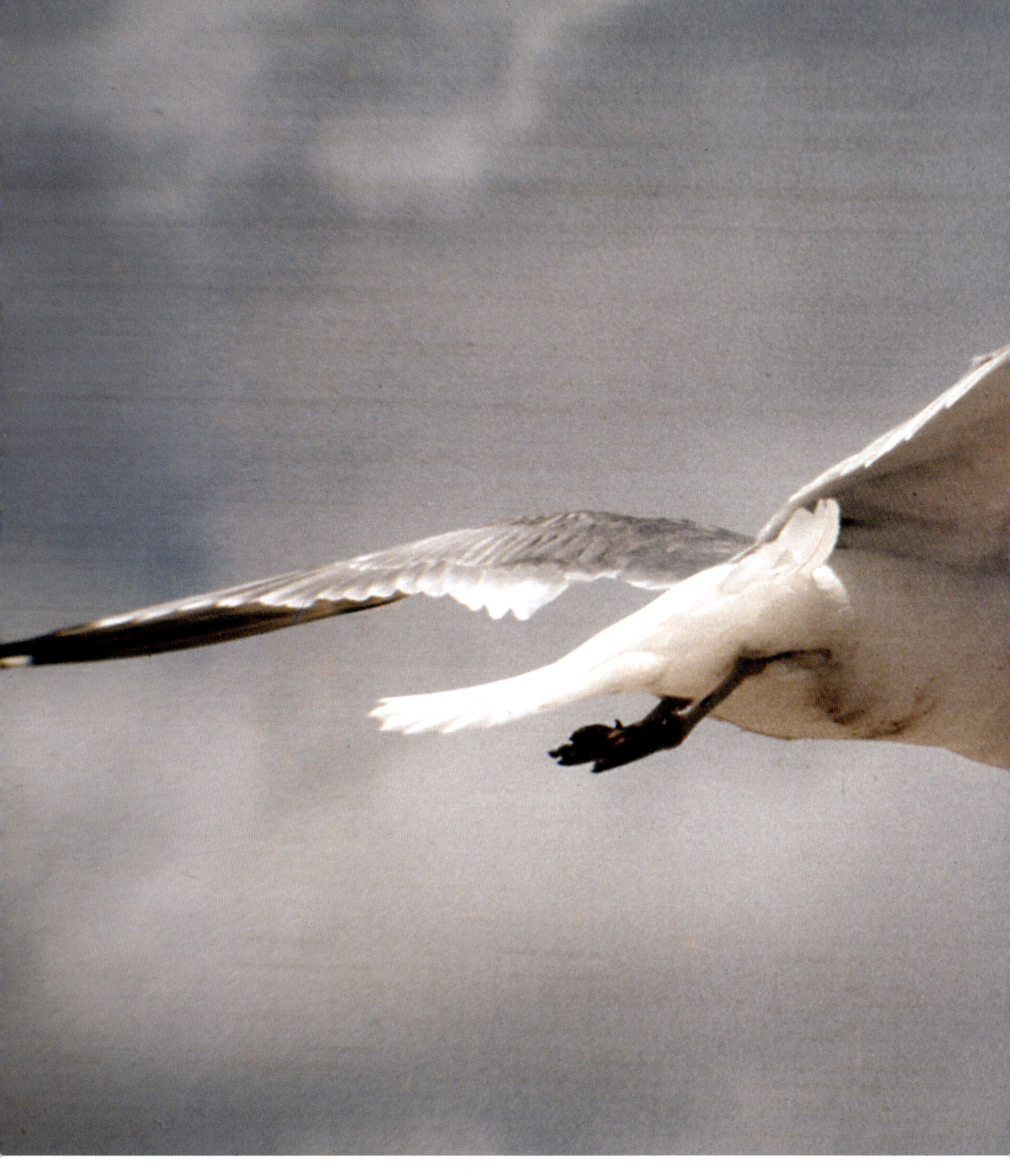

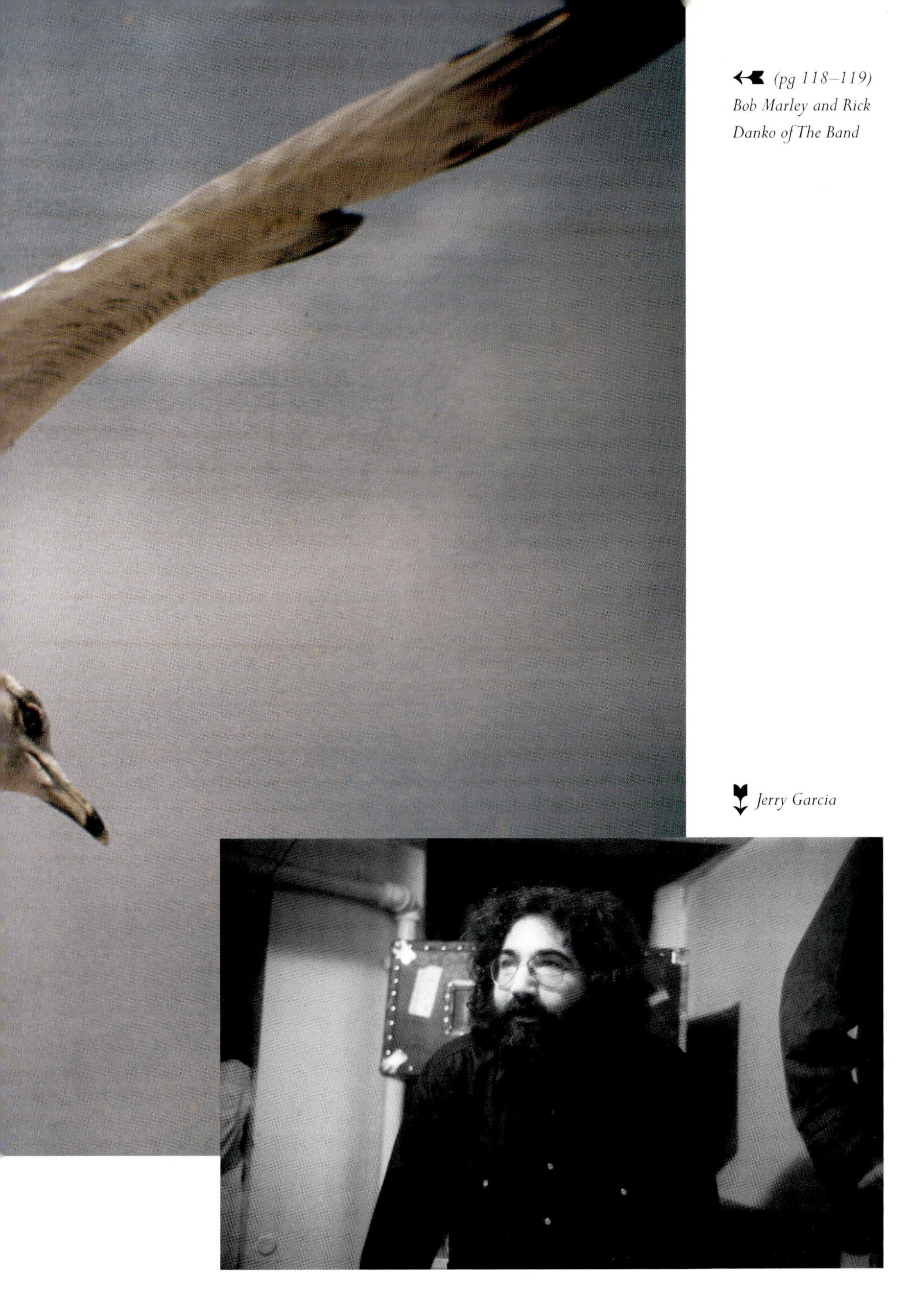

(pg 118–119)
Bob Marley and Rick Danko of The Band

Jerry Garcia

Acknowledgments

For decades I grieved that my photos, taken while on staff at Warner Brothers, had been tossed by a photo librarian. Pat Thomas brought me the crucial clue to their rediscovery, which led to a subsequent search assisted by Kristan Crossley, who helped me for hours and hours by pulling my photos from the WMG archives. And the book itself was Pat's idea. Without Kristan and Pat there would be neither photos nor book.

Thank you Jonathan Hyams, first at Michael Ochs and then at Getty Images, for keeping me in touch with what photos had escaped loss and coaching me over the years in the use of the photos that survived.

Thanks to Sky's dad Carl
who made me toss as a loss ~
out of focus eyes ~
in all photos I took.

Thank you Maria.
This is really OUR book.
Beyond a voice, your words
equal the music we've heard!

Son Sky
for the tech to deliver!

Daughter Daryl & her Tom
for the cheers to keep on.

Diana "Aunt Dinny" Muldaur Dozier
for the space and the grace!

Thank you Jessica Hundley and
Nic Taylor who made it all click!

Thank you dear reader.
Through you
these photos
come alive and survive!

With love and a grin ;)
Yours truly—Giniwin

Pat Thomas wants to thank Jessica, Nic, and Sky for their extreme efforts to bring this book to completion, Mike Johnson for introducing me to Ginny several years ago, Maria for writing the introduction, Jon Klages for eyeball editorial assistance, and Ginny for just being herself.

ISBN: 978-1-68396-975-4
LCCN: 2023947291
FU080

Edited and Written by Pat Thomas & Jessica Hundley
Design by Thunderwing
Scans and Images facilitated by Sky Esser
Proofreading and Editorial Assistance by Jon Klages
Production by Kristian St. Clair

Printed in China

First Edition: January 2024
Published by Fantagraphics Underground
7563 Lake City Way NE
Seattle, WA 98115

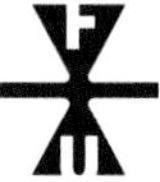

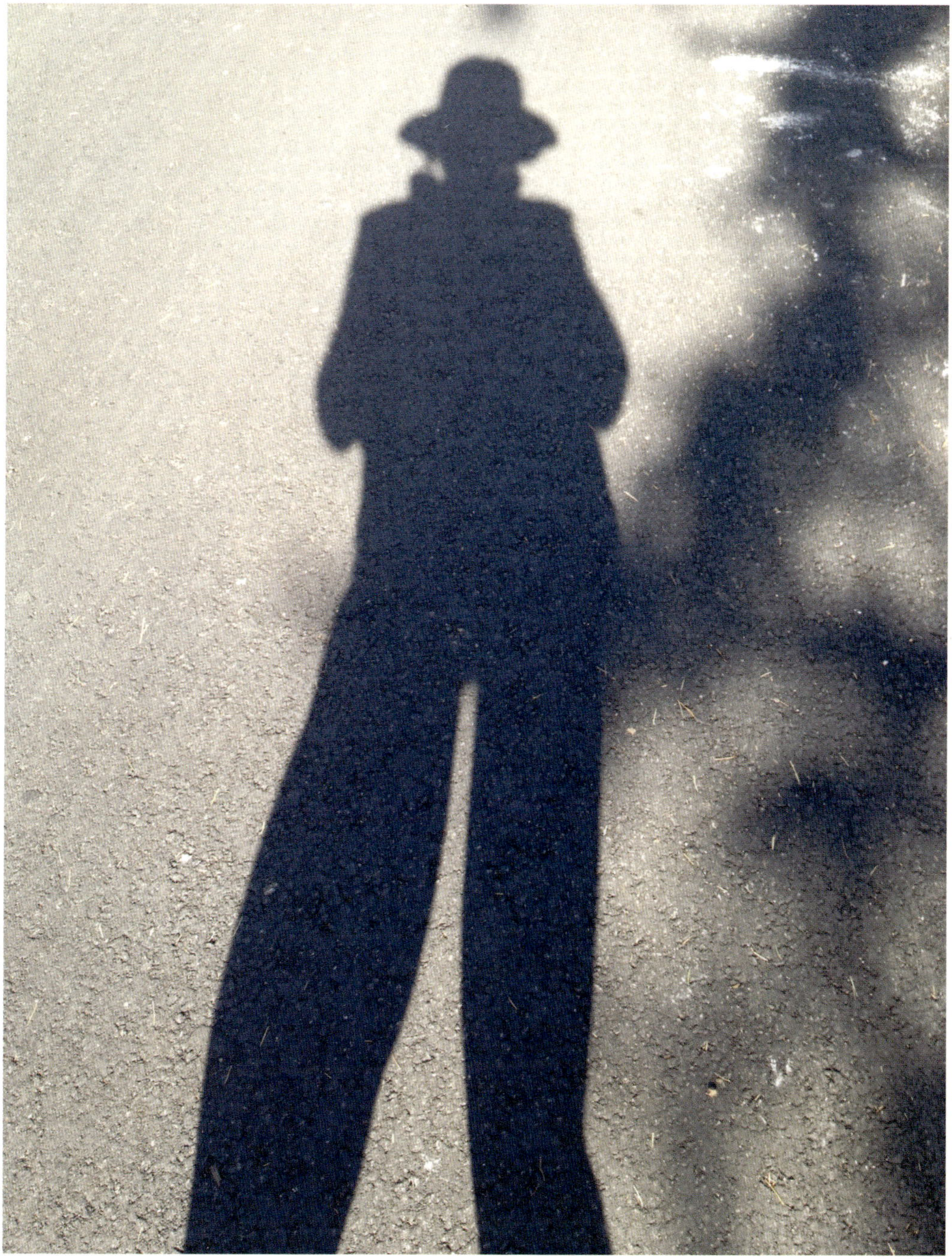

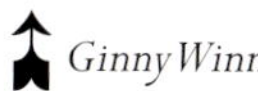

Ginny Winn